to know the leading figures in the hierarchy of the Roman Catholic Church. He will delight in the anecdotes and amusing sidelights exchanged at the Vatican's coffee bars. And he will suffer in suspense over unresolved issues concerning the inner renewal of the Church.

But above all, this smooth, swiftly moving narrative will provide the layman with a clear understanding of the basic challenges that face the Church fathers and a guide to the deeper meaning of the major issues under debate.

Because this book is derived from Dr. Brown's personal journal, with entries written each night while the day's proceedings were still fresh, OBSERVER IN ROME has an unusual immediacy and contains rare insights into the nature of modern Roman Catholicism. The insights are those of a Protestant who recalls the words of Cardinal Bea to the non-Catholic observers: "We ask you to grant us complete confidence and consequently to tell us frankly . . . everything you dislike, to share with us your positive criticisms, your suggestions, your desires."

OBSERVER IN ROME

Subject:
Vatican Council, 2d.

Books by Robert McAfee Brown

AN AMERICAN DIALOGUE (with Gustave Weigel, S.J.)

THE SPIRIT OF PROTESTANTISM

THE SIGNIFICANCE OF THE CHURCH

THE BIBLE SPEAKS TO YOU

P. T. FORSYTH: PROPHET FOR TODAY

OBSERVER IN ROME

*A Protestant Report
on the Vatican Council*

by

ROBERT McAFEE BROWN

1964
DOUBLEDAY & COMPANY, INC.
GARDEN CITY, NEW YORK

To Sydney

(who, after ten weeks of letters
about the Vatican Council, will
not be surprised by a Latin
quotation)

UXORI CARISSIMAE
qui domi
flammas amoris domestici splendide ardentes
curabat
dum ego Romae
flammas dissensionis ecclesiasticae paulatim extingui
spectabam. *

---

* Translation, for the benefit of those who didn't have ten weeks of letters
about the Vatican Council: "Dearest wife, who kept the flame of family love
burning brightly at home, while I observed the flame of ecclesiastical misunderstanding being extinguished bit by bit at Rome."

Contents

"We must welcome the criticisms which surround us with humility, with reflection, with recognition. Rome has no need to defend herself by being deaf to suggestions that come from honest voices, and all the less so, if the voices are those of friends and brothers."

— POPE PAUL VI, to the Curia
September 21, 1963

"We ask you to grant us complete confidence and consequently to tell us frankly . . . everything you dislike, to share with us your positive criticisms, your suggestions, your desires. Of course, I cannot promise you to find a solution for every problem. But I do assure you that we shall be grateful for your confidence, that we shall try to consider everything sincerely in Christ, in order to do, as far as we are permitted, everything that can be done now and in the future."

— CARDINAL BEA, to the non-Catholic observers
October 18, 1963

OBSERVER IN ROME

Preface

The telephone call was unexpected.

Would I be willing to accept appointment as the North American representative of the World Alliance of Reformed and Presbyterian Churches, to attend the second session of Vatican Council II as one of the Protestant observers?

As a result of the telephone call, I spent every weekday morning from September 29 to December 4, 1963, sitting under the statue of St. Longinus in the observers' tribune in St. Peter's. I spent most afternoons and many evenings talking with, eating with, discussing with, and sometimes praying with, Roman Catholic bishops, theologians, journalists, and laymen. I spent the remaining afternoons and evenings trying to write down what had happened while it was still fresh in mind.

Since this was a privilege few non-Catholics (let alone Catholics) have ever had, it has seemed worthwhile to try to share as widely as possible, and in as readable a form as possible, the nature of that experience. The purpose of these pages, therefore, is to help the reader catch something of the "feel" of what it was like to be a part of the most important event of recent Roman Catholic history. I have purposely cast my comments in the form of a day-to-day diary, so that the reader can share my discoveries, my anticipations, my disappointments, my bafflements, and also my appreciation of the genuine movements of the Holy Spirit that could be discerned in the words and actions of the Council fathers. I have tried to record the things that were exciting, amusing, clarifying, and revealing, so that the reader, when he finishes, may have something of the feeling that he was there too. The claim for these pages is, therefore, a modest

one. They represent one observer's reactions as they were recorded in the heat of the battle, from day to day, sometimes
from hour to hour, trying to indicate "what it was like while
it was going on."

*   *   *

I have always been skeptical of books containing the disclaimer that "what follows was not originally intended for
publication," but I must insist that the disclaimer is appropriate in the present case. When I got to Rome I decided
to keep a full diary for just three reasons: (a) as a basis
for the official reports I had to send to the World Alliance of
Reformed and Presbyterian Churches; (b) as a resource
for the inevitable talks and articles I would have to prepare
after my return; and (c) as a means of keeping my wife
informed from day to day of what I was thinking about
what the Council fathers were doing.

About three quarters of the way though the sessions, however, I reread what I had accumulated, and experienced
that hypnotic and fatal moment when a thought flickered
into my consciousness: "I wonder if there's a book
here. . . ." By the end of the Council I had not succeeded
in stifling the thought.

In editing my original notes, I have had to cheat at two
points. First, I have had to cut my entries down to about a
third of their original length. This means that a lot of summaries of speeches are omitted, as well as a lot of incidental
material of interest to me but not necessarily to anyone else.
Furthermore, to keep the finished product within reasonable
size, I have had to identify leaders of the church in ways
that may seem staggeringly informal to fastidious Catholics.
I know that "His Eminence Leo Joseph Cardinal Suenens,
Archbishop of the Diocese of Malines-Brussels in Belgium"
should be so identified when he is referred to, but for purposes of brevity, "Suenens" has to do.

Second, as a Protestant observer I was privileged to share

in many conversations that were conducted with a candor and frankness that would have been impossible had I been a journalist. Consequently I have deleted the names of Roman Catholic partners to these conversations whenever the public use of their names would have betrayed a confidence, let alone gotten somebody in trouble.

There is one point, however, at which I have tried very hard not to cheat. In the editing I have done, I have refrained from introducing the hindsight of later wisdom, either to show myself a clever prophet or to get myself off the hook from speculation later proven false. If these notes have any value in an assessment by someone else of the "meaning" of the Council, it will be precisely because they do *not* have the artificial stamp of later perspective imposed upon them, but genuinely indicate "what it was like while it was going on."

*   *   *

I have made some criticisms of the Council, particularly during the entries for the last couple of weeks. I was initially tempted, for the sake of ecumenical relations, to edit these out. But I finally left them in precisely "for the sake of ecumenical relations." If the situation were reversed, and a Catholic onlooker were observing a Protestant gathering, I would want him to tell me as honestly as possible where he felt we were going astray. Indeed, the closer I got to various of the *periti* and bishops, the surer I was that they wanted me to speak my mind, and the freer I felt to do so. Roman Catholics with ecumenical concerns do not simply want to hear nice things about themselves; they want to know the inmost heart of the "separated brethren," and this I have tried to show, in the spirit of the requests by Pope Paul and Cardinal Bea, cited in the front of this book.

I am not eager to score points for Protestantism at the expense of Catholicism. I am eager only that divided Christians somehow be brought closer to one another. I believe

the Council is an instrument God has given us by means of
which we *can* be brought closer together. I therefore have a
personal stake — as do all Christians, whether Catholic or not
— in the Council being the most authentic reflection of the
Holy Spirit that mortal men can produce. I do not expect
Vatican II to issue "Protestant-sounding" statements. I do
expect it to issue the very best "Catholic-sounding" statements it can, and I know just enough about contemporary
Catholic theology to know that the Council can, if it chooses
and the Holy Spirit is willing, rise to heights of unimagined
greatness. It is because I have seen this greatness within the
deliberations of the unfinished Council that I want it to be
embodied within the achievements of the finished Council.

So if it occasionally seems that this particular observer is
shouting too many critical suggestions from the sidelines,
let it be clear that he does this not because he wishes to confuse the participants, but only because he wishes to spur
them on. Shallow praise can be a betrayal of love; criticism
that proceeds from, and may occasionally give rise to, pain
can be an exercise of love. It is meant to be so here.

*   *   *

The terms "progressive" and "conservative" (or "reac-
tionary") will be found liberally sprinkled through the following pages. I concede that these terms are misleading at
best, but they are the only convenient shorthand terms
available. There are differences of opinion within the Council, and it would be naïve or dishonest to pretend that there
are not. But it should be clear that the terms I have employed do not refer to theological positions so much as to
over-all attitudes. The "progressives" are not theologically
suspect; they are those whose minds are open to the modern world and to the non-Catholics and to the future, and
who are trying to state the unchanging substance of Catholic thought in ways that take account of those three real-
ities. The "conservatives" are not villains nor are they any

more theologically correct; they are simply those whose orientation is to the past, and particularly to past formulas. The terms are meant to be descriptive; I realize that in many contexts they will appear (and probably are) evaluative.

Latin terms also recur from time to time. They are not employed to impose a veneer of scholarly profundity that these pages make no claim to possess, but are employed simply because the flavor of Vatican II could not possibly be communicated without them. Appendix A contains a glossary of Latin phrases that recur without being translated each time.

❖ ❖ ❖

I must conclude by expressing appreciation to all the members of the Secretariat for Christian Unity for their great kindness to me during my stay in Rome, coupled with the assurance that they are absolved of all responsibility for the comments that follow; to the World Alliance of Reformed and Presbyterian Churches for sponsoring my sojourn in the Eternal City, coupled with the assurance that I do not commit them to responsibility for any of my reactions; and to Stanford University for granting me a leave of absence to attend the Council, coupled with the assurance that I will not transform my courses into a series of anecdotes on "what it was like in Rome." My greatest debt, to my wife, is indicated on another page.

ROBERT MCAFEE BROWN

Stanford University
Stanford, California
December 31, 1963

Note: A few portions of the material that follows were adapted out of my original notes for publication in *Christianity and Crisis, The Commonweal* and *Presbyterian Life.* I am grateful to these journals for permission to reincorporate those portions into their original context. I am also grateful to Mrs. William Daily, without whose expert typing we never would have made the deadline.

By Way of Background

The calling of the Council – Vatican I and Vatican II – the Secretariat for Christian Unity – the first session – the death of John XXIII, good shepherd of all the sheep – Pope Paul VI makes "the legacy of John XXIII his own"

The events recorded in this book took place at the second session of Vatican Council II in the fall of 1963. This second session was preceded by a first session in the fall of 1962, which in turn was preceded by over three years of intensive planning. Readers who are unacquainted with any of this background may find the following paragraphs useful. Those who are already among the *illuminati* can skip them and plunge immediately into "The Opening Session."

❖   ❖   ❖

In January of 1959, Pope John XXIII surprised the non-Catholic world by announcing his intention to convene a Council of the Roman Catholic Church. He made clear that his decision was not the result of long premeditated deliberation; the inspiration came during a time of prayer. The time was that period particularly devoted to prayers for the reunion of Christendom, the Christian Unity Octave of January 18–25.

On October 11, 1962, the pope's original impulse received fulfillment as he formally convened the Second Vatican Council in Rome.

The First Vatican Council was held in 1869–70, and Protestants had assumed that it was the last such Council that would ever be held. For at that time Pope Pius IX promulgated the dogma of the infallibility of the pope, and the realization that irreformable truth would henceforth come from the pope himself invited the inference that no future Council would ever be needed to help the pope reach dogmatic decisions. When Pius XII took the initiative, in 1950, without recourse to a Council, of proclaiming the dogma of the bodily assumption of the Virgin into heaven, it seemed even clearer that church Councils had become an anachronism.

If Protestant reaction was one of open surprise, Roman Catholic reaction was at least one of veiled surprise. For in spite of all the power that the pope possesses in principle, it has almost invariably been papal custom to make important decisions only after wide consultation with bishops, theologians, and trusted advisers. But in the case of the calling of this new Council, the pope did not follow such custom, but solely on his own initiative issued his now famous call.

With a skill born of centuries of experience, the Roman Catholic Church quickly adjusted to the new fact that a Council would be held. After all, there had been twenty authorized Councils in the past, and there was no reason why another Council could not be convened. After recovering from their initial surprise, if not shock, Roman Catholic forces rallied marvelously to set in motion the machinery necessary to make the Council a notable event in Catholic history. If conservative forces within the Vatican tried to discourage having the Council soon, more progressive forces outside the Vatican looked upon the Council in precisely the terms of Pope John, as an opening of the windows of the church to let in some fresh air, and as an opportunity for (and the Italian word soon became a commonplace) *aggiornamento,* a bringing of the church "up to date."

The first news releases described the Council as an "ecumenical council." This term has a special meaning in Catholic theology, referring to a meeting of accredited representatives of the Roman Catholic Church throughout the world, with power of representation being vested in the bishops, cardinals, patriarchs, abbots, and heads of religious orders. But the term "ecumenical" has come to have a much broader meaning in Christendom since its adoption by the World Council of Churches and other Protestant groups, referring to all Christians throughout the inhabited world.

Thus the initial impression was given that the pope was calling for a Council of the heads of all the churches in Christendom. This was not, and never has been, the case, and unnecessary misunderstandings followed in the wake of the original announcement. The misunderstandings were in part justifiable, however, because the pope had explained that one of his reasons for calling the Council was to show the rest of Christendom the true nature of the Catholic Church, so that the "other sheep" would feel more ready than before to return to the sheepfold from which they had strayed so many centuries before. In other words, the Council, while not "ecumenical" in the sense that non-Roman Christians use the term (since it was to include only Roman Catholics), was "ecumenically oriented" in the sense that it looked to a future in which divided Christendom would be reunited.

Pope John's later designation of the Council as "the Second Vatican Council" resolved these initial ambiguities. The designation is a happy one. It puts the Council in the tradition of the other Councils of the Roman Catholic Church, and it also puts it in a continuity with the First Vatican Council. The latter fact is of considerable importance, since the First Vatican Council adjourned with a large portion of its agenda unfinished. The dogma of infallibility, in particular, did not receive *full* formulation; the teaching authority of the bishop of Rome (the pope) was defined, but not the teaching authority of the other bishops. This remained a major bit of unfinished business with which the Second Vatican Council has had to concern itself.

The Second Vatican Council must be seen, therefore, as concerned primarily with the inner life of Roman Catholicism, and with the reform, renewal, and *aggiornamento* of that branch of Christendom. Since, however, what happens within one branch of Christendom affects all the rest, not only Catholics but non-Catholics have had a considerable interest in what happened in St. Peter's. The Catholic Church has recognized that what it does in the Council will have an impact far beyond its own borders, and one of the first indications of this recognition was an invitation to people all over the world to send in suggestions about topics the Council should discuss. The invitation was sent not only through the regular Catholic channels, but to many *non-Catholic* groups as well. This was an almost unprecedented step, since in recent decades the Catholic Church has not given the impression of caring very much what non-Catholics thought about it.

    ✿   ✿   ✿

But more unprecedented steps were to follow, the most important of them being the creation of the Secretariat for Christian Unity.

It was clear that some organ within Roman Catholicism would be needed both to interpret the Council to the non-Catholic world and to deal with those matters within the Council that impinged on the relations of Catholics and non-Catholics. For several decades there have been individual Catholics concerned about relations with non-Catholic groups, but until recently they have been somewhat suspect. When Pope John created the Secretariat for Christian Unity, however, he made clear that, henceforth, ecumenical concern would not be an avocation of "fringe" Catholics but would be a central concern of the entire church. The men whom he appointed to serve on the Secretariat were the very best among the ecumenically minded Catholics. Cardinal Bea, the head of the Secretariat, is a renowned Biblical scholar whose spirit has endeared him to the Protestant world. Others appointed to the Secretariat — men like Msgr. Willebrands and Frs. Weigel, Tavard, Baum, Thils, and Dumont — are precisely those Catholic theologians whose writings have given most encouragement to non-Catholics. No

Protestant, charged with choosing the membership of such a
Secretariat, could have selected a group of men more capable
of symbolizing this new concern within Roman Catholicism
for the "separated brethren."

To continue the recital of "unprecedented steps," it was
through the Secretariat for Christian Unity that invitations
were accorded to non-Catholic groups to send accredited
"observers" to Vatican Council II. Through the agency of
the World Council of Churches, various world confessional
groups of non-Catholic Christians — Presbyterians, Method-
ists, Lutherans, Episcopalians, and others — were invited
to choose observers to represent them at the meetings of the
Council fathers. They were not, of course, allowed to participate directly in the debate, but they were admitted to all
the sessions, given copies of all the *sub secreto* documents,
asked to voice their reactions to the debates and the documents, and overwhelmingly made to feel that the Catholic
Church really wanted to know what they felt. The importance of such a step in breaking down walls of division, misunderstanding, and insularity can scarcely be overestimated.

❋   ❋   ❋

When one surveys what took place at the first session of the
Council in the fall of 1962, it is clear that not a great deal
actually "happened." Few votes were taken, few items on
the agenda were completed. But something much more important "happened" than the completion of a given body
of work. What "happened" was that an atmosphere was
created, an air established that will characterize the subsequent sessions of the Council — when many votes will be
taken and many items on the agenda will be completed.

It is hard to describe this atmosphere without being misunderstood. One way to describe it would be to say that the
Council made clear that it was not going to be a rubber
stamp. From the opening day there was insistence on full
discussion of all issues, and in many cases there was an un-

willingness meekly to accept proposals submitted to the Council by the very conservative Curia officials who dominated the preparatory meetings. A more pointed way to describe the atmosphere would be to say that what have been called the progressive or "open-door" bishops were more numerous and powerful than anyone had anticipated, and that they, rather than what have been called the conservative or "closed-door" bishops, dominated the mood. Pope John's desire to open the windows and let in some fresh air was a desire that was found to be lodged also in the hearts of the great majority of his episcopal brethren.

Differences in viewpoint between the Council fathers must not be overstressed, but they certainly existed from the start, and the difference can be symbolized by the attitudes taken toward the *schema* dealing with Scripture and tradition. The document presented for discussion was a conservative and conventional treatment of the problem, stressing the relative independence of Scripture and tradition from one another (the "two sources" view), and it downgraded the tremendous strides that have recently been taken in Catholic Biblical scholarship. It would have solidified *one* interpretation of the teaching of the Council of Trent in such a way as to jeopardize creative Catholic scholarship, and it would have dealt a serious blow to further Catholic-Protestant cooperation in the area of Biblical studies.

This *schema* was roundly criticized from the start, not because the more progressive of the fathers wanted to "change" Catholic teaching, but because they wanted a *fuller* explication of the totality of Catholic teaching than the *schema* made possible. The *schema* looked only to the past; they wanted to take account of the present and also look to the future. And when an impasse developed in which the progressives had a majority of the votes but not the requisite two thirds, the pope himself intervened, withdrew the *schema* from discussion, and appointed a new commission to rewrite it. (This was the point at which one of the Protestant observers was heard to comment, *"Now* I see why they have a pope.")

The incident not only demonstrated certain procedural advantages to having a pope; it demonstrated that the majority of the fathers did not simply want to repeat past formulas, and it also demonstrated that they could engage, with full freedom, in an honest and open airing of differences of opinion. The latter fact was not something for which monolithic images of the Catholic Church had prepared non-Catholics.

But there was a partial "achievement," even at the first session. With only eleven dissenting votes, the fathers gave approval to an initial chapter dealing with reforms of the liturgy. Although the document remained *sub secreto* until it was officially promulgated over a year later, the word got around that it was a far-reaching document breathing the very spirit of reform and renewal. It put a new emphasis on the place of Scripture in Catholic worship, exalted the place and importance of the sermon, gave more attention to the place of the laity as participants *in* the mass rather than observers *of* the mass, greatly increased those portions of the mass that could be said in the vernacular, and gave more power to bishops to approve local changes in the liturgy without having to appeal every decision to Rome for ratification.

Another impression the first session of the Council highlighted was that (if it can be said without sounding condescending) many of the bishops received a second theological education. For the first time, many of them discovered what was going on in other parts of the Catholic world. They discovered the extent of the "dialogue" that has been going on in Europe between Catholics and non-Catholics since the end of World War I. They were exposed for the first time to such prophetic theological voices as Karl Rahner, Hans Küng, Yves Congar, and Jean Daniélou. They celebrated the mass each morning in ways that illustrated how limited is the belief that "the mass is always said in Latin," for they heard it said in Greek, in Russian, in Coptic, and they even celebrated it to the accompaniment of African jungle drums. Those bishops who had quiet concerns about the importance of Scripture discovered others who had outspoken concerns about the same thing. Those who wanted more stress on the vernacular in the liturgy not only found others who shared this concern, but all of them discovered that they were in an overwhelming majority — a fact none of them would have dared believe before the Council convened.

As a result, almost all of the bishops (one would hazard the guess) now have a vision of the church much wider than that of a diocese primarily plagued with the need to pay off the mortgage on the new parochial school.

* * *

Even before the Council had recessed, it was clear that Pope John was ill. It gradually became common knowledge that he was suffering from cancer. After a painful illness, he died a gallant death on June 3, 1963, leaving the entire world, and not only the Roman Catholic world, bereft at the loss it had sustained. It is impossible to understand the spirit of Vatican II without understanding the spirit of John XXIII.

There are many stories about Pope John. One that is particularly well authenticated, and captures the spirit of the man, is the account of his audience with a group of Jews shortly after assuming the pontificate. When the delegation entered the room, the pope, rather than waiting for them to approach him, rose from his chair, walked into their midst, held out his arms, and, using his Christian name, said to them, "I am Joseph, your brother."

The incident serves as a good symbol of the impact Pope John made on the non-Catholic world. The papacy has always been an area of the life of Roman Catholicism from which non-Catholics have felt more than ordinarily separated. Part of the reason for this may be that, with whatever

other gifts they had, recent incumbents of the papal chair
have not given the impression of outgoing warmth in personal relations. That Pope John was able to overcome, and
indeed to destroy, this image of austerity and aloofness in a
space of less than five years is one of those facts of history
that could never have been predicted in advance. In the
past, the death of a pope has not been a fact about which
non-Catholics felt any particular sense of personal involvement. But the death of Pope John was the death of "Joseph,
our brother," and we felt his loss as the loss of a member of
our family.

The important thing is not simply that Giuseppe Roncalli
was this warm human being, our brother, but that it was the
Supreme Pontiff of the Roman Catholic Church who was
this warm human being. There have been many periods in
papal history when the splendor of the Holy See was tar-
nished in comparison to the simplicity of the Holy Family.
At times it has not been clear that the pope was *servus
servorum Dei* (servant of the servants of God), and some
popes left an image of human pretension rather than divine
condescension. Pope John was different. Once, receiving a
group of Roman Catholics who knelt before him, he urged
them to rise. They stayed on their knees, one of them asserting, "You are the Vicar of Christ." To which Pope John responded, "You do not kneel before the Vicar of Christ. You
kneel only before Christ."

The Protestant theologian Karl Barth once remarked, after
surveying the history of the papal see for several centuries,
"I cannot hear the voice of the Good Shepherd from this see
of Peter." That remark now sounds curiously dated, as Karl
Barth would probably be the first to acknowledge. For during
the pontificate of John XXIII, non-Catholics did hear the
voice of the Good Shepherd, solicitous not only for those in-
side, but for those outside the sheepfold as well.

It would not be correct to credit Pope John with the initiation of concern for those outside the sheepfold, as though
the present surge of ecumenical interest from the Roman

Catholic side were his creation alone. But what he did, and what was so important, was to give his blessing to the ecumenical forces already tentatively at work within the Roman Catholic Church, encouraging them and supporting them, so that ecumenical Catholics soon came to realize that they were not merely being tolerated, but that they were articulating precisely those emphases that the Holy Father wished to have at the center of the church's life and concern. John did not originate the term "separated brethren" to describe those outside the visible structure of the Roman Catholic Church. But he did give the phrase popular currency within Catholic life, and for him the noun rather than the adjective was basic. To him we were first of all "brethren," and only secondarily, if tragically, "separated."

Pope John beckoned the Catholic Church to move out toward the "separated brethren" as far as she could, in fidelity to her own convictions, and to engage in that renewal which is always the church's task, and the task in which Christians are always most loathe to engage. It has therefore become the prayer of Catholics and non-Catholics alike that the concerns of Pope John, so manifest in the atmosphere of the first session of Vatican II, will be brought to fruition in its succeeding sessions. The completion by his fellow bishops of that which he initiated will be the most signal mark of honor his own church can bestow upon him.

* * *

On June 21, 1963, Cardinal Montini of Milan succeeded to the papacy as Paul VI. The main question of both Catholics and non-Catholics alike was easy to frame: How would the new pope stand in relation to the reforms initiated by his predecessor?

Within the first weeks of his pontificate, Paul VI made clear that he intended to maintain and even to strengthen those emphases and directions that had characterized the reign of John XXIII. His prompt setting of an early date for reconvening the Council was a symbol of this. Had he wished, he could have postponed it for a year or two, even indefinitely, and thereby dissipated the momentum it had gained. But he chose to call the fathers back to Rome only three weeks later than the date John had originally set.

Three other actions gave cause for great hope that Paul would stand in spiritual as well as chronological succession to John. The first of these was the decision to invite Roman Catholic laymen to attend the meetings of the Council as "auditors." To be sure, they were not given the privilege of speaking on the Council floor, but they were assured that their advice would be sought, and their presence in the *aula* of St. Peter's became an important symbol. The door to the laity has been opened, and, the layman's foot now in it, we can be sure that the door will not again be closed.

Second, Pope Paul decided to put the task of presiding over the Council sessions in the hands of four cardinals, rather than the rotating body of nine that served during the opening session. The important thing in this decision is the outlook of the cardinals named by Pope Paul. Cardinal Lercaro, the only Italian of the four, has been an outspoken advocate of the newly emerging consensus on religious liberty. Cardinals Doepfner of Munich and Suenens of Malines-Brussels are likewise clearly and unmistakably identified with the progressive wing of the Council. Cardinal Agagianian comes from the ranks of the Eastern churches, whose presence at the Council is an important symbol of the fact that Roman Catholicism is not merely the Latin church of the West.

The choice of these particular men is therefore a good indication of what Pope Paul wishes the temper and tone of the rest of the Council to be.

The pope's third move is in some ways the most important of all. On September 21, little more than a week before the opening of the second session, he met with the Curia, the group of ecclesiastical leaders in Rome who are assigned to carry out the pope's bidding, but who in actual fact often delegate to themselves decisions for which the pope must then bear responsibility. Although he began by giving the members of the Curia a raise in salary, he then went on to make quite clear that they were not to engage in obstructionist tactics during the Council. He described himself as "the Pope who today has made the legacy of John XXIII his own, and has also made it a program for the entire Church." He asserted that the Curia is out of date and that it must be modernized and internationalized. "Various reforms," he pointed out, "are therefore necessary."

While it is not yet clear what the nature of these reforms will be, it is of great importance that the pope has gone on record as determined to reform the Curia. The bishops can vote all kinds of reforms at the Council, but unless the Curia helps carry them out, the reforms will come to naught. And the Curia in the past has shown no enthusiasm for the notion of reform.

Perhaps the most important thing Paul stressed was the need to internationalize the Curia. It is no secret that for generations it has been dominated by an almost exclusively Italian mentality. There is nothing wrong, *per se*, with an Italian mentality, but when that mentality becomes ingrown and parochial, seeing the church almost exclusively in terms of the Italian situation, then the time has come for the winds of change to blow more briskly. Pope Paul has made clear that they will.

* * *

It was hard on the heels of this hard-hitting speech that 2300 bishops, several hundred Catholic theologians, and about fifty non-Catholic observers gathered in Rome for the opening of the second session of Vatican Council II, on September 29, 1963.

The Opening Session
(*September 29*)

The Council convenes – the papal allocution: four points, each giving cause for ecumenical encouragement

Sunday, September 29

Since the first gathering of the Council fathers is an "open session" to which the public is admitted, and also a ceremonial session of great solemnity, the observers were asked to wear ecclesiastical vestments proper to their own traditions. Consequently, as we gathered in the Columbus Hotel at 7:45 A.M. we were a more colorful crowd than I would have anticipated. The extremes ran from the Quaker observer, Douglas Steere, in a simple business suit, to representatives of various Eastern groups, such as Syrian Orthodox and Copts, wearing most elaborate garments. In between were Episcopalians, in cassock and surplice, and representatives of the Taizé Community in France wearing their white habits. Professor Skydsgaard, of the Danish Lutheran Church, wearing the wide white ruff around his neck, looked like a kindly pastor right out of Franz Hals. I had a minor catastrophe at 7 A.M. when the new clerical collar I had purchased for the occasion turned out to be the wrong size. Bill Wolf, one of the Episcopalian observers, came to my rescue with another collar, appropriately called "Pontiff." This is Ecumenically Okay. One of the Catholic priests at the session informed me that he was wearing a style called "Canterbury."

We were escorted to St. Peter's by members of the Secretariat for Christian Unity, including Msgr. Willebrands, who speaks very good English for a native of Holland, Msgr. Arrighi, who speaks very good French for a native of Sicily; Fr. Stransky, who speaks very good English for a native of America; and Fr. Long, who speaks very good American for a native of Brooklyn.

After being escorted past any number of Swiss guards, a colorful relic of the former Papal States, we were marched down the full length of the nave of St. Peter's. This was my first glimpse of the interior, and although it is not in an architectural style to which I am instinctively attracted, there is something undeniably impressive about its sheer size and sweep and color, accentuated by all the TV floodlights. Along each side of the nave is a high tier of substantial seats. The word "bleachers" has been used to describe these, but it is hardly an adequate word; one gets more the impression of box seats on the first-base line than of being far out in left field. Each bishop has his assigned place, designated by date of consecration, so the farther back one goes, the younger are the inhabitants. There is a large altar at the head of the nave, behind which is the papal throne. We were given, as some bishops have said, "the best seats in the house," and we were indeed the nearest people in the entire *aula* to the pope and all the events of the morning.

All of this had been accomplished by 8:15, with the opening mass scheduled to begin at 9:00. Having sat out many Protestant ecclesiastical events that were tardy in getting underway, I took a certain comfort in the fact that not even the efficient machinery of the Vatican was able to engineer a prompt start. The procession did not begin at 9 A.M. as scheduled. It began right on the dot of 9:48. A printed program identified the many participants in the procession which culminated, of course, in the person of the pope, who *walked* down the center aisle, rather than being carried in the huge throne (*sedia gestatoris*) that is often used. I rather liked this disavowal of regal pomp on the pope's part, though the entire ceremony had considerably more of both

regality and pomp than is customary to Protestant eyes
and ears.

The program also included the full text of the mass, in
parallel Latin and French columns — a great help to bum-
bling Latinists such as I. A mixed choir ("mixed," that is, by
Roman standards, e.g. men and boys) sang beautifully at
many points during the mass. I had not realized the relatively
small degree of participation by the people in such an act
of worship, and can already see why the liturgical reforms
discussed at the last session, giving more part to the laity,
are so important. I am astonished at the nonchalance with
which photographers wander around during the mass, pop-
ping flashbulbs at the pope while he prays, and making quick
end runs around the altar to get a better shot of the celebrant.

The formal opening of the Council began immediately
after the mass. Pope Paul made his own confession of faith,
reciting the creed and the relevant portions from canon law,
and then all bishops who had not made similar profession
last fall did so. Following this was the act of obedience —
first the cardinals, one at a time, came forward and knelt
before the pope, followed by the heads of the religious orders
and delegated representatives of the bishops. The mind
boggles at how long it would have taken to parade all 2300
bishops out of their seats, up the steps to the throne, down
on their knees, up again, down the steps on the other side of
the throne and back to their seats.

          *   *   *

Pope Paul's allocution followed. It was a long speech —
twelve single-spaced, folio-sized typewritten pages in translation, and forty-three printed pages in a Latin pamphlet —
but, I am already sure, a very important one. For the pope
indicated that the allocution was not simply an opening
to the second session of the Council, but an opening to his
entire pontificate. Indeed, he suggested that if the reconven-

ing of the Council had not provided the occasion for his remarks, he would probably have cast them in the form of an
encyclical, a type of papal declaration that, while not infallible, has a high degree of teaching authority behind it.

It seems to me, both in hearing the allocution (with the
help of a translation provided by the Secretariat for Christian Unity) and in thinking about it since, that to the
degree that it comes to represent the mind of the Roman
Catholic Church, it gives cause for hope in the ecumenical
dialogue in each of its four main points. I am sure that as
the Council proceeds there will be speeches that will cause
me moments of pessimism and gloom, but such emotions
have no place in reflecting upon the papal speech itself. Each
of the main points opens windows that Pope John had
begun to open, and opens them yet further.

1. Pope Paul reminded the fathers that their first business
was to proceed to a clearer understanding of the meaning
of the church. A great many Protestant concerns about Roman Catholicism center around what we have felt to be
the one-sidedness of the treatment of the church at Vatican
I, in which the church is understood almost exclusively in
terms of papacy. But at Vatican II, those one-sided implications are, hopefully, to be corrected, at least in terms of the
relationship between the bishop of Rome and the other bishops. The Council which Pope John originally convoked, and
in conformity with whose intentions Pope Paul has clearly
allied himself, is to banish "the fear wrongly deduced from
that Council [Vatican I], as if the supreme power conferred
by Christ on the Roman Pontiff to govern and vivify the
church were sufficient, without the assistance of the Ecumenical Councils." It is clear, in other words, that the pope desires
the present Council to clarify the way in which the teaching
authority of the church is shared among all the bishops, and
not concentrated so exclusively in the bishop of Rome that
ecumenical councils are an unnecessary luxury.

To whatever degree the Council acts in this direction, then,
there will be a clarification of the doctrine of the church at

the point of the role that the bishops occupy within it. This is helpful ecumenically, not because it does away with certain theological difficulties Protestants will continue to have about *any* definition of infallible teaching authority, but because it clarifies an area that has been much misunderstood. In a dialogue, clarification of issues is basic, and must precede any spelling out of the differences and similarities of point of view that then remain for the two participants. And in this instance, while (as must constantly be reiterated) the clarification will not remove theological problems, it will at least put the discussion on a clearer plane, and also, I feel, move it in a direction that is relatively more, rather than less, congenial to a Protestant understanding of the church.

2. The pope's plea for renewal and reform strikes an immediately responsive note, of course, in any Protestant breast. While the allocution made perfectly clear that from a Catholic standpoint such a plea did not involve an admission that the Catholic Church had been basically unfaithful "to her divine Founder," it did make clear that renewal there must be if the church is to present herself to the world as a vehicle through which the world can see Christ. The Christocentric emphasis here and throughout the allocution was particularly impressive. When we hear the pope say, as he did in his allocution, "May the living church be conformed to the living Christ," we realize that in principle all has been said that needs to be said about the way by which the church — Catholic, Protestant, or Orthodox — is to become a more faithful transmitter of her heritage. We Protestants have often claimed a kind of corner on the notion of reform, as though the idea were somehow inadmissible within a Roman Catholic framework, and it is most heartening to the ecumenical dialogue that the principle of reform is not only implied by the calling of a Council, or stated with such remarkable vigor by a Hans Küng, but expressly insisted upon by the Holy Father himself.

3. The third area of the allocution was the area of most immediate interest to the observers present, for here Pope

Paul was dealing with the unity of the church. Until fairly recently, many Catholics have represented the idea of the reunion of Christendom as though it meant that the sinful Protestants would return to the sinless Mother Church, who was waiting patiently for them, but not reaching out toward them. A good many recent Catholic theologians have given the lie to this point of view, and Pope John certainly emphasized the need for reciprocal repentance as a basis for working toward reunion. But I do not recall any single statement by any Catholic that puts the matter as directly and forthrightly as did Pope Paul, or any statement previously that occupies such a formally important place as the statement he made to those of us sitting so close to him in St. Peter's on September 29. The key paragraph, dealing with the separation of Catholics and non-Catholics, cannot be heard too many times by Protestants — or Catholics:

"If we are in any way to blame for that separation, we humbly beg God's forgiveness and ask pardon too of our brethren who feel themselves to have been injured by us. For our part, we willingly forgive the injuries which the Catholic Church has suffered, and forget the grief endured during the long series of dissensions and separations."

I predict that this statement will become a kind of charter to characterize the atmosphere that must inform future ecumenical discussion, not only because of its source, but because it is so forthright in stating the two essential ingredients that must be present in any genuine reconciliation: (a) a plea for forgiveness for wrongs that one has inflicted, and (b) a granting of forgiveness for wrongs that one has suffered. I would hope that in comparable situations on the Protestant side, our own leaders can make statements that are as generous and gracious. As long as this attitude prevails, there are no barriers too strong to exclude the visitation of the Holy Spirit in our ecumenical endeavors.

The pope's treatment of Christian unity, however, did not run any danger of evaporating into sentimentality. It was kept firmly in the context of reality by his recognition of the grievous problems that still remain, and by the acknowledgment, which it seems to me must always inform discussions of Christian unity, that although with men it seems impossible, with God all things are possible.

4. The final theme of the allocution, the concern of the church for the modern world, is ecumenically significant not only because it is morally right, but because it also opens certain doors for joint activity. Protestants as well as Catholics are concerned about the poor, about culture, about the leaders of the nations, about adherents of other religions. And while doctrinal unity is denied us at present, civic solidarity and mutual concern for the world are not. There are many areas in which even now we can make common cause one with another.

To the degree, then, that the Catholic Church wishes, in the pope's magnificent words, to approach the world "with the sincere intention not of conquering it, but of serving it; not of despising it, but of appreciating it; not of condemning it, but of strengthening it and saving it," she will find that there are many points where Protestants can be comrades in arms rather than separated ecclesiasts. One can even entertain the hope that disgruntled Protestants will begin citing the above words to describe the Catholic attitude to the world rather than always resorting to Pius IX's *Syllabus of Errors*.

* * *

As we left St. Peter's, a crowd was gathered in the large square to receive the papal blessing. The pope finally appeared in his Vatican window, many floors above the street level. I could not help feeling how very small he looked, so high and so far away. And then it occurred to me that this smallness was not a bad symbol for the man who had just told us that he was "the least among you," that in him "there is no intention of human predominance, no jealousy of exclusive power," and who had only a few minutes before compared himself to the figure of Honorius III in the Basilica of St. Paul's, "a humble worshipper, tiny and prostrate, kissing the feet of a Christ of gigantic dimensions."

The First Week
(*September 30 – October 4*)

Daily procedure – the coffee bars – discussion of *De Ecclesia* – the first vote – "briefing sessions" with the Secretariat for Christian Unity – the banning of the books – "collegiality" – married deacons?

Monday, September 30

Every Monday and Friday at 8:15 A.M. the observers will worship together at the Methodist Church just across the Tiber from the Castel Sant' Angelo. This gives us a chance to express the unity we have despite our denominational differences, and it also gives us an opportunity to pray together for the work of the Council. The Right Rev. John Sadiq, the Anglican bishop of Nagpur, based his brief sermon this morning on the Christocentric emphasis of Pope Paul's allocution yesterday.

Today we took our permanent seats in the "tribune," the raised tier of seats reserved for the observers in the very front of the *aula* under the statue of St. Longinus. The furniture has been rearranged since yesterday. Behind the altar is a desk with four seats, for the four cardinal-moderators who will chair the sessions. Behind them is a much longer table with twelve seats for the twelve cardinal-presidents, whose main job seems to be to ensure that the moderators don't break the ground rules. Numerous other desks for secretaries, clerks, and so forth fill up most of the remaining space.

The procedure this morning was typical of the usual order of things. Each session starts at 9 A.M. with a dialogue mass, in which the fathers recite the responses, and the celebrant says his portions aloud, save for the central portion of the mass (the "canon"), which is said silently. The amplification is very good (usually one priest has nothing to do but trail after the celebrant, microphone in hand) and it is not hard to follow what is being said.

After mass, the gospel is "enthroned." Each day a different bishop brings forward a beautifully illuminated manuscript which he places on the altar to remind the fathers of their proper business, which is to embody the gospel in all that they do or say. When this has been done, usually to the accompaniment of a hymn or a sung version of the creed, Cardinal Tisserant, the head of the cardinal-presidents, leads the fathers in the *Adsumus,* a prayer written specially for the Council:

We are present [*Adsumus*], Holy Spirit of God; we are present, conscious indeed of the burden of sin, but gathered together especially in Thy name. Come to us, and be with us: deign to enter into our hearts. Teach us what to do and how to proceed; and show us what we should accomplish, that with Thy help we may be able to please Thee in all things. Be Thou the beginning of our judgments and bring them forth, Thou Who alone has the name of God, along with the Father and His Son. Do not, Thou Who lovest order above all things, permit us to undermine justice in any way. Let not ignorance lead us astray. Let not the desire to please turn us aside from our duty. Let not bribery or favoritism corrupt us. Unite us, instead, effectively to Thyself with the gift of Thine Own grace. Grant that we may be one with Thee and that we may not deviate from the truth. As we have gathered together in Thy name, so may we maintain in all things a proper piety and a fitting moderation that here our thinking may not fail Thee in any way and that hereafter we may obtain the reward of eternal life for the faithful fulfillment of our responsibilities. Amen.

I am greatly impressed by the recognition of human failings in this prayer and by its exclusion of the "triumphalism" that has often seemed to characterize the church. Except for the last two lines, which stress a kind of "works-righteousness" uncongenial to Protestants, there is nothing in this prayer that could not be said by any Christian.

When the *Adsumus* has been completed, Archbishop

Pericle Felici, the secretary-general of the Council, says sternly, *"Exeunt omnes!"* and any who do not have official credentials must leave. Photographers, choir members, priests, visitors, the Swiss guard — all must vacate the *aula.* Those who remain are the bishops, cardinals, theological experts, official clerks — and Protestant observers. That we are exempted from the *Exeunt omnes* is, as Professor Cullmann has remarked, "almost a miracle." Even a few years ago our present privilege would have been almost unthinkable.

After a few minutes of scurrying around (observers gathering around a translator, tardy bishops finding their seats, Archbishop Felici conferring with the moderator of the day, clerks distributing lists of the morning's speakers, somebody taking a last flash photograph) Felici mounts the *ambo,* or pulpit, and makes the announcements for the day. Today he discussed rules of procedure, noted the presence of the Catholic laymen (technically known as "auditors" to distinguish them from the non-Catholic "observers"), and urged with some feeling that bishops speak in the name of as many other bishops as possible in order to cut down on the number of speeches. The suggestion brought immediate applause. He urged with even greater feeling that a bishop, hearing his arguments given by someone else, relinquish his speaking time rather than repeating what had already been said. This suggestion brought even greater applause. The fathers obviously have no interest in wearisome repetition.

An important distinction was then made. The meetings of the smaller commissions are under the rule of secrecy, but the events of the council sessions themselves are to be guarded only by "great discretion." This means, in effect, that what is said in the *aula* can now be legitimately discussed outside of it, which will make things considerably easier for the press, and will also make it easier for the observers to comment on the proceedings.

In order that no one misunderstand, the instructions on procedure were repeated in six different languages — Spanish,

French, English, German, Arabic, and Greek. Here is where
the myth of the "universality" of Latin is exploded. Theological discourses are all in Latin, but when it comes to voting
procedures and the like, Latin isn't trusted. I am reminded
of Hans Küng's dictum that the language for worship should
be the same language that is employed in announcing the
offering.

When the announcements have been completed the
cardinal-moderator for the day takes over (the task rotates
daily among the four moderators) and introduces the
speakers. To save time, when one speaker is announced a
second is told to go to the microphone so that when the first
speaker concludes the second can begin immediately. Thus
the formula is, "*Loquatur nunc Excellentissimus Dominus
So-and-so, et accedat ad microphoniam Excellentissimus
Dominus So-and-so.*" Ten minutes is allotted to each speaker.
The speeches continue all morning unless there is to be a
vote on some matter, in which case the speeches are interrupted to give the necessary information.

The speeches (or "interventions" as they are properly
called) almost invariably begin with the words *Venerabiles
patres* (venerable fathers) — a salutation sometimes expanded to include *carissime observatores* (esteemed observers), depending on the ecumenical predilections of the
particular bishop. The signal that an intervention has been
completed is the word *Dixi* (I have spoken).

Shortly after twelve, the moderator cuts off discussion for
the day, Felici makes any further announcements, and the
fathers adjourn after Cardinal Lisserant has led them in the
Angelus.

※   ※   ※

That, briefly, is the format to which we will be exposed
five times a week for the next nine and a half weeks. But
there is one part of the daily activity that is not covered by
the official rubrics. This is a trip to one of the coffee bars.

From 10:30 on, coffee, soft drinks, and rolls are available off the side aisles, supplied in unending profusion for the participants in the Council. Within the course of the morning, most of the fathers (and most of the observers) make their way either to "Bar-jonah," on our side of the nave, or to "Barrabas," on the other side. The nickname "Bar-jonah" was one of the first Council jokes last year and a pretty sophisticated one at that. It is pun on the Hebrew for "son of Jonas," the designation in the gospels for St. Peter, in whose church the Council meets. "Barrabas" was a robber, and the fact that this bar is on the side where the cardinals sit is presumed to have some veiled symbolism behind it. The bars provide a splendid opportunity to "mingle," and to meet bishops and *periti,* and will serve, I imagine, as a source of real information about what is going on. The only catch, of course, is that the speeches go on all the time, and one never knows what he might miss. That is simply a chance one has to take.

Playing it safe, I took no chances this morning, and ducked out during the translation of the rules of procedure, assuming that I could pass up the Greek and Arabic translations without losing the pulse of the Council as a whole. The bar was jammed since several hundred bishops had had the identical thought, and it was necessary to "push boldly that drinks may abound." I'm still not used to elbowing bishops out of the way in order to get a crack at the Coke machine.

When I returned, Cardinal Agagianian, moderator for the day, announced that the fathers would first discuss the *schema De Ecclesia* (On the Church) in general, after which they would vote on its acceptability as a suitable basis for detailed discussion, chapter by chapter.

The discussion of the church is by all odds the most important topic the Council will deal with. Other matters, such as religious liberty, may have more immediate impact, but nothing in the long run is as basic as further reflection by Roman Catholicism about its own inner reality. It is from the doctrine of the church that Catholicism's similarities to, and differences from, other sectors of Christendom are defined.

The printed text is divided into four chapters. The first deals with "The Mystery of the Church" as growing out of the mystery of the triune God, and relies heavily on Biblical imagery. Chapter Two deals with the hierarchy, particularly the bishops and their relationship to the bishop of Rome, the pope. Chapter Three deals with the people of God as a whole, and then with the laity, while the final chapter discusses the "call to holiness" as something laid not only upon members of religious orders, but upon all Christians. However, it has been proposed to change the structure as follows: Chapter One on the mystery of the church will be followed by a treatment of "the people of God" as Chapter Two. Chapter Three will deal with ecclesiastical offices, and especially bishops. Chapter Four will deal with the laity, and Chapter Five with the call to holiness. This is an important shift. It means that the church is not defined primarily as "the hierarchy" plus the leftovers (e.g., the laymen), but is defined primarily as *the whole people of God*, within whom are various groups, such as bishops and laymen, all joined to one another by their common designation as the people of God.

*   *   *

Cardinals have first chance to speak each day, and are listened to carefully, as their opinions carry great weight. Cardinal Frings of Cologne, one of the twelve Council-presidents, initiated the discussion, speaking in the name of sixty-five bishops. Frings, one of the leaders of the "progressive" forces last session, is truly "venerable" and almost blind, but his speeches, given without notes, are clear, precise, and direct. He approved the *schema* as a fit basis for detailed discussion. He felt that it demonstrated the pastoral tone Pope John had asked the council to manifest, and he approved the dependence on Scriptural imagery. There was need, however, for more stress on the church's calling to a life of suffering and poverty.

Cardinal Siri, of Genoa, another of the Council-presidents,

likewise gave general approval, but with many more qualifications. More detail is needed, many phrases are ambiguous, important doctrinal elements are lacking.

These interventions set the pattern for the discussion. Frings and Siri are at opposite ends of the theological spectrum as well as at opposite ends of the presidents' table, and each is ready to accept the *schema* for detailed discussion, but each is serving notice that it will need modification. The bishops who subsequently spoke had variants of a similar formula, and even today I can begin to distinguish phrases like *Schema mihi in genere placet* (I approve the draft in general) followed by the *attamen* (but, or however), after which the qualifications are introduced.

Some want more stress on the basic equality of all the people of God; others want more stress on the inequalities, created by ordination and subordination, that remain. Some emphasize "*universal* priesthood"; others insist that such a formula must not gloss over the *different* kinds of priesthood. Some argue, "Although the tone of the *schema* should be pastoral, due attention must be given to the juridical structure of the church"; others argue, "Although the church has a juridical structure this should not be allowed to obscure pastoral concerns." Where one bishop applauds an initial chapter stressing "mystery," since no definition of the church is ever fully adequate, another bishop feels it unwise to begin with the concept of "mystery," since this is fuzzy and will only confuse the faithful.

No doubt such polarities will be focused more sharply as the discussion proceeds. After ample discussion, the *schema* will be remanded to the Theological Commission for revision in the light of whatever consensus the fathers' comments have produced.

If today's session is any sample, the consensus won't come quickly.

Tuesday, October 1

I am not going to overload these pages with ten-line summaries of ten-minute speeches, but I will comment on a few of those given today, since they pinpoint sensitive spots that will be crucial in the later discussion.

Cardinal Silva Henriquez of Chile spoke for thirty-eight South American bishops. In their name he gave strong approval to the proposed shift in chapter sequence, making "the people of God" the basic concept for understanding the church and the hierarchy. He also suggested that material from the now separate *schema* on Mary be included within *De Ecclesia* since many people in South America develop a devotion to Mary which is independent of their understand ing of the church, and which leads to excesses that distort the true nature of the Catholic faith. He felt, quite rightly, that a separate *schema* on Mary would not foster ecumenical understanding.

Cardinal Rugambwa of Tanganyika spoke on behalf of many African bishops. He accepted the *schema* in general, but felt that it was deficient in its attention to the *missionary* purpose of the church, which is to evangelize the world, not only on the "so-called 'mission field'" but wherever the church finds itself.

Archbishop Hermaniuk of Winnipeg, who represents the Ukrainian rite in Canada, raised an issue about which we will hear much more, when he gave strong approval to the principle of "collegiality" in the *schema*. To speak of "collegiality" is a shorthand way of affirming that Christ gave rule in the church not only to Peter, but *to the other apostles as well*, so that as a group or a "college" they, and their successors, would bear rule in the church.

The lines will be drawn pretty clearly on this one. Extreme papalists will have nothing to do with it, since it seems to diminish the absolute power of the pope. The more forward-looking groups will assert that "collegiality" is simply an area in the understanding of the church's authority that has not previously been clarified, but that the time is now ripe to effect such clarification. Hermaniuk went on to ask for the removal from the *schema* of phrases like "Roman pontiff" and "vicar of Christ," since these are scholastic terms whose meaning is blurred and whose implications are offensive to non-Catholics. Later in the discussion a missionary bishop gave similar support to the "collegiality" principle.

Other bishops pointed to various gaps in the *schema:* Bishop Garonne of Toulouse agreed with Cardinal Silva that Mariological material should be incorporated within it, and also asked for clarification of the relationship of Scripture and tradition. Bishop Gasbarri, an Italian, wanted a treatment of church and state, and a discussion of matrimony. Bishop Elchinger, of Strasbourg, spoke in terms congenial to Protestant ears when he suggested that the *schema* begin with a treatment of the Word of God, since it is the Word of God that creates the church. He, too, favored inclusion of Mariological material within the *schema.*

While none of these speeches contained real fireworks, they indicated that a couple of significant differences of opinion have already emerged: (a) the place of Mary in conciliar statements and (b) the concept of "collegiality," dealing with the relation of the authority of the pope to the authority of the rest of the bishops.

*　　*　　*

At eleven o'clock general discussion was closed and a vote was taken on accepting the *schema* in general as a basis for detailed discussion. Voting is done on special cards which are marked with a metallic pencil, and fed into computors so that the votes of 2300 bishops can be tallied and announced within a few minutes. The voting procedure was explained in six languages, so everybody should have gotten the word about those metallic pencils. Only two votes were possible: *placet* (an affirmative vote) or *non placet* (a negative vote). On some questions, but not on this one, a third vote is possible, *placet juxta modum* (an affirmative vote with "modifications"). Three of the fathers nevertheless voted *placet juxta modum,* and fifty-four marked their ballots improperly

—not too bad a batting average for the first time around with metallic pencils and computor cards. To nobody's great surprise, *De Ecclesia* was approved as a basis for detailed discussion, 2231 fathers voting *placet* to only 43 voting *non placet*. The fathers who haven't yet caught up with automation obviously didn't affect the outcome.

*   *   *

The voting procedure took about forty-five minutes. It was a welcome intrusion for ears not yet attuned to the steady stream of Latin speeches. But once the vote was announced, the moderator of the morning, Cardinal Lercaro of Bologna, who is not one to waste valuable minutes, directed the fathers to begin a detailed discussion of Chapter One. The first speaker was Cardinal Ruffini of Palermo, one of the Council-presidents and one of the strongest voices of the "conservative" group. It was immediately clear that he had been holding his fire during the preliminary discussion, for he launched into a series of detailed objections to the first chapter. He immediately joined the issue on "collegiality," by emphasizing that Peter is far above the other apostles and that authority to rule in the church was given exclusively to him. Ruffini sees vestiges of "Modernism" in the *schema*, "Modernism" apparently meaning anything that questions the absolute, sole, sufficient, and final rule of the pope.

I must confess to a certain difficulty in understanding this point of view. Grant, with Ruffini, that the pope has supreme and absolute authority, shared by none. One must then take everything the pope says with radical seriousness. Day before yesterday, in his opening allocution, the pope asked the fathers to proceed toward a clarification of "collegiality," and asserted that the pope rules in conjunction with the college of the bishops. If the pope is for it, who can be against it?

Somehow I'm sure this is not the only point at which Cardinal Ruffini and I have differences of opinion.

*   *   *

At 4:30 this afternoon the Secretariat for Christian Unity sponsored the first of its weekly "briefing sessions" for the observers. These are going to be among the most valuable experiences of the entire Council. One of the Catholic *periti* who has helped write the *schema* under discussion on the Council floor gives a brief introduction to the material, after which Protestant reactions are elicited. The discussions are conducted in English and in French, save for Professor Schlink of Heidelberg, who prefers to speak in German, and whose remarks are translated by the omnicompetent Father Weigel, who has already spent the morning translating Latin speeches for us in the *aula*.

I am impressed with the genuineness of the Secretariat's desire to know what we think. To observe people of the stature of Père Congar, one of the most eminent of living Catholic theologians, busily taking notes for over two hours on Protestant comments to *De Ecclesia* has been a somewhat humbling experience. Obviously, the Council is not going to produce Protestant documents, but it does wish to produce Catholic statements that are as ecumenically oriented as possible. Often certain phrases, ideas, or even certain nuances have a grating sound in our ears that was not intended by the writers, and it helps them to know what *we hear* when we listen to what *they say*.

The briefing sessions are begun and ended with prayer by Msgr. Willebrands, the secretary of the Secretariat for Christian Unity. When he prays, we are not divided by liturgical differences, but more closely joined than before. He prays in English with just enough of an accent so that I can imagine myself — and I mean this as the highest compliment — in the congregation of a devout German evangelical pastor who is really ministering to my impoverished spirit. That the life of Catholic devotion can produce this kind of transparent piety is something any critic of Catholicism had better remember before he is too quick to anathematize the Catholic Church.

When I glance around the room and see men of the caliber of Oscar Cullmann, the New Testament scholar of Basel and the Sorbonne; Edmund Schlink, the Lutheran theologian of Heidelberg; G. C. Berkouwer, the Dutch Calvinist theologian; Albert Outler, the foremost American Methodist theologian; Douglas Horton, former dean of Harvard Divinity School; George Caird of Mansfield College, Oxford; Alexander Schememann, dean of St. Vladimir's Orthodox Seminary; Kirsten Skydsgaard, a Danish Lutheran theologian who has pioneered in Lutheran ecumenical involvement; Max Thurian, subprior of the Taizé Community in France; George Lindbeck of Yale Divinity School; Hébert Roux of the French Reformed Church — I realize that probably never before has there been such a concentration of non-Catholic minds dealing with ecumenical issues under Catholic sponsorship and I wonder if I shall ever have the nerve to speak up in such a gathering.

Although these Tuesday afternoon discussions are "off the record," it will not be cheating to indicate the general area of the observer's concerns as the Council moves into a discussion of *De Ecclesia*. Here are the kinds of questions we discussed:

Does the *schema* give sufficient attention to the prophetic task of the church, and to the fact that the church itself is always under judgment? Is the *schema* sufficiently clear in its acknowledgment of the reality of sin within the life of the church? Does the *schema* really acknowledge the presence of the Holy Spirit outside the structure of the Roman Catholic Church in a way that does sufficient justice to evidences of grace in the lives of non-Catholic Christians? Is it possible for the *schema* to acknowledge the reality of the *church* in the corporate lives of non-Catholic Christians?

The latter point arises again and again in discussions among the observers. Catholic theology acknowledges that the Holy Spirit works among individuals who are not Roman Catholics. It even acknowledges that by baptism non-Catholic Christians are mysteriously linked to the Catholic Church. But can Catholic theology acknowledge that the Holy Spirit works through what we call our *churches*? Can these be seen as more than voluntary associations of like-minded people who have elsewhere been individually exposed to the working of the Holy Spirit? Is it possible for Catholic theology to affirm that God has used our churches as vehicles of His Word and Spirit?

These are questions on which the *schema* still seems unclear. They are crucial questions for the future of the ecumenical dialogue. Dr. Schlink has put the point as forcibly as anyone. "Non-Roman Christendom consists not merely of individual Christians, but of churches. Non-Roman Christians are certain of salvation as members of their own churches. It is not through the Roman Church, but through their own church, that they have received baptism, and that they have come to the faith through the Gospel."

❅   ❅   ❅

We have already been given one informal bit of advice by the observers who were here last year. There is at least one thing an observer does not do. If he is (a) married (b) has his wife with him, and (c) wears a clerical collar, he does not (d) walk the streets of Rome holding hands with his wife since this (e) causes scandal to the faithful who are likely to mistake him for (f) a Roman Catholic priest.

Wednesday, October 2

Another bit of advice observers must take seriously: Always have your passport with you. Between the end of the Via della Concilazione and the observers' tribune there are at least four "checkpoints" at which one must either be garbed as a bishop or produce the appropriate credential. In our case the latter is a red Vatican passport, complete with photograph, signed by Cardinal Bea. There is a story going the rounds of a journalist who wanted to crash the secret sessions. He borrowed a cassock and clerical collar, attached himself to a bishop, explained that he was a priest who wanted *very* much to get into the Council for just one day.

The bishop finally got him in as his official chaplain. After
mass the reporter's conscience began to get the better of him
and so he finally said, "Your excellency, I have a confession
to make. I'm not actually a priest, I'm a newspaper reporter."
To which his companion replied, "Well, one confession deserves another. I'm not actually a bishop. I'm a newspaper
reporter too."

*   *   *

Three cardinals and a steady stream of bishops devoted a
full two and a half hours to discussion of Chapter One on
"The Mystery of the Church." The cardinals were all outstanding, which is no reflection on the bishops.

Cardinal Barros Camara of Rio de Janeiro announced that
he spoke on behalf of 153 Brazilian bishops. (A speech with
an opening like that is always greeted with pleasure, since
it eliminates 152 potential orations. At ten minutes a speech
that is a sizable gift.) Their concern, obviously widespread
in South America, is to have more stress on the church's
identification with the poor. In so many areas of poverty,
the church is identified solely with the rich landlords. The
schema, Cardinal Camara insisted, must emphasize the fact
that the church shares with Christ in His suffering and not
just in His glory, and it must also acknowledge that God can
work outside the boundaries of the visible church.

Much the same stress was made by Cardinal Gracias of
Bombay, who speaks with forcefulness, passion, and even
wit — a saving grace among highly placed ecclesiastics. He
says precisely those things that comfortable churchmen
— whether Catholic or Protestant — need to hear from missionary areas. The church must renounce all ambition
to dominate, and can have ambition only to serve. It exists
not for itself, but for others. It must *show* the moral quality
it claims to possess, and this insistence must be more explicitly stated in the *schema*. Cardinal Gracias brought all heads
up with a start when, objecting to the style of the *schema*

occasioned by its composite authorship, he said it illustrated the truth that (and the words came forth in booming English) "too many cooks spoil the soup."

Cardinal Alfrink of Utrecht, one of the Council-presidents, spoke on behalf of the Dutch bishops and took issue directly and forcibly with Ruffini's rejection yesterday of the notion of collegiality. Where Ruffini tried to separate Peter as much as possible from the other apostles, Alfrink insisted that while Peter is the foundation of the church the other apostles are also. There is something ambiguous about referring to "Peter and the apostles." The proper reference is "Peter and the *other* apostles." This makes clear both that Peter is an apostle, and that authority is given to the other apostles as well.

Clearly, the cardinal-presidents have not been chosen for their unanimity of theological opinion.

The rest of the speeches indicated a wide range of opinion. Another Dutch bishop opted for collegiality (the Dutch are well organized) and wanted more emphasis, along with Barros Camara, on the gifts of Christ that can be found outside the church. A French bishop who wanted more stress on the mystery of the church was followed by a Spanish bishop who wanted less on mystery and more on hierarchical structure, and insisted that power to rule in the church is given only to the pope. Later in the morning Bishop Carli, one of the most articulate of the Italian papalists, put the latter point with great eloquence. The pope has the full plenitude of power and the other bishops occupy a very subordinate role in relation to him. Any other teaching challenges the infallible pronouncements of the First Vatican Council. But before one could assume too easily that Spanish and Italian bishops are all alike, along came Bishop Guano, an Italian, asking for more stress on the sense of mystery, more stress on the image of the church as the people of God, rather than the hierarchy, and more stress on the image of the pilgrim church, i.e., a church which has not yet achieved fullness and completion.

If viewpoints in the Council are not neatly characterized by nationality, they do reduce themselves to fairly consistent positions. Those who stress an extreme *papalism* also stress the visible structure of the church, downgrade any acknowledgment of sin within it, and are pretty clear about where its boundaries (and therefore the boundaries of God's grace) are to be found. Those who stress the *collegial principle* see the church in less static, structural, and juridic terms, recognize that it is in movement, that it looks forward to a consummation it cannot yet fully claim, and that it must not be too quick to deny the gifts of the Spirit to those beyond its visible walls.

*   *   *

The last two speeches of the morning dealt directly with matters raised at our "briefing session" yesterday afternoon. (This is not an example of *post hoc ergo propter hoc*, since the fathers have to submit their speeches three days in advance, but it does illustrate the fact that Catholics are also concerned with questions that perplex us.) Bishop Primeau, of Manchester, New Hampshire, the first American to speak at this session, wanted more stress in the *schema* on the fellowship non-Catholics can enjoy with God. He distinguished between a fellowship and a society. A rigorous definition of the church as a society means, of course, the Roman Catholic Church. But non-Catholic Christians do not approach God simply as individuals; they are united in a fellowship with one another and with God and this corporate dimension of their life must be more fully acknowledged.

If this represented a step in our direction, Christopher Butler, the abbot of Downside, took a gigantic stride. Speaking in pure Oxonian English that just happened to come out in Latin words, he insisted that provision must be made for the reality of the *communal* life non-Catholics share before God. Such Christians live in communities and are joined in churches. The latter are not just "natural societies," but are somehow supernaturally joined together, even though incompletely, and "therefore the nature of the church can be found in these communities."

It is too soon to tell how widely such a view would be shared by the other Council fathers, but these speeches make clear that our concerns of yesterday are valid concerns, and that we can expect further attention to them as the Council proceeds.

Abbot Butler provided a splendid note on which to end the morning, and encourages me to feel that many questions that have been regarded as "closed" are not nearly as closed as either side has tended to believe. My general good feeling was enhanced by a later conversation with Fr. Godfrey Diekmann, one of the *periti* for the Liturgical Commission. He reports that the liturgy *schema* is just about ready for presentation to the Council fathers. If this is adopted during the present session it will represent an important victory for the cause of *aggiornamento* — the "bringing up to date" of the church, which was Pope John's reason for convoking of the Council.

Thursday, October 3

A curious episode is being buzzed about Rome today. Within the last two or three days, the main religious bookstores have been told not to display or sell Xavier Rynne, *Letters from Vatican City*, Robert Kaiser, *The Pope, The Council and the World*, or any of the writings of Hans Küng and Teilhard de Chardin. The stories vary. Some bookstore managers got phone calls. Others were shown a letter giving the order and asked to sign a statement that they had seen the letter, after which the letter was recovered from the shopkeeper. Others were simply told to remove the books from display. The order seems to have come from the Vicariate of Rome, i.e., the local authority rather than the Vatican, although it appears to have been done with the approval of the Curia's Holy Office and of Archbishop Parente, second in command under Cardinal Ottaviani. One source alleged that the ban was imposed so that bishops "from far-away territories" would not have their faith shaken by such dangerous writings. At all events, whatever the reasons and whatever the extent of the ban (some say Küng's books were not included), it has backfired spectacularly. Sales of all the books are zooming as a result, and if they are unavailable in some stores it is only because the ban has called such attention to them that the bookstores have exhausted their present stock.

I am interested in how unperturbed my Catholic friends are about the episode. Nobody is worried, nobody takes the move seriously, nobody feels that it will do anything except give some excellent publicity to some excellent books. This childish attempt to "protect" the faith of grown men will only give fresh impetus to reforms that will update an attitude that fears and therefore seeks to suppress the printed word.

* * *

The printed word, I must add, is a great boon to me in following the mass. Having gotten a copy of the *St. Andrew Missal* (the closest I can come to identifying locally with my Presbyterian heritage) I am able to enter a little more fully each day into an understanding of the central act of Catholic worship.

There is great difference among the observers concerning a proper degree of participation in mass. Almost all come for mass, and only a very few arrive, rather obviously, at its conclusion. A good many simply "observe," taking no part even in such things as the Lord's Prayer. Others, mostly Orthodox and Anglicans, participate to a high degree, and join with the Roman Catholics in kneeling during the act of consecration. I find an increasing desire to participate in all those parts of the mass which I can repeat without either compromising my own Protestant convictions or appearing to Roman Catholics to be profaning what is sacred to them.

Thus I join in all the responses that have a Biblical origin, and in such affirmations as the *Kyrie*, the *Gloria*, the *Credo*, the *Sanctus*, the *Agnus Dei*, and the *Pater Noster*. These are part of the liturgical heritage of all of Christendom and I have no difficulty affirming them, even though I am still stumbling into familiarity with the Latin versions. (Just about the time I finally feel at home in Latin, the liturgy will begin to be celebrated in the vernacular.) I do not join in the prayer of confession that is addressed to *"beatae Mariae semper Virgini, beato Michaeli archangelo . . ."* and so on, but when the celebrant addresses me with the words *"Dominus vobiscum"* (The Lord be with you), I do not see anything improper in responding, *"Et cum spiritu tuo"* (And with your spirit).

I have the feeling that I will learn more about Roman Catholicism by this degree of participation in Catholic worship than I will from reading any number of books *about* Catholic spirituality.

❖   ❖   ❖

Discussion continued today on Chapter One of *De Ecclesia*. There were no less than six cardinals, followed by thirteen bishops. Nineteen interventions is a lot of interventions, and already there is a good deal of repetition. The cardinals were mainly concerned to introduce missing emphases into the *schema*. Cardinal Lercaro wanted more stress on the Eucharist; Cardinal Arriba y Castro, speaking for sixty Spanish bishops, wanted more stress on Mary, who, since she is the mother of the church, is greater than the church; Cardinal Confalonieri wanted more stress on Pentecost; Cardinal Richaud wanted the concept of the church to draw more directly on Ephesians 1; and Cardinal Ritter of St. Louis, speaking a very clear (and very American-sounding) Latin, urged that more stress be given to the importance of preaching. Unless the *schema* stresses the efficacy of the preached word, he went on, all other reform will be empty. The *schema* must be based on a theology of the Word, for Word and Sacrament together are essential to the life of the church.

To hear an intervention like Cardinal Ritter's is to realize how much closer we can be drawn together by a recovery of our common heritage. Past Catholic emphasis on the Sacrament is now being balanced by concern for Sacrament *and Word*. Past Protestant emphasis on the Word is now being balanced by concern for Word *and Sacrament*. Each has had an imbalance in the past and as we recover the lost emphases we are drawn closer to one another than we were before.

Cardinal Bea, the head of the Secretariat for Christian Unity, was the last cardinal to speak. Bea looks very old — as he has every right to at eighty-three — and is stooped with age. But when he begins to speak, the age disappears, and a young and vigorous mind asserts itself. A Biblical scholar of note, one of the drafters of *Divino afflante spiritu* (the encyclical of Pius XII that gave a new freedom to Biblical scholars), Bea is now putting his whole lifetime of study at the service of ecumenical concern. Thus it was entirely in character that his two points this morning had ecumenical import. First he called attention to places in the *schema* where Biblical texts had been improperly used and warned that nothing is gained by pulling Biblical passages out of context. Secondly, he suggested that, when appealing to tradition, the *schema* should use the earliest sources possible, so that appeal could be made to a heritage shared by both Catholics and Protestants. For ecumenical purposes it is better to buttress a passage by reference to one of the early fathers than by quoting recent provisions of Canon Law.

The interventions of the bishops were uniformly good. German, Brazilian, and Swiss bishops echoed Cardinal Ritter's concern for more emphasis on preaching. Van Velsen of South Africa and Van der Burgt of Indonesia underscored the importance of the image of the people of God, and Pildain of the Canary Islands asked for more emphasis on the fact that the church must not seek her own glory. Van der Burgt also pointed out that the *schema* must not appear to identify the Kingdom of God and the church, since the church is still the pilgrim people, conscious of its own failings and its own sin.

Archbishop Heenan, just enthroned as Archbishop of Westminster in England, had a stricter approach to ecumenism than some of the fathers we have heard. He pointed out a discrepancy between the sections on non-Catholic Christians and non-Christians. The *schema* urges Catholics to evangelize the latter but not the former. Surely, however, Catholics must preach to non-Catholic Christians as well, and seek to bring them back to the true church.

Heenan is a member of the Secretariat for Christian Unity, and his speech indicates the diversity that exists even within such a group. The difficulty a Protestant has with this sort of approach is that it seems to suggest that movement is called for on only one side; the Catholic Church is simply waiting for the others to "return" to it. Protestants would reply that we are both called to enter upon the ecumenical dialogue without being too sure exactly where it will lead, recognizing that in the course of our confrontation both, in various ways, are going to change. Of course, the notion that the church can "change" is repugnant to those Catholics who are fond of quoting phrases like "without spot and wrinkle" to describe the church. But surely the very calling of a Council is an indication of the need for "change," and in the process, particularly in confrontation with non-Catholics, the change may go in directions originally unforeseen.

The last speaker, Archbishop Martin of Rouen, indicated that he was a man of compassion and understanding. He began his intervention with the words, "Venerable fathers, I will make my remarks brief, for charity's sake. . . ." And what is even more remarkable, he did.

*   *   *

This afternoon I crashed the press panel for the American newsmen. Every day at 12:30 the journalists are given a running summary of all the morning's interventions, and then at 3 P.M. they meet in the basement of the USO building to ask questions of a distinguished panel of *periti* and bishops. The sessions are chaired by Fr. John Sheerin, of the Paulist fathers, who opened the session with some important information I hadn't yet heard: "Koufax struck out fifteen for a new series record."

Archbishop McGucken of San Francisco and Bishop Zuroweste of Belleville have arranged for the panel, and they see to it that Council fathers are present as well as a group of experts — including such luminaries as Fr. Weigel, the real pioneer in American ecumenism; Fr. McCool, a very creative Jesuit Biblical scholar; Fr. McManus, an expert on canon law who is also closely involved in the revisions of the Liturgy *schema;* Msgr. Higgins of the National Catholic Welfare Conference, an expert on the church and social problems; Fr. Tavard, an outstanding French ecumenist now teaching in the United States; Fr. Haering, a German Redemptorist who is an authority on moral theology; Fr. Baum, a German now teaching in Canada, who is one of the most creative ecumenical theologians; and Fr. Stransky, a Paulist father who is a member of the Secretariat for Christian Unity. The Catholic seminarians in Rome also turn up in droves, for this is an unparalleled opportunity to supplement one's theological education. The questions are very probing (the newsmen are professionals, and know how to track down what they want) and the answers are very honest. It is clear that the church is not trying to hide anything, but simply wants information about the Council to be as accurate and informed as possible.

Friday, October 4

Mass this morning was rather touching. Today is the Feast of St. Francis, so the mass was celebrated by a bishop named

Francis who was ordained fifty years ago today and has spent
his life in a mission diocese working among the poor.

After some concluding discussion of Chapter One, the interventions were directed, quite bombastically, to Chapter
Two of *De Ecclesia*. Although nothing really new emerged
on Chapter One, a number of important points received further emphasis. Cardinal Gerlier and Bishop Himmer, for
example, picked up the note a number of missionary bishops
have stressed, emphasizing that the church belongs to the
poor, and must identify with the poor. Speaking for many
missionary bishops, Archbishop Grauls of Africa asked for
greater recognition of the diversity that can exist within the
unity of the church, arguing that there must be possibilities
for greater adaptation to non-Christian cultures than the
present *schema* makes possible.

Archbishop Baudoux of Canada amplified Abbot Butler's
point made yesterday. It is not enough, he insisted, to speak
of non-Catholic Christians only as individuals. There are, in
fact, Christian communions which proclaim the Word of God
and have at least some of the Sacraments. It is the communions themselves that bring salvation to their members. The
Catholic Church should acknowledge this openly and freely.
Furthermore, since it is the sin of the Catholic Church that
has led many away from it, there should be more open acknowledgment of this side of the church's reality. Baldasarri
of Italy also stressed that those who are baptized are already,
in some sense, in the church; they love Scripture, tradition,
and many other things that Catholics love, and the Catholic
Church must be more forthright in confessing its share of
responsibility for the ills that have divided Christians from
one another.

*   *   *

Most of the speeches on Chapter One, then, have supported its main concerns, urging only that it go further in
certain directions. But Chapter Two, dealing with the

hierarchy, is not going to get such amiable treatment. The first three interventions, all by cardinals, were critical especially at one point. This concerns a kind of sleeper clause which, in urging the restoration of the permanent diaconate to fulfill certain functions that now cannot be performed by laymen, suggests that where appropriate the deacons could be married.

Cardinal Spellman of New York led off on this one. He objected very much to the diaconate, whether married or not. The diaconate became obsolete and there is no reason to revive it. It became obsolete because there was need for priests who could perform *all* sacerdotal functions and not just some. What the church needs today is more priests, not more deacons. Reviving the diaconate will not swell the depleted ranks of the priesthood.

Cardinal Ruffini, content to leave the diaconate to Spellman, save for an assertion that celibacy must not be taken away from the deacons, went on to attack the chapter on many other grounds. There is absolutely *no* evidence of collegiality in the New Testament. The church is *not* founded on Peter and the other apostles, as Alfrink says, but solely on Peter. Christ did *not* give power to an episcopal college but to Peter alone. The pope does *not* need a college of bishops when he is representing Christ. To be sure, he can consult with experts if he wishes before making an infallible pronouncement, but his infallibility is not in the least infringed if he fails to do this, or even if he defines something imprudently.

Cardinal Bacci of the Curia took up the cudgels next, expressing a particular horror of a married diaconate. Unless they are forbidden to marry, deacons will marry; if they marry, the church will have to support their families, seminary education will become more complicated, and vocations to the priesthood will diminish. The section on the married diaconate is thus the thin edge of the wedge against clerical celibacy.

After these vigorous perorations urging the church not to

move forward, I made my way to the coffee bar. On previous mornings it has been so crowded that conversation has been almost impossible. I have now discovered that after elbowing one's way into the crowd, either to the Coke machine or the coffee counter, one then goes out to the Chapel of the Blessed Sacrament (from which the consecrated host has been removed) where he can engage in leisurely and informative conversation. One Italian bishop told me this morning that he couldn't understand the furor against the diaconate. After all, Stephen had been a deacon, and since he had become a saint, perhaps the diaconate wasn't a bad idea after all. I also discovered from a lot of the *periti* circulating around the bar that the initial blasts against the diaconate will be countered when the missionary bishops get the chance to speak. To them the married diaconate is a sheer necessity for ecclesiastical survival.

This morning I also met one of the many men reputed to be "Xavier Rynne." He blandly denies all identification with the mysterious *New Yorker* author who gave such phenomenal coverage to the first session of the Council. Since it is clear that "Xavier Rynne" is a composite of several men who pool their information, any priest can in good conscience, say quite honestly, "I am not Xavier Rynne." When I pointed out that those who deny a share in the Xavier Rynne plot usually say in print, "I cannot *claim* to be Xavier Rynne," he responded, "Ah, you're beginning to think like a Catholic!" I have had helpful *entré* into various groups this week because of a tongue-in-cheek article I wrote for *The Christian Century*, establishing that Xavier Rynne is really Phyllis McGinley. I had no idea *The Christian Century* was so widely read in Catholic circles, but at all events the article has been a great help in making new acquaintances. Indeed, the purported facsimile of Xavier Rynne whom I met this morning (wild horses wouldn't drag the name from me), greeted me with the words, "Ah yes, you're Phyllis McGinley."

I returned from various other exhilarating exchanges to hear the last speaker of the morning pointing out that dangerous ideas were afoot in the church, with which the Council must deal. Heresy is rampant and must be condemned. Reference was made, as the press release later put it, to "unspecified volumes which have appeared with ecclesiastical approbation and which have been found to contain error. Steps must be taken to counteract the influence of such books lest the impression be given that the church is tolerating error or becoming less exacting in matters of doctrine." The actual speech was more pointed: the books contain a repetition of "Protestant errors" and therefore are particularly dangerous.

On this ecumenical note we concluded the morning and adjourned for the weekend.

* * *

The press panel today was particularly good. One of the Biblical scholars on the panel gave a clear account of the New Testament basis for collegiality, pointing out that he had prepared his remarks before Cardinal Ruffini had informed the Catholic world that no such basis existed. But this claim did not deter the presentation. Indeed, it gave it extra vigor.

Sunday, October 6

I have spent the entire weekend recovering from the cumulative effects of my first week of Italian food.

The Second Week
(*October 7 – 13*)

"Collegiality:" crucial concept of conciliar concern – married deacons?? – pope and Council – lay communicants

Monday, October 7

Collegiality and the married diaconate got pretty rough treatment on Friday. But the progressive forces were out in vigor this morning, and as soon as the names of the cardinals were announced it was clear that rich fare was in store. After Cardinal Siri, who would probably find both collegiality and the married diaconate uncongenial, the lineup went: Leger, Koenig, Doepfner, Meyer, Alfrink, Lefevre, and Rugambwa. These are all strong names, any of whom could be expected to defend both notions. The words "heavy artillery" were murmured by some of the Catholics in the tribune with us.

However, Cardinal Siri, whose location at the cardinal-presidents' desk is next to Ruffini both geographically and theologically, didn't take as extreme a position as Ruffini had done on Friday. Where Ruffini had denied any Biblical basis for collegiality, Siri acknowledged that there has always been a college of bishops, but insisted that it must be so structured that the college is absolutely dependent on the pope. With explicit safeguards, making clear that papal primacy is not jeopardized, a notion of collegiality might be admissible.

The interesting thing about this speech is that it indicates a decision to discuss *within* the notion of collegiality rather than to deny that such a notion is valid at all. If this stance is accepted by other conservative bishops, it means that Chapter Two should receive approval, and that the notion of collegiality, however it is defined, should find *some* place in the future thinking of the church.

Cardinal Leger, archbishop of Montreal, is one of the most impressive members of the cardinalate. He has been a missionary, a staunch opponent of barren theologizing, and in recent years an equally strong proponent of ecumenism. It was Leger who delivered the memorable address to the members of the World Council in their meetings last summer at Montreal. While acknowledging that episcopacy is decisive for an understanding of the church, he went on to say that an old truth is always open to newer and deeper understanding. Collegiality is not a denial of papal primacy but complementary to it. Bishops must be characterized not by the desire to grasp power but to serve. The *schema* should underline this point by limiting the adornments and titles a bishop may have. To retain these today is an anachronism, harking back to the days when bishops were also secular princes.

Cardinal Koenig of Vienna is another ecumenically minded cardinal who has been active in the Secretariat for Christian Unity. He stressed the fact that the doctrine of the power of pope *and bishops* is no new doctrine at all, and in no ways denies the privileges of the pope. To argue against collegiality is really to argue against councils! To insist that the church is founded on Peter *and* the other apostles is merely to be underlining what the pope said in his opening allocution.

Cardinal Doepfner countered the repudiations that had been offered of the diaconate, pointing out that even the Council of Trent had affirmed its sacramentality. The restoration of the diaconate is needed in many areas of the world. It is forced on no one, but is merely offered to those bishops for whom it will be helpful. It in no way prejudices the issue of clerical celibacy.

Cardinals Meyer, Alfrink, and Lefevre all stressed that

Christ gave power not only to Peter but to the other apostles as well, and Rugambwa added that the bishop does not only rule in his diocese, but, through the college of bishops, has responsibility with the pope for the church everywhere.

His Beatitude Maximos IV Saigh, the patriarch of Jerusalem, joined with considerable enthusiasm in this chorus. Vatican I's teaching on the authority of the pope has been misunderstood, and must be completed by relating the doctrine of the pope's primacy to the doctrine of collegiality. The real head of the church is Christ. Peter, as one of the twelve apostles, was the head of the apostolic college, but the position of privilege given to Peter and his successor (the pope) does not destroy the position of authority given to the apostles and their successors (the bishops).

I wrote last week that all of the business of the Council was conducted in Latin. I reckoned without Maximos. He refuses to speak Latin, which is not the language of the Eastern church, but only of the Western church. Last year he offered to speak in Aramaic, which was the language Christ spoke, but he feared the fathers would not understand him. So defying the rules — and getting away with it — he speaks in French. After he finished this morning, the speech was translated into Latin. During this interval I headed for the coffee bar. So did about 1100 other people. The bar is small, and few bishops are advocates of girth control.

❋ ❋ ❋

The role of the patriarchs, such as Maximos, is a difficult one for Western non-Catholics to understand. In the early church there were a number of centers of great importance, known as the patriarchal sees. In each see certain rites, patterns, and ecclesiastical laws developed, often in considerable independence of one another. Each see had a patriarch, and many of them viewed the pope as simply the patriarch of the Western church, ruling from the Roman See. In the schism of A.D. 1054, a good many of the sees retained their own autonomy — these we now know as the Orthodox churches — but some stayed in communion with Rome, or, after a period of independence, returned to communion with Rome, acknowledging the pope as, so to speak, the chief patriarch, but still retaining their own customs, rites, canonical law, and so forth. It is these groups that are headed by the patriarchs, and it is their liturgies that are being referred to when mention is made of "Eastern rites" liturgies. Mass before the Council each morning will frequently be celebrated according to one of the liturgies of the Eastern rites.

*   *   *

I returned in time to hear Bishop DeSmedt of Bruges, another ecumenically minded bishop, make a strong case for collegiality, understood as the bishops gathered together with the pope to enrich the life of the church. The more the pope is helped by the bishops the more he can fulfill his own function and mission. In the modern world it is quite possible to gather the bishops together. Indeed, with the help of modern transportation, pope and bishops can maintain close contact with one another in a way that has not been possible in the church since Pentecost.

Bishop Beck of Britain, dealing with a slightly different problem, opened up some ecumenical doors by suggesting that a true understanding of priesthood should start with the priesthood of Christ; this should be the basis from which to talk about the priesthood of the laity. All attempts to understand the various levels of human priesthood must start from this point.

Bishop van Dodenwaard, speaking for the Dutch hierarchy, clarified a point that is always getting muddled in the discussion. He pointed up the fallacy of differentiating too much between bishops and pope, or between pope and Council. The bishops and the pope actually exercise their power together. The pope, when he acts, acts in the name of all the bishops of whose college he is head; the bishops, when they act, do so only in conjunction with the pope, who is their head.

* * *

After the session, Msgr. Francis Davis, one of the translators in our tribune, took several of us to lunch at the English College, where the British hierarchy is staying. This was my first contact with a sizable number of bishops, and it was good to discover that they are human beings like everyone else, particularly when they get rid of the finery they wear to the Council sessions. A visit to the English College also gives one a new picture of the hostilities of the Reformation. We think of Catholics oppressing Protestants, but there were long periods in England when the shoe was very much on the other foot. Since Roman Catholic theological education was forbidden in England, priests came to Rome for their training, and would gather in the chapel to sing the *Te Deum* each time word came from England that another of their number had been martyred by the non-Catholics.

Tuesday, October 8

Mass is always an education for the observers. Today it was an education for the Council fathers as well. It is the custom to have mass about once a week according to one of the Eastern rites that I mentioned yesterday, and today it was celebrated according to the Syro-Antiochene rite. Nothing could do more to explode the myth that Rome is everywhere one and the same than such services. One of the Council fathers had to explain each step in Latin, since the rite was celebrated in Aramaic to the accompaniment of quavering oriental music. The bread and wine were brought in by laymen who also received communion — the first time this session anyone but the celebrant has received.

We were introduced to a new Council procedure this morning, simultaneous voting and discussing. The Liturgical Commission has returned a revised text of Chapter Two of *De Sacra Liturgia,* with emendations growing out of suggestions by the fathers. These emendations, nineteen of them, are voted on one at a time while discussion continues on *De Ecclesia.* After every speech or two Felici announces a vote on the next emendation. Votes are recorded, the cards are fed into the computors, and pretty soon the results are known.

The process sounds more complicated than it actually is, and makes efficient use of time, since the bishops receive a pamphlet explaining the changes several days before the vote is called for, and have plenty of time to make up their minds.

* * *

The strong support given yesterday both to collegiality and the diaconate has carried over to this morning, so that in spite of a couple of "anti-" speeches, the general atmosphere remains favorable.

Cardinal Gracias reminded the fathers of some of the implications of collegiality. Since the last two days had clearly established the principle of collegiality, to speak more about that would be (and once again a booming English phrase) "slaying a dead horse." But if the bishops really share rule in the church, then they must be concerned for *all* of the church, and those with means and resources must help those without.

The diaconate also received attention. A spokesman for a large number of South American bishops stressed the importance of restoring the permanent diaconate where it can be useful. Even though other areas of the church do not wish to restore it, the missionary areas cannot really survive without it. Cardinal Suenens, one of the four cardinal-moderators, close friend of Pope Paul and an acknowledged leader of the progressive forces, also emphasized that those who do not need the diaconate need not restore it, but that it would be useful in the overcrowded urban areas which suffer from a shortage of priests. Like others who support the restoration of the diaconate, Suenens took strong issue with the notion that vocations to the priesthood would drop if the diaconate were restored.

When the discussion shifted back to collegiality, both Bishop Heuschen and Bishop Charue argued that the church is founded on Peter *and the apostles*, and both gave extensive documentation from the New Testament and the early fathers to support the claim. Such speeches as these emphasize that collegiality is not "new," but is merely a part of the total faith of the church that is now ready for more precise definition.

Opposition to collegiality has not, however, disappeared. Gori, the Latin patriarch of Jerusalem, was worried that the idea would lead to excessive local autonomy and a disregarding of the voice of higher authority, while Archbishop Staffa of Italy gave a straight "Vatican I" papalism talk: all power belongs to the pope and to him alone. He exercises it quite apart from the other bishops. He can consult with them if he chooses, but the power of decision is solely his.

*   *   *

No one attending our observer's "briefing session" this afternoon could have felt that anyone was wearing kid gloves. *De Ecclesia* was subjected to considerable criticism, much of it searching, only a little of it carping.

Some went so far as to deny the ecumenical importance of the document, since it is dealing only with an internal Roman Catholic problem posed by the Vatican I assertion that the pope has supreme power, and that when he defines a matter of faith and morals he does so quite apart from the consent of the rest of the church. Ruffini, Siri, Staffa, and company say that this is the end of the matter. The other voices in the Council want to relate the supreme power of the pope to that of the other bishops, who share rule with the pope by virtue of the fact that all are members of the episcopal college.

Just how this adjustment is to be made is not easy for the

non-Roman Catholic to see. I agree that the problem is *immediately* a Roman Catholic problem, for Catholics must work out the manner of stating their own conviction, but I do not agree that it is *exclusively* a Roman Catholic problem, for the ecumenical overtones are immense. Only as some principle of collegiality is established is there a way beyond the extreme papalism that cuts Roman Catholicism off from the rest of Christendom. As I hear the speeches pro and con, and note that the forces favoring collegiality seem very much in the ascendancy, I sometimes have the feeling that we are witnessing the beginnings of a revolution of incalculable magnitude — a revolution that slowly and quietly will transform the whole face and structure of the Catholic Church. If the bishops are given more power, this means that more and more decisions will come up *to* Rome for ratification, rather than emanating down *from* Rome.

On the other hand, a victory for the forces of collegiality may not necessarily be an overwhelming one. The shadow of Vatican I looms large over every speech, whether by progressive or conservative. Conservatives defend it to the hilt, while progressives insist that belief in collegiality *in no way* challenges the definition of papal authority. I cannot escape the feeling that the Catholic Church is — and I don't mean this invidiously — "stuck" with Vatican I, since it is an irreformable definition, and that it must find ways to *amplify* an apparently constricting definition without in any way denying it. This is a very delicate task.

We cannot expect this Council to give us the moon. Indeed, one Council can probably do little more than get off the launching pad. But that is certainly preferable to remaining inert.

Wednesday, October 9

The debate today featured new voices repeating familiar arguments, and it is clear that the issues have been joined already. So important are the issues, however, that I can understand the reluctance of the cardinal-moderators to cut off debate prematurely. The only interruption to the flow of oratory was the frequent interspersing of votes on emendations to the liturgy *schema*, all of which continue to pass by overwhelming margins.

The first intervention, however, by Cardinal Lienart of Lille, another of the "venerable fathers" who is venerable in years but young in spirit and outlook, provided a handy summary of the outlook of the pro-collegiality group. This group — and Lienart spoke for sixty-three of them — sees no conflict between the supreme power of the pope and the supreme power of the collegiality of bishops. These are two ways of talking about the same thing. Lienart ranged over the experience of the early church to indicate that the power of Peter and the power of the twelve were not in opposition. Christ chose twelve, not one, and He did this after a night of prayer. Peter addressed the apostles as brothers, not servants. All of them, not just Peter, received their commissions from Christ. Together they chose the deacons. The foundation of the church, then, is Christ, and Christ manifests Himself through Peter *and* the other apostles.

There was, however, one new emphasis in the morning's discussion. Bishop Conway of Galway called attention to the *schema's* inattention to the priests: there are nine pages on the bishops, seven pages on the laity, and less than half a page on the priests. Surely they deserve at least a chapter! A Spanish bishop went so far as to suggest that collegiality should be extended to include the priests as well.

I have a distinct feeling that the latter sentiment is an appropriate one, but I have an even more distinct feeling that it is being voiced about fifty years too soon. A proposal to extend collegiality to include the laity is probably about a century away. I will not be surprised if these emphases are voiced in the future, and it is probably just this that the opponents of collegiality fear. There is, after all, the story of the camel's nose. . . .

We had interventions on the diaconate as well. It is clear that no matter how strong may be the feeling for a permanent diaconate, a large group of the fathers will draw the line at married deacons, for fear of its effect on a celibate priesthood. There is, after all, the story of the camel's nose. . . .

Another story is also going the rounds. If both collegiality and the married diaconate are approved, the new situation in the church will be as follows: the bishops will have all the power, the priests will have all the work, and the deacons will have all the fun.

*   *   *

This afternoon the English-speaking observers met with *periti* from the Secretariat for Christian Unity. In these smaller language groups there can be better give and take than when fifty or sixty are gathered together amid a profusion of tongues. Today, with Frs. Weigel, Baum, Stransky, Bevenot, and Davis on hand, we had an average of one third of a *peritus* apiece, which is batting extremely well in any ecumenical league.

The main area of discussion was the relationship of collegiality to papal infallibility. We tend to see the problem in terms of the relationship between the power of the Council and the power of the pope. As I try to pull together a lot of discussion on this matter, both this afternoon and on other occasions, I find a number of considerations emerging, and will set them down here, even at the risk of some repetition. For one thing, the pope himself must call a Council of Roman Catholic bishops, and in this sense it is *his* Council, since the bishops cannot meet unless he directs them to do so. Indeed, if a pope dies while a Council is in session, the Council cannot be resumed unless and until a new pope reconvenes it. Thus if Pope Paul had not announced a second session of Vatican II, that would simply have been the end of the matter. For another thing, the decisions made in a Council by the bishops do not become an official part of Catholic teaching unless and until they have been formally approved by the pope. Thus, technically, all the decisions the bishops are now making could be lost and forgotten if the pope chose not to promulgate the *schemata* they pass.

Does this not suggest, therefore, that a Council does not really "mean" anything, and that the real power in the Catholic Church is vested purely and simply and exclusively in the pope himself, regardless of Councils? To put the question this way is, I am discovering, a "Protestant" way of putting the question, and not the best way to come to an understanding of the Catholic answer. There is, however, some excuse for Protestants putting the question this way, since the decrees of Vatican Council I in 1870 appeared to give exclusive and total power to the pope, quite apart from any consensus in the rest of the church. Protestants had thought, indeed, after Vatican I, that there would never be another Council, since that Council had seemed to invest the pope with power to make all decisions unilaterally.

Vatican II now being in session, however, perhaps the prime theological issue with which it must wrestle is an attempt to define how the power of the pope, the bishop of Rome, is to be related to the power of the other bishops. In facing this problem Catholics now freely admit that the Vatican I decree, seeming to leave all power in the pope's hands, was "one-sided." That Council had, in fact, intended to go on and deal with the power of the bishops in the church. But for various reasons, Vatican Council I never completed its agenda, with the result that since then there has been a *partial* teaching in Catholic theology, a teaching that states the supreme power of the Roman pontiff, but does not state how that power is related to the power of the other bishops who also, in some way or other, bear rule in the church.

The extreme papalists, of course, would like to leave it that way. But, as we have seen this week, there is growing sentiment in the Council to define the "collegiality" of the bishops, to insist that Christ left power not only to Peter, but *to the other apostles as well,* so that just as Peter and the other apostles shared in the governing of the church, so today (according to Catholic teaching) their successors, pope and bishops, share in the governing of the church.

It would be premature to suggest just how the relationship of pope to bishops will be stated, since the matter is still under discussion. But Pope Paul himself set the tone for a new direction in his opening allocution. Speaking to the name and memory of his predecessor, Pope Paul said, "You have gathered the broken thread of the First Vatican Council, and by that very fact you have banished the fear wrongly deduced from that Council, as if the supreme powers conferred by Christ on the Roman Pontiff to govern and vivify the Church, were sufficient, without the assistance of the Ecumenical Councils." That is about as forthright a statement as one could find of the belief that the papacy of the future is not to act unilaterally, but in conjunction with the bishops assembled in Council.

Protestants must avoid looking at the matter simply in terms of two power *blocs* vying with one another. Catholics believe that pope and bishops together represent the voice of the church, and they further believe it to be inconceivable that the Holy Spirit would permit the two to be in conflict with one another. Perhaps the matter could be stated this way: when the *bishops* speak, they speak in concert with the bishop of Rome, the pope, who is one of their number, albeit pre-eminent among them. When the *pope* speaks, he speaks the mind of the whole church, the governance of which has been assigned pre-eminently to himself but also to the other bishops as well. Each speaks for both and there is therefore only one voice.

Thursday, October 10

Handy summary of today's discussion:

Some bishops favor collegiality; some do not.

Some bishops favor restoration of the diaconate; some do not.

Some bishops desire a married diaconate; some do not.

Of course issues are never quite that simple, particularly in an ecumenical Council, and even this late in the discussion new notes continue to creep in. One such note was provided by Bishop Schick of Germany. He strongly urged more attention to the local church, which receives too little attention in discussions of the universal church. Such attention is basic for the cure of souls in our time. Bishops cannot begin to do all they should for the cure of souls, and the task devolves on the priest in the local parish. The New Testament, after all, uses the term *ecclesia* not simply as a broad concept but as a descriptive term for the concrete, specific, local unit gathered together in somebody's house. The whole church is somehow present there.

How much a speech like this disturbs our stereotypes of Roman Catholicism as concerned mainly with structure, hierarchy, power, and pomp! Here is a bishop turning not to theological manuals to find out what the church is, but going back to the New Testament, and discovering there a note that is being overlooked in all the conciliar debate. What more can we ask in principle from the Catholic Church than that it engage in just this kind of investigation, an investigation in which we must be willing to join since it draws us both to the common source we share despite our differences, namely the Holy Scriptures?

Archbishop Yago, speaking for forty African bishops, made a fervent plea for the married diaconate. The voice of Africa must be heard, he said, because Africa has particular need of the married diaconate. Otherwise the church will not have the resources to engage in its proper task of ministry. The diaconate was needed in the primitive church, and this is precisely why it is needed in the African church, which mirrors the New Testament situation of a small minority group struggling in a culture that is profoundly un-Christian. Bishop Maurer of Bolivia, speaking for over fifty South American bishops, made the same point.

To hear these fervent pleas from missionary areas is to realize the high degree of parochialism contained in speeches that argue in effect, "We don't need the diaconate where *we* are, so let's not restore it at all." To this the missionary bishops must reply, "All right, perhaps you don't need it, but *we do.*"

The entire discussion dramatizes the impact the missionary bishops are having on the life of the church, which parallels in an interesting way the impact that representatives of the "younger churches" of Asia and Africa have had on the European and American groups in the World Council of Churches. And it is always hard for the old centers of power — whether in Rome, Geneva, or Canterbury — to realize that the creative voices are coming from elsewhere.

*   *   *

When so much of the speaking is repetitious, I discover that I learn at least as much in the coffee bar as in the tribune. In Bar-jonah I can ask a *peritus* his views on the relationship of papal and conciliar authority, discuss "religion in the university" with a Midwestern bishop, and even get a line on who polished up the Latin for Bishop So-and-So's intervention. As I was inching my way toward the Coke machine this morning I was surprised to have a hand reach out and offer me a full glass. This gesture led to an acquaintance with Bishop Arcilla of the Philippines, who is a very charming person — all five feet of him. He told me that when the Philippine bishops had their audience with the pope he was almost lost in the shuffle until the pope called him up to the front with the salutation: "*Episcopo bambino!*"

In all of the overcrowded conditions of the bar, there is at least one consolation: this is the only place in Rome where one can be in a dense mob without worrying about pickpockets.

Friday, October 11

The Roman Catholic laymen at the Council are called "auditors." This means that they hear, but do not speak, and that their presence is more a *symbol* of the church's new concern for the laity than an actual working expression of it. Nevertheless, there are more ways to "speak" than simply by making sounds, and the lay auditors "spoke" this morning through what they did. Four of them, at their own request, came forward to receive communion during mass. It has been a strange phenomenon for the observers that (save for the one morning with the Syro-Antiochene rite) nobody has received communion at mass except the celebrant, when communion is, both etymologically and theologically, supposed to be an act of sharing. Nothing could be more appropriate as the fathers continue to approve emendations to the liturgy *schema,* many of which establish more active participation of the faithful in the sacraments, than a demonstration of the corporate nature of the liturgy. So the fathers have already learned something from the "silent" auditors, and it is an indication of ecclesiastical health not only that the request came, but also that it was granted.

*   *   *

Cardinal Lercaro announced that, because of the importance of the topic, there would be no premature closing of debate. But in view of the fact that twenty-eight speakers were announced he requested the fathers not to repeat and reminded them that it was sufficient to state one's agreement with a previous speaker. When this plea brought forth hearty applause, Cardinal Lercaro had to remind the fathers that the Council rules forbid applause – a rule that was broken twice before the morning was over, but in each case with the moderator's tacit approval.

Both outbursts were interesting. One occurred when Archbishop Slipyj, a metropolitan of the Ukraine, was announced to speak. As a result of lengthy negotiations, Slipyj has just been released after serving *seventeen years* in a Siberian prison for his religious convictions, and it would have been a heartless man who tried to stop applause for him. The other outburst came at the very end of the morning after the intervention of Bishop Bettazzi, who was consecrated only four days ago, and who made a speech noteworthy for the fact that it was by an Italian and yet did not represent an extreme papalist line. The performance was even more astonishing for the fluency of its rapid-fire Latin. I'm sure Bettazzi got at least twenty minutes' worth into his allotted ten, although Lercaro may have given him a minute or two of grace. I'm not quite sure whether the fathers were applauding (a) his delivery, (b) his content, (c) his recent consecration, or (d) the fact that they had just heard their last Latin speech for the next sixty-nine hours.

The Third Week
(*October 14 – 20*)

The patriarchal relocation – cloture – the "four questions" – sin in the church? – the laity, con and pro – the papal audience – an evening of open discussion – the bishops and Bach

Monday, October 14

The Catholic Church does some things quietly and some things ostentatiously. The things that are done quietly are frequently more important than the things that are done ostentatiously, and I have been in Rome just long enough now to have discovered that a symbolic action can be of the highest significance. We have just gotten a good example of this.

When we came into the *aula* this morning we discovered that over the weekend a very important symbolic change had been effected in the seating arrangements. There are clear seating priorities in the Council which reflect relative importance within the church at large. They go: moderators, presidents, cardinals, patriarchs, and bishops. For centuries the patriarchs have argued that their precedence should be above that of the cardinals, since the patriarchs represent the ancient sees of the early church, such as Antioch, Jerusalem, and Alexandria, whereas the cardinals are merely recent papal appointees whose main concern is with the affairs of the Western church.

Today, at last, the complaint of the patriarchs was answered. No longer do they sit "below" the cardinals. A special seating area has been built for them directly opposite the cardinals, so that they are at least on an equal with the cardinals. If one wants to put a fine point on it (which one can always do with symbols), one can argue that the patriarchs are now nearer than anyone else in the entire *aula* to the statue of St. Peter, who symbolizes the power and rule in the church that the patriarchs claim to share.

Although I find it hard to see why ecclesiastics should be so concerned about matters of rank and privilege, I also see that for the patriarchs a *principle* is at stake, and an ecumenical principle at that. And the pope's gesture in changing the seating arrangement is an important symbol of the fact that the one, holy, catholic, and apostolic church is not just or even primarily the Latin wing of it (which the cardinals tend to represent), but the Eastern churches as well (which the patriarchs very definitely represent). The gesture, then, is one that emphasizes greater catholicity and de-emphasizes Western ecclesiastical imperialism.

⁂   ⁂   ⁂

The first order of business this week was a vote on the revised Chapter Two of *De Sacra Liturgia*. Rather surprisingly, it did not get the necessary two-thirds majority due to the fact that 781 *placet juxta modum* votes were recorded. The word around the coffee bar was that many of these came from bishops who want even more use of the vernacular than the present *schema* allows. Presumably further revisions in this direction will be offered later.

The interventions again centered on Chapter Two of *De Ecclesia*. Many more things were said about collegiality and the diaconate but they were not particularly new. Two cardinals, however, Frings of Cologne and Ritter of St. Louis, helped to clarify what the discussion is really about. Frings said that arguments against collegiality on grounds that it is not developed in ancient texts would be devastating if applied to papal primacy or Mariological dogmas since the latter are not found there either. The practice is clear from earliest times even if a juridical concept supporting the practice grows slowly. Ritter's point was that discussion should focus on the *doctrinal* understanding of collegiality and the diaconate, and that *practical* problems could be discussed later. Whether or not the presence of married deacons would diminish vocations to the priesthood is not germane at present.

The next speaker was Archbishop Parente, an opponent of collegiality, married deacons, modern Catholic theologians, and all things contemporary. No sooner had he begun than the loudspeaker in the observers' tribune went dead and we missed a strong attack on collegiality. Even if members of the Secretariat for Christian Unity had been cutting the wires, they would have been hard put to keep us "protected" this morning, since there were at least four other interventions along the same line: no diaconate except under exceptional circumstances; no married diaconate under any circumstances; no collegiality if it suggests in any way any diminution of any powers of any pope.

Bishop Kemerer of the Argentine, however, gave an impressive and impassioned plea for the restoration of the diaconate, since in missionary situations deacons are an absolute necessity for the survival of the church. He closed with a ringing plea: People are perishing for want of the bread of life. We cannot give it to them without the help of deacons. Don't take away the hope for their restoration. The *schema* opens the door for that restoration. You need not go in the door if you don't wish to. But don't shut the door on us for whom the diaconate is a desperate necessity. We want to go in!

This sincerity and passion of this plea brought forth a rousing burst of applause — the most encouraging moment in a discouraging morning.

Tuesday, October 15

In introducing the third chapter of the liturgy *schema* Archbishop Hallinan of Atlanta called attention to a couple of important emendations. One of these extends the use of the vernacular in the rest of the sacraments, and the other suggests that the sacrament known as extreme unction can "also and better" be known as "the annointing of the sick." This change is suggested to make clear that it is available as a resource during illness, and also to circumvent the notion that it must be postponed until the moment of death. Both changes were overwhelmingly approved.

Back, then, to more of the same on collegiality and deacons. Cardinal Siri gave the speech we have already heard so often stressing the absolute and exclusive power of the pope. Vatican I must not be touched. His Beatitude Paul Meouchi of Antioch gave the speech we have already heard so often stressing the sharing of power between pope and bishops. Vatican I must be completed.

After hearing both speeches a couple of times more, I went adventuring to Barrabas, the other coffee bar. It is much larger, but I really missed all the friendly jostling and the familiar faces of Bar-jonah. I did run into Père Congar and discovered that, whatever we may disagree about, we agree completely in our assessment of the past two days — too much repetition.

I do not think we should claim credit for what happened next, but when we returned to the *aula* and heard the speaker proposing the arresting notion that if deacons married this might lead to priests wanting to marry, it was reassuring to hear Cardinal Suenens, moderator for the day, announce that if all those still wishing to speak were given the opportunity, the debate on Chapter Two would take at least three more days to finish. *Would* the fathers entertain a motion to close debate? The question was no sooner put than the *aula* was filled with the sound of clapping hands, "like the rush of a mighty wind," which in an earlier situation indicated the descent of the Holy Spirit. When the question was put, the entire assembly was on its feet with one motion. Never has unanimity among the fathers been so great. Never has collegiality been more manifest.

❊   ❊   ❊

Suenens then announced that tomorrow the moderators would present four questions to the fathers on which they would take a preliminary, though not binding, vote, in an attempt to sum up Council sentiment on Chapter Two, where there have been such strong differences of opinion. The idea behind this, he went on, was to ease the work of the Theological Commission which must revise the *schema* in accordance with the will of the fathers.

Since we have heard from only a fraction of the members of the Council, but have had all possible viewpoints expressed, this procedure sounds like a good way of determining Council sentiment. I also have a slightly Machiavellian reaction to the proposal, which goes like this: Suppose the vote should indicate a strong preference for, say, a doctrine of collegiality; in this case, the Theological Commission could hardly revise the *schema* in a way which would not reflect that fact, even though it is well known that neither the chairman nor vice-chairman (Ottaviani and Browne) believe in collegiality. This is not a matter of "forcing" the commission's hand so much as instructing it. For the commission does not exist to transmit its own view of doctrine, but simply to summarize the doctrine of the Council as a whole. A vote such as Suenens has proposed should therefore help to speed the process of revision in line with the convictions of the majority.

It becomes clearer and clearer that the Theological Commission is crucial to the Council's success. Ottaviani and Browne represent a position that was defeated in almost every vote last year. Although they do not have anything like a majority within the commission, they do have control over how often it meets, what is on its agenda, and so forth. They can prolong debate on theological differences within the commission, even though the mind of the fathers as a whole may be quite clear. Even a united commission would have difficulty writing Chapter Two in more explicit "collegial" terms without seeming to undo the papalist orientation of Vatican

I. What will happen under the present circumstances is something I'm glad I don't have to predict.

But, in light of the decision to close discussion on Chapter Two, at least I can predict that there is now going to be fresh debate in the *aula*.

*　　*　　*

Our "briefing session" this afternoon covered a lot of territory. The main emphasis behind many of the observers' comments was a feeling that *De Ecclesia* does not yet come to grips with the reality of sin in the church. The church it describes is not the church as it actually is, but only the church as it ought to be. The *schema* starts with the mystery of the church, but the deepest mystery of all, as Professor Skydsgaard put it, is the mystery of the forgiveness of sin. And sin must be acknowledged before it can be forgiven. The great mystery — and the great hope — is that Christ dwells in the midst of a sinful people. As another observer put it, the *schema* must not hide the fact that God works *through* the imperfections of man.

I think this discussion points to one of the traditional differences between the Catholic and the Protestant. The Catholic can say, "The church is a community of sinners," but he draws back from saying, as the Protestant must say, "The church is a sinful community." To the Catholic it is abhorrent to say that the church, as the body of Christ, is sinful, for this is like calling Christ a sinner. But to the Protestant it is abhorrent to assert that a human institution is sinless, for this identifies it too unambiguously with the sinlessness of Christ. If the Protestant can assert the sinlessness only as an unrealized possibility, the Catholic can and frequently does claim that the possibility has already been realized. This is why we are encouraged by reminders on the Council floor that the church is a pilgrim people that has not yet "arrived" and that must confess its sin — for these suggest a dimension of Catholicism that is moving beyond "triumphalism" and uncritical self-adulation.

Commenting on the forthcoming discussion of the place of Mary, I suggested that the ecumenical dialogue would be helped if Mary were included within the *schema* on the church, and hindered if a separate *schema* gave encouragement to continued independent development of Marian doctrine. I suggested that a chapter in *De Ecclesia* ought to be both brief and Biblical: *Brief*, to keep a sense of proportion, and because the main Marian doctrines have been thoroughly stated in recent times, and *Biblical* in order that we might have a common ground on which to open up the Marian question once again.

*   *   *

A reception given by the American hierarchy for the Council fathers and the observers followed our "briefing session." To comment on it can only sound like name-dropping, but thanks to Fr. Quinn of the Paulists I was able to chat briefly with Bishop Wright of Pittsburgh, Cardinal Gracias, Cardinal Koenig, and Cardinal Lercaro. I told the latter how much use we had made in America of his pamphlet on *Religious Liberty,* since it was one of the few unequivocal statements by a member of the hierarchy, but I had the uneasy feeling afterward that, in spite of his gracious smile, he doesn't understand a word of English.

Wednesday, October 16

Mass today was according to the Coptic-Alexandrian rite. Most of it was in the vernacular, both Coptic and Arabic, with music chanted by a special choir. The music was accompanied by a pair of cymbals struck in such a way as to establish an oriental rhythm that was almost hypnotic.

Cardinal Agagianian announced that, although cloture had been voted yesterday, a number of fathers had appealed to the ruling allowing them to speak beyond cloture if they have obtained the approval of five bishops. Presumably because we had reverted to Chapter Two, there was no further mention of the "four questions" Cardinal Suenens had promised for today.

Most of the interventions were simply rehashes of old, familiar material, but two were unusual enough to deserve mention. Bishop Ammann of Germany exploded something of a bombshell when he attacked the whole system of papal nuncios and political representatives from the Vatican. Such political representation, if it needs to be done at all, can be done just as well by laymen. To use bishops in this capacity is to imply that the church is trying to regain secular power.

The other bombshell was ignited by Archbishop Zoghby, a Melchite from Egypt, who minced no words. The *schema*, he said, is far too unilateral; it makes so much of papal primacy that little place is left for the bishops, while the patriarchs are practically ignored. The powers of the bishops must be increased rather than restricted. The church is founded on Christ rather than Peter, but the authors of the *schema* seem to have an obsession with Peter. Unless more attention is given to the patriarchs, and to the significance of the local church, it will never be possible to enter into significant dialogue with the Orthodox Churches.

I wonder how much impact such a speech will have. Zoghby is right, as far as the Orthodox are concerned, and he is also right as far as the rest of us are concerned. Extreme papalism *is* the point at which our relationship with Catholicism is most difficult, and any moves that acknowledge patriarchs, bishops, presbyters, and local congregations are moves that help rather than hinder.

*   *   *

The discussion finally moved on to Chapter Three, which deals with the laity. Here is an area of particular interest to Protestants as well as Catholics, for both groups have been engaging in independent reassessment of the place of the laity within the church. If fresh thinking is to come out of Vatican II, here is one place that is absolutely bursting with possibilities.

The first speaker, predictably, was Cardinal Ruffini, and he was, predictably, dead set against giving the laity more power in the church. Ruffini is a powerful speaker and he never bluffs — one knows exactly where he stands. His presentation was well organized, well presented, and hopelessly out of date. He acknowledged that the laity exist, but he did not acknowledge that they have any such "mission" as the *schema* implies. They do not share in the task Christ laid upon His apostles, for that task has been bequeathed to the hierarchy. The laity can help the priests, but only in a subordinate role. To give them more status would introduce disorder into the church.

Cardinal Cento, who is head of the Apostolic Penitentiary, seconded these sentiments and insisted on a clear distinction between laity and priesthood so that there would be no possible confusion between them. Cardinal Bueno y Monreal of Seville interjected a positive note by rejoicing that the chapter represents the beginning of an exaltation of the laymen, who have been too passive in the past and have allowed themselves to be thought of as sheep. But the final speaker, Cardinal Bacci of Italy gave little comfort to the layman's camp; even though laymen have a kind of priesthood, the *schema* must make clearer that they are at all times subordinate to the hierarchy.

Score for the morning: 3 – 1 against the laity. This is the general pattern when new material is introduced. Ruffini speaks first and attacks change. Other cardinals of ample years follow him, by virtue of their seniority, and also attack change. Thus the opening comments are usually negative. But the tenor of discussion soon shifts, and within a day or so, the initial objections have been answered and positive material is being presented. From all signs and portents, therefore, tomorrow should be a good day.

Thursday, October 17

At mass this morning there were no cymbals, no chanting, no incense, no mysterious Eastern language; we were back to what I can now refer to as "the stark simplicity of the Latin rite." This was followed by Archbishop Felici's usual announcements. We waited to hear about the "four questions" held over from yesterday, but no word was forthcoming. Instead we were told that during the morning everyone would get a packet of Vatican stamps.

*   *   *

The discussion was on the role of the laity and it struck me as one of the best days so far. At the end of the morning I felt more encouraged about the Catholic Church's concern to speak to the modern world than I have in some time. I must comment on a few of the interventions to indicate the flavor of the discussion.

Bishop Rastouil of Limoges pointed out that the laity share in the universal priesthood which is conferred on them by baptism. The incarnation of Christ is the basis of all priesthood and *all* have a part in this. There is a special exercise of priesthood by ordination, but this is only a *different kind* of priesthood.

Bishop Hengsbach of Germany, who has worked with laymen in the Ruhr Valley, urged the fathers to consult with the laity themselves in rewriting the *schema*. The present text seems fearful that the laity will be given too much responsibility in the church. The *real* danger will come if they are not given enough responsibility. At Pentecost, the Spirit came to all who were present, not just to the twelve, and the Spirit will be hampered today if the laity's role continues to be as restricted as it has been in the past.

Bishop Wright of Pittsburgh made his first intervention of the entire Council. On the basis of what he said, one wishes he would speak more often. He felt that the chapter was a good beginning, but that it should be much stronger. For years the church has waited for a conciliar statement on the laity. There have been statements by popes, theologians, and individual bishops, but divine providence has now given the full church a chance to speak its mind. It cannot leave to the churches of the Reformation the task of developing a genuine theology of the laity. Since the present chapter defines the layman simply as one who is not a priest or a "religious," a more positive approach must be found.

Later on, Bishop Hannan, auxiliary bishop of Washington, spoke of the need for the *schema* to have concrete application. Laymen must be active in social and economic life, and cannot be content just to do "church work." They must join societies that exercise influence on public life: P.T.A.'s, labor unions, professional associations, welfare organizations. In these ways, the spirit of Christ can begin to be intruded into public life. Bishops, moreover, must be persuaded to ask the laity for advice in areas where the laity have competence.

Two distinct ideas about the role of the laity are emerging in the discussion: (a) Some of the fathers want the laity to "help the priest" with church work, and take some of the burden off the priest's back. This theme is usually accompanied by a stress on the subordination of laity to clergy; (b) others insist that the layman must go out into the world to exercise a dangerous but crucial apostolate for which he must be nurtured and prepared by the church. The *schema* seems to be weak in the latter area, and if the Theological Commission draws upon the resources of the lay auditors, this gap can be closed.

The whole discussion was admirably summarized by Bishop Philbin of the diocese of Down and Connor in Ireland. The church, he said, is often accused of being interested only in the afterlife; unless the *schema* is changed, the accusation will be justified. The *schema* gives the impression that the church is concerned only with "remedial charity," i.e., binding up the wounds of those who have been injured by the world and offering them future consolation. On the contrary, the church must be concerned with "constructive

charity," it must seek to change the world so that men will
not be harmed by it. When creation is abused, the church
must protest. The improper distribution of goods, for example, is an offense against God and man. Consequently,
technology, international means of communication, and the
like must be affirmed for the good of human society. A religious vocation is not merely one that spurns the world, but
one that accepts concern for the world.
    Amen.

                        *   *   *

    Our entrance to the Vatican for our papal audience was
through a door that was inscribed, quite appropriately, JOH.
XXIII, and was, even more appropriately, wide open to receive
us.
    This was the first time I had been inside the Vatican, and
I was not prepared for the sheer ornateness and the vast
wealth that have accumulated in it over the centuries. Every
room had tapestries, marble floors and walls, and priceless
art treasures. I commented to a fellow observer, "Not very
reminiscent of Nazareth," to which he replied, putting me in
my place, "No, quite an improvement." I know that many
Roman Catholics find this splendor hard to understand, but
accept it as part of the price that must be paid for a sense of
history and tradition. It is as though they had to grit their
teeth and say, "Be it ever so splendid, there's no place like
Rome."
    We were finally shown into the consistory, where papal
audiences are usually held, a room with amazing carved, gold
ceilings and a huge papal throne. But Msgr. Willebrands informed us that the holy father was going to meet us in his
private library instead. This meant going through more and
more rooms, in one of which was a throne above which were
the words, *Ubi Petrus ibi Ecclesia* (Where Peter is, there is
the Church) — a tag I had always thought Protestants in-
vented for purposes of disparaging contrast to the phrase,

Ubi Christus ibi Ecclesia (Where Christ is, there is the Church).

I mention the flamboyance of the surroundings, so apparently in contrast to the one who is supposed to be "least among all," "the servant of the servants of God," to emphasize the degree to which the person of Paul VI overcame whatever negative feelings I might have had from the surroundings of our meeting.

We were ushered into the pope's private library right on the dot of six. The pope greeted each one of us in person. After Cardinal Bea had introduced us, our delegated spokesman, Professor Kirsten Skydsgaard, addressed the pope in French. He expressed satisfaction that the pope had recognized both the possibilities and problems of ecumenical life, and he suggested that further attention to Biblical studies, particularly to "salvation-history," would be a useful area in which Catholics and Protestants could work together. "Is there a better way," he went on, "for us to meet each other than that of going out from ourselves in the assurance of the forgiveness of sins, without concern for our preferences or our merits, in order to live in the world and with men in the world? It is thus that we shall be truly the disciples of Christ who did not desire to exist for Himself but solely for the world." He concluded with the prayer, "May God bless Your Holiness in the heavy burden and responsibility of your ministry, and may He spread His Spirit of repentance and truth upon all the churches of the world."

Pope Paul then responded in French. He emphasized that we were meeting not in a formal gathering, but for a private audience, due to "Our desire to receive you not merely on the threshold of Our home but in the very heart of Our intimacy." He thanked us for coming to the Council, and, so there could be no mistake, he repeated the main point of his opening allocution: "In Our speech of September 29, We ventured to give the first place to Christian forgiveness, mutual if possible. 'We grant pardon and ask it in return.'" Picking up on Skydsgaard's quotation from Augustine that we must "seek in order to find, and find in order to seek still more," he acknowledged that Christians cannot rest content with "immobilism," but must always seek better possession of divine truth than they yet have. He accepted Skydsgaard's suggestion of further Biblical studies centered on the history of salvation, and intimated that this would be stressed in Catholic institutions even if it meant the creation of a new center of study. He concluded, "Permit Us to say farewell with the very words of the great Apostle whose name We have made Our own: 'The grace of our Lord Jesus Christ be with you; I love you all in Christ Jesus. Amen.'"

He then came down from his chair and presented each of us with a medal of the Council showing Christ, the twelve apostles, and Pope John kneeling before Christ.

There are at least three things that make this audience significant: (1) We were received in the pope's private library as friends rather than as visiting dignitaries; (2) we were not just given a little lecture — the event was a genuine dialogue (Skydsgaard spoke first, and the pope in speaking, *replied* to what Skydsgaard had said); (3) at the end of the audience, instead of concluding with a papal blessing as is customary on such occasions, the pope came down into our midst, and suggested that all of us, as fellow Christians, say together the Lord's Prayer, each in his own tongue. So there we were, united one with the other for a moment at least, across barriers of language, race, theology, and ecclesiology — not Protestants in the presence of a Catholic or vice versa — brethren in Christ, praying together the prayer our common Lord had bequeathed to us all. This wiped out any negative impact the grand and ornate buildings had produced and confirmed the genuineness of Pope Paul's closing words to us, "*Je vous aime tous dans le Christ-Jésus.*"

There are those who say that Paul VI is "reserved" in comparison to John XXIII. It is unlikely that twice in a single generation will God grant as ebullient and outgoing a personality as Pope John. But Pope Paul has what may turn out to be an even greater asset for effecting genuine reform in contemporary Catholicism — knowledge of, and experience in, the ways of the Curia. And, as his speech to the Curia has already made evident, he not only has a stout heart, but also a strong right arm.

Friday, October 18

We have not yet gotten the "four questions." There begin to be rumors of trouble behind the scenes, hard to track down, but nevertheless cropping up everywhere. The most persistent one is that Ottaviani, chairman of the Theological Commission, has not taken kindly to the notion that his commission is to be given a mandate by the Council.

The discussion on the laity continued with good speeches, but no strikingly new material. The difficulties with the material in the *schema* center around a feeling that the laymen are seen too negatively and are not given enough sense of their mission to the world.

Cardinal Gracias, for example, was fearful that the present *schema* leaves the laity in the position of doing only those things the priests will let them do. Laity must not be looked upon as intruders into the priestly preserve, even if "frictions" should result. "Frictions" are the price of growth. Cardinal Doepfner, moderator today, indicated that he meant business, for he cut Cardinal Gracias off after ten minutes — something that rarely happens to a cardinal. Gracias was gracious.

Cardinal Rugambwa wanted more emphasis on the laymen in the world. It is good to have lay auditors in St. Peter's, but this must not obscure the way in which laymen can represent the church outside of St. Peter's. Bishop Picachy of India feared that the *schema* would leave the impression that laymen were merely to be obedient to the priests, and Bishop Schroeffer of Germany feared that the laity would assume that they were supposed to feel like clerics, rather than developing the fullness of their laicity.

❈   ❈   ❈

The *placet juxta modum* habit is catching on. Chapter Three of *De Sacra Liturgia* was voted on today and had over 1000 such qualifying votes. This slows things up a bit, but indicates that the fathers aren't prepared to be a rubber stamp for anybody.

* * *

This afternoon Cardinal Bea gave a reception at the Columbus Hotel for observers and members of the Secretariat for Christian Unity. When Bea salutes us with the words, *"Mes très chers frères en Jésus-Christ,"* one knows that he really means it and that this is not just polite talk. He spoke briefly, thanked us for our help, and asked us to continue to make our comments and criticisms, repeating his invitation on a similar occasion last year (see the front of this book for his statement). The Very Reverend Archpriest Vitalj Borovoj of the Russian Orthodox Church responded for the observers. His speech took somewhat longer since it had to be given in Russian and then translated into French. Bea, all eighty-three years of him, stood throughout this response, but departed soon after. Nobody begrudges him an early departure. We want him to save his energy for the important battles on the Council floor.

* * *

I had a rare evening of conversation with a number of Roman Catholics at the Council. I am always amazed by the frankness and honesty of such discussions, and without betraying that trust I think I can record some of the things about which we conversed.

1. A number of people feel that the theological depth of the various *schemata* is limited due to the small number of *periti* who are actually Biblical scholars. The best theologians in the church are here, but the Biblical people are not fully enough represented. A few Biblical scholars like the amazing Barnabas Ahern of the Passionist Fathers can't be expected

to carry the whole Council on their backs. Theology must be Biblically grounded, and to do this properly demands the help of the Biblical experts.

2. More and more there is open talk of difficulties within the Theological Commission. The majority of its members are reasonably open to new currents of thought, but they are under the control of a chairman, vice-chairman, and secretary who are closed to anything but their own point of view. This is a real thorn in the commission's flesh, and it will become more and more of a thorn in the Council's flesh if the commission fails to produce documents reflecting the opinion of the Council as a whole.

3. A specific example of this problem may shortly confront us. The commission is divided as to whether the material about Mary should be in a separate *schema* or incorporated in *De Ecclesia*. It may be proposed that two members of the commission speak on the Council floor, one advocating each location, after which the fathers can take a vote. This would be an interesting and possibly significant procedural breakthrough.

4. One member of the group pointed out that Hans Küng's book *The Council in Action* is oriented primarily to the European situation, in which genuine reform will lead to closer dialogue with the mainline Reformation groups — Lutheran, Reformed, and so forth. But in other areas of the world, particularly the missionary areas, reform makes possible the beginning of a dialogue, not with Lutherans, but with modern man as such. Only by genuine reform can the church make contact with men of the twentieth century. This does not invalidate Küng's thesis about the importance of reform, but simply indicates that it can lead in many directions.

5. There was an interesting reaction to the reading of papal and conciliar documents. Those who have been writing the latter now realize full well what patchwork affairs they are. To get a new idea included, a drafter may have to swallow three old ideas he doesn't like so well, and the document

will always be overloaded with references to past documents, so that a proper sense of continuity will be maintained. The thing to look for, consequently, in reading such a document, is not the material with which one is already familiar, but the one sentence or two that is genuinely new and fresh — *this* represents the foundation on which the church's advance in thinking must be built.

Saturday, October 19

I have just come from one of the most heart-warming experiences of my life. I have been sitting for two and one-half hours in company with hundreds of bishops, dozens of cardinals, and one pope. We have been spiritually nourished and refreshed by listening to a setting of the mass written by a Lutheran. That the fathers of the Roman Catholic Church should devote an afternoon to Johann Sebastian Bach's *Mass in B Minor*, one of the greatest musical products of the Reformation, is a fact of considerable ecumenical significance. One might have expected them to patronize a concert of Gregorian music, or a work by some great Roman Catholic composer, in which Catholicism's contribution to sacred music could be extolled. Instead they gathered to hear the music of one who was not seeking to bring glory to the Roman Catholic tradition, or indeed to any tradition, but who wrote, as he inscribed at the top of each of his manuscripts, *Soli dei gloria* — to the glory of God alone.

Around me were purple skull caps, in front were red ones, and to one side was a single white one, on the papal throne. On the stage was a German chorus, joined by soloists from America, Britain, Hungary, and the Netherlands. Here, gathered around Bach's musical offering, were all kinds of Christians, indeed, all kinds of human beings, of different races, nationalities, colors, churches. Although the pope sat on a throne, he was not the center of attention. Although the musicians sat on the stage, they were not the center of attention either. Nor was the music the center of attention; it was simply the means through which all of us were enabled to share in a corporate act of praise. Five mornings a week at mass we say all the words the chorus and soloists sang this afternoon, but never have they brought us so close together as they have just now.

We have heard a lot of theology in the *aula*. I have talked with a lot of theologians in Rome. But since theology itself must finally be an act of praise, perhaps the best theology is the theology that can be sung. Today I have been exposed once again to the unearthly beauty of the *Qui tollis,* and to the amazing vigor and vitality of the *Cum Sancto Spiritu,* which is a better representation of the sheer power of the Holy Spirit than any theological treatise ever written. I have shared in the awe and wonder of the *Incarnatus Est,* the affirmation of which can only be uttered in awe and wonder. I have heard the aria in which the Holy Spirit and the one, holy, catholic, and apostolic church are linked together, which is the only way either one of them can properly be understood. I have felt the anguished pleading in the *Agnus Dei,* and I have heard the same musical setting used for both the *Gratias Agimus Tibi* and the *Dona Nobis Pacem,* which is the only proper way to do it, since only those who have given thanks to God for his glory can really ask for his peace.

And when I reflect on this, and ponder what I have heard, I come to the conclusion that the greatest theologian of them all is not Athanasius, or Augustine or Anselm or Thomas, or, again, Congar or Küng or Daniélou or Rahner, but rather (as I think they might also acknowledge), one who simply signed himself "Joh. Seb. Bach."

The Fourth Week
(*October 21 – 27*)

The *periti* attacked and defended – laymen in church and world – where are the "four questions"? – the location of material on Mary – simultaneous translation in the offing – the call to "holiness" – "Reformation Sunday" in Rome

Monday, October 21

Mass this morning was in the Byzantine Roman Rite, fortified by wonderful music. Although this meant little "congregational participation," at least there was dialogue between the celebrant and the choir. Since mass took an hour, and forty minutes more were consumed describing emendations for Chapter Four of *De Sacra Liturgia*, there was time for only eight interventions.

Cardinal Meyer of Chicago, one of the cardinal-presidents, spoke on what Hans Küng has referred to as the "peccability" (i.e. the sinfulness) of the church. Since this is an unpopular theme in certain Catholic circles, the speech was particularly noteworthy. The prayer of the church, Cardinal Meyer said, must always be, "Forgive us our trespasses." Life on earth is always a struggle against evil, and churchmen must see themselves as sinners more than as saints. The fathers individually acknowledge their sin each morning at mass, and do so corporately in the *Adsumus*, the prayer of the Council. Before talking so glibly, then, of the church as "without spot or wrinkle," it should be recognized that the church is the community of the fallen.

Nothing could have spoken more helpfully to our discussion at the "briefing session" last week. Some indication of this theme in the *schema* will remove from it the false tone of "triumphalism" that at present pervades it.

The next speaker was Cardinal Ottaviani, head of the Holy Office, chairman of the Theological Commission, and symbol of the forces of conservatism within the Council. He is an excellent linguist who speaks Latin extemporaneously. He had two points, neither of which was strictly in order, but he spoke less than ten minutes and was not called to account. With a good deal of feeling, he first attacked the *periti*, the theological experts of the Council. They have, he said, been distributing materials to the bishops on the subject of the married diaconate. It is not their business to do this sort of thing. They are on hand to be consulted if the bishops wish to consult them, but they should not take initiative to influence the Council's mind. (Although no names were named, it was clear that one of the *periti* so indicted was Karl Rahner, a German Jesuit whose theological orientation is as far removed from Ottaviani's as east is from west, and who is probably the most creative thinker in contemporary Catholic thought.) Ottaviani's second point did not relate to Chapter Three, now under discussion, but back to Chapter Two. He made a brief but forceful objection to the notion of the married diaconate. How could there possibly be situations in which a celibate diaconate would not be proper? If there is a shortage of priests, let acolytes take over some of their tasks, and let them be married if need be, but marriage must never invade the ranks of the ordained.

What with a long mass and a long introduction to the liturgy chapter, it was now well past eleven o'clock. Everybody had stayed to hear Ottaviani's first intervention this fall, so immediately following it there was a mass exodus for the coffee bars. This meant that a lot of the fathers missed a very pointed intervention by Archbishop Tchidimbo of Guinea, who must have been voicing the complaints of many missionary bishops. The implication of his talk was that people from Rome try to "tell the natives how to run things," without any knowledge of local problems, so that the church, while it condemns political colonialism, itself practices ecclesiastical colonialism.

Later in the morning, Archbishop Hurley of Durban, South Africa, one of the few white churchmen in South Africa who has taken any stand against *apartheid,* aligned himself with Bishop Philbin in asserting that the human condition of the laity is not sufficiently stressed in the *schema.* The church's concern must not be simply with the "state," but with "human society" as a whole, or else the impact of the church will be unnecessarily restricted.

The rest of the interventions did not add much to the discussion, but a very pointed bit of repartee was produced by Bishop Kozlowiecki of Northern Rhodesia. To the salutation, *Venerabiles patres,* at the beginning of his speech, Kozlowiecki, speaking not long after Ottaviani's blast against the *periti,* added the further salutation, *carissime periti* (beloved *periti*). The point was lost on no one, and to his credit it must be said that even Ottaviani joined in the laughter.

* * *

I am tremendously impressed by the caliber of the *carissime periti.* For a number of years I have been reading a certain group of Catholic theologians, to my great profit and excitement. But when I have quoted them to make a point before some Protestant group, I have almost always been confronted by the charge, "Oh, but they're not typical. They don't really speak for the Church." Among this group I would include such men as the following: Fr. Yves Congar, a French Dominican who wrote the first important book on ecumenism from the Catholic side; Fr. Jerome Hamer, another Dominican who wrote one of the first Catholic studies of Karl Barth; Fr. Godfrey Diekmann, a Benedictine who has been the real motivating force behind the Liturgical Movement in America; Fr. Bernard Haering, a German Redemptorist who has broken new ground in the field of moral theology; Fr. Hans

Küng, a Swiss theologian whose treatment of "reformation" makes him perhaps the most creative voice on the Catholic scene; Fr. George Tavard, a French Augustinian who has explored Catholic-Protestant theological issues in half a dozen books; Fr. Gustave Weigel and Fr. John Courtney Murray, Jesuits on the faculty of Woodstock College in Maryland, who between them have thrust American Catholicism into the ecumenical dialogue; Fr. Karl Rahner, a German Jesuit whose *Quaestiones Disputatae* series is forcing Catholics to re-examine questions that are not yet "closed"; and Fr. Jean Daniélou, a French Jesuit, whose studies of the early church can be ignored by no serious scholar.

"Time would fail me" to tell of others, but the point is that every one of these men is now here at the Council as an official *peritus*. They are the ones, in company with many others of course, who have been chosen to help guide the Council to its proper conclusions. Not many years ago most of them were in trouble with the Curia and the Holy Office. Some of them have had their books withdrawn from circulation, many of them have been forbidden to publish, and a few have been removed from teaching positions because their ideas were presumed dangerous. But today they are all here at the Council being consulted by bishops, lecturing for the bishops, and — as is no secret at all — writing interventions for the bishops. (One of our favorite indoor sports, indeed, is the attempt, after a particularly good intervention, to try to guess which *peritus* had the biggest hand in its composition.) These theologians, in other words, have a platform unparalleled in the past history of the church, which, considering who they are, is yet another indication of new winds blowing through the windows that Pope John opened such a short time ago.

Last year the administrative authorities at Catholic University in Washington, D.C. denied permission to Hans Küng, Godfrey Diekmann, John Courtney Murray, and Gustave Weigel to speak on the campus. The incident provoked much outcry, and it is important to realize how little the attitude of the administration there reflects what is really going on in the church. For this fall, all of the men who were too "dangerous" to speak to university students, are official *periti* at the Council.

The Benedictines, the European Dominicans, and the Jesuits have been the leaders of this theological renewal. I am sometimes criticized for extrapolating too much hope from the creative currents among the Jesuits.

To this charge I can only reply: Some of my best friends are Jesuits. But I wouldn't want my daughter to marry one.

Tuesday, October 22

The reception of communion by the lay auditors is now clearly established and each day a significant number go forward to receive. The first time this happened there was, of course, a delay before the celebrant went on to the next part of the mass. Some of the bishops at the far end of the *aula* couldn't see what was causing the delay, and according to the story now going the rounds, the following exchange took place.

First Bishop: What's going on up there?

Second Bishop: I can't quite see, but it looks as though some of the younger bishops are making their first communion.

This is undoubtedly a variant on last year's story concerning the day mass was celebrated according to the Ethiopic rite, complete with jungle drums. As the drums began to sound, another conversation took place:

First Bishop: What's going on up there?

Second Bishop: I can't quite see, but it looks as though they're fixing to boil a cardinal.

The same pattern of discussion is manifesting itself in relation to Chapter Three as was evident for the previous chapters. Ruffini and Company begin with a blast against the proposals; these are followed by a day or so of creative interventions; these, in turn, are followed by interventions that are good but almost sheerly repetitive. For the last few sessions we have, in effect, been having little homilies on the laity, and, as Henri Fesquet recently pointed out in *Le Monde*, sixteen sermons a morning is a stiff dose, even for bishops.

Only two interventions this morning were of real significance. The first of these was by Cardinal Suenens, one of the truly prophetic voices in contemporary Catholicism. He was answering a position voiced by Ruffini that while "charisms" (manifestations of the Holy Spirit) were normal in New Testament times, we must not look for them any more, since the Spirit now works through the hierarchy. But to think in these terms, Suenens replied, is simply to stifle the Holy Spirit. The direction of the church is not solely in the hands of hierarchical administrators, but has been given to all, laymen included, by baptism. The Spirit can act in many ways, and can give His gifts to whom He chooses. There is no assurance that He will work only "through channels," and bishops must be open to the fact that the Spirit can speak in many unexpected ways. All of this means, Suenens concluded in very practical vein, that the Council should not assume that the Spirit works exclusively through males. Women are, after all, half the human race, and they should be represented among the auditors in the *aula*.

It is a speech of this sort that gives me hope about the future of Roman Catholicism. So often in the past the structure has dominated the Spirit and even stifled the Spirit. But here is a cardinal reminding the fathers that the Spirit has His own ways of working, and that He may sometimes use unconventional means in order to reassert His power among churchmen who have become closed to the reality of His presence. With this kind of openness, there is no limit to the new creativity that could enter into the Roman Catholicism of today or tomorrow. As encouraging as the speech was the response of the fathers, for when Suenens had concluded they broke into sustained applause.

The other encouraging intervention was by Auxiliary Bishop Mark McGrath of Panama City, speaking in the name of more than forty Latin American bishops. Their dissatisfaction with the *schema* stems from the fact that it does not give sufficient attention to the life of the layman within the world. The impression created is that the laity simply exist under the hierarchy. The present situation in St. Peter's is a good example: The laity are silent, while bishops talk about the laity! Lay work in the world must not be downgraded by priests because it does not seem "ecclesiastical" enough. In Latin America, the church's first task must be to help renovate society, for unless the church is willing to minister to men's bodies, it cannot properly claim to minister to their souls.

The hope must be, of course, that sentiments like those of Suenens and McGrath can be incorporated into the *schema* itself. The fact that Bishop McGrath is a member of the Theological Commission gives cause for hope that they can.

* * *

At our "briefing session" this afternoon many of us were still basking in the glow of Cardinal Suenens' remarkable intervention, but this did not lead to undue euphoria. Indeed, fortified by Suenens' theme, many of the observers pressed home the degree to which true acknowledgment of the free working of the Spirit is absent from the *schema*. Attention was also paid to the rather negative approach to the laity. Just before 6:30 P.M., our official closing time, there was one speaker still to be heard from. He began a treatment of St. Paul's teaching about the gifts of the Spirit. When, after thirty minutes, he got to "sixth and last point," we gathered ourselves together for his conclusion. After "sixth and last point," however, there was a brief pause, followed by, "So much for the facts. Now I will draw some systematic conclusions from the facts." It was a brilliant performance, even though the "systematic conclusions" took another fifteen minutes, and it left me wondering whether this might not be an indication that the Spirit *does* indeed operate outside of

humanly defined structures — such as the human agreement
that meetings beginning at four-thirty ought to end by six-
thirty.

*   *   *

We had an evening reception at the Waldensian Theological Seminary that was most pleasant. When I totaled the
number of speeches that I had heard since morning, however, I was not too surprised to discover that it came to
forty-one.

Wednesday, October 23

I am making an important discovery: What goes on *in the
Council* is not necessarily what *goes on* in the Council. To
put the matter less subtly, one can sometimes learn more in
the coffee bar than by listening to the speeches. For the first
couple of weeks I felt guilty every time I missed a speech.
Now, particularly when the speeches are so repetitious, I am
spending more and more time in the coffee bar, and it is not
the coffee that attracts me but the conversations.

It is clear from such conversation that the Council has
gotten bogged down, and that important things are happening behind the scenes. The issue is focused by the fact that
we have not yet heard a single word about the "four questions" Cardinal Suenens promised over a week ago. Apparently some of the cardinal-presidents challenged the
authority of the cardinal-moderators to propose the "four
questions," and Archbishop Felici, the secretary-general, has
also protested.

The question boils down to: "Who's in charge here?" When
the pope appointed the four moderators their powers were
apparently not clearly defined. A "summit conference" of
the various leaders of the Council is scheduled for this evening to iron this out. So far the moderators have not exercised
leadership. Their role has been mainly that of announcing
speakers, calling time (not very rigorously), and reminding
the fathers (not very imperiously) to stick to the subject.

Now that they have taken some initiative in proposing the four questions, they are being challenged. Should the pope intervene? Here is a nice dilemma. If he does intervene, this is "papalism," just when a doctrine of collegiality is being hammered out. But if he does not intervene, a stalemate is likely and one that could work only to the advantage of the forces of reaction. It is a curious paradox that those most opposed to collegiality in principle, the conservatives, really practice it all the time by going to see the pope and trying to influence him, while those most in favor of collegiality appear to wait for the pope to make up his own mind.

I cannot avoid the feeling, however, that a crisis is in the making, and that it converges more and more on the matter of procedures. If the temper of the Council is really "progressive," should not this receive clearer expression through the admittedly "progressive" moderators, as long as the minority has its rights of speech, debate, and vote safeguarded? If the pope genuinely wants to carry through the reforms of Pope John, should he not be able to do so? If the leadership of the Theological Commission is definitely in the minority, should not that leadership be reconstituted so that it will be reflective of the Council as a whole?

One of the Curia bishops has said, "Popes and councils come and go; the Curia goes on forever." The problem could not be stated more clearly. Is the Curia, with its entrenched conservative viewpoint, really the church? Can it thwart the will of pope, bishop, council? I have the feeling that such questions as these are either going to kindle an explosion *ad majorem gloriam Dei,* or that the fuse lit by the notion of reform will fizz out to gloomy extinction. Many Catholics tell me that this is a "typically Protestant" attitude of wanting too much too soon, and that (in those blessed words) "the Church moves slowly." But I am not the only man in St. Peter's these days who is impatient.

This state of affairs may influence what happens to the proposed statement on religious liberty. The American bishops have studied a proposed statement to which they have given their approval, which would not only guarantee inner freedom of conscience but also outward expression of faith through witnessing, preaching, evangelizing, and public worship. There is a move on foot to add this to the *schema De Oecumenismo,* along with a chapter on the Jews that is already prepared. This is certainly preferable to attaching it to "Schema Seventeen" on The Church and the Modern World, which will not be debated for many years, if progress continues to be as slow as it has been so far. . . .

❖   ❖   ❖

The English-speaking observers met this afternoon and most of our time was devoted to further discussion of matters like the above. All agree that this is the critical point so far in the Council. Either there must be a real breakthrough, so that the moderators can exert authority, or the Council will wander aimlessly and ineffectively through repetitious speech after repetitious speech.

There was one nice ecumenical gesture at the end of our meeting. It was suggested that we close by repeating together the Lord's Prayer. As we are reminded every morning in mass, the Roman Catholic version ends after *Sed libera nos a malo* (But deliver us from evil), whereas the Protestant version includes a final doxology, "For thine is the kingdom, and the power, and the glory, forever." This afternoon, however, the Protestant observers stopped after "But deliver us from evil," while the Catholic *periti,* went on to pray, "For thine is the kingdom and the power, and the glory forever." It was most revealing of the intention of each group to make the other feel spiritually at home, and I don't think its impact was lost on anybody.

But then, as Fr. Weigel commented later, "Why *shouldn't* we say, 'For thine is the kingdom and the power and the glory, forever'? After all, it's nothing but a Catholic addition to the original text."

❖   ❖   ❖

There were, after all, interventions this morning. One of the patriarchs made the interesting suggestion that since the observers come to the Council five days a week, they should be heard from at least once a week. Perhaps by Vatican III . . . ? And Bishop Larrain of Chile, speaking for more than sixty South American bishops, asked for more emphasis on the *prophetic* mission of the church. There is much emphasis on obedience to the pope, but little emphasis on preaching the word of God. The *schema* is also too lacking in self-criticism. The church must be more forthright in acknowledging its sin, and must realize that Christ's word "Repent!" is spoken *to* the church and not only *through* the church.

This kind of thing is being heard more from South Americans than I would have expected. Indeed, the greatest surprise of the Council to me is the large number of creative voices that are being heard among the South American hierarchy. New winds are blowing there that I knew not of, and all my stereotypes about South American Catholicism are crumbling as a result.

Bishop Przyklenk of Brazil began by saluting the "venerable fathers, the auditors, the observers, and even the *periti*." The latter have been greatly appreciated in the last few days and should appreciate the attack by Ottaviani which has called such attention to their labors.

Archbishop Shehan of Baltimore asked that the adjective be deleted from the phrase "unhappy separation of church and state." The American bishops, he said, want this eliminated, since they do not believe that separation of church and state is a bad thing. Bishop Primeau of Manchester, New Hampshire, gave a forthright speech on behalf of the laity that indicates the kind of contribution Americans can make at the Council. The laity, he insisted, must not be treated like "dumb sheep." They can give intellectual help in the life of the church, and the present text relegates them too much to a role of "obedience." They must be allowed to do more than "obey, pray and pay." If all this is true, then the lay auditors in the *aula* should have a chance to speak and not merely listen.

This, I think, could happen even at Vatican II. It is only a question of time until the logic of admitting lay auditors in the first place will lead to the extension of speaking privileges for them. Bishop Primeau is still ahead of the church, but it will catch up to him before long.

Thursday, October 24

The announcements this morning gave no indication that anything had been resolved at last night's "summit conference," though there was a significant departure from usual procedure at the end of the morning. But there was not a word about the "four questions." Voting continued on emendations to the liturgy *schema*. Votes on emendations are only *placet* or *non placet* votes. Although Felici makes this clear before every vote, there is always one vote which he has to announce as *placet juxta modum* and therefore invalid. This is becoming a matter of great curiosity. Last year the mystery was: "Who is Xavier Rynne?" This year it is: "Who is the bishop who votes *placet juxta modum?*"

Cardinal Siri, the first speaker of the morning, certainly made clear that the laity question is far from settled. The *schema* must give more stress to the laity's submission to the hierarchy. To talk of a "universal priesthood" in which the laity share is a dangerous way to talk and must be handled with great prudence. Indeed, more rather than less control over the laity is needed, for too many strange conclusions are liable to be drawn from a doctrine of universal priesthood. The notion of "charisms" in the church is a dangerous one and the activity of the Spirit must be understood as under the authority of the hierarchy. Otherwise scandal will result.

Later in the morning there was another heartening indication that the American hierarchy is beginning to get more actively involved in the Council. Bishop Tracey of Baton Rouge, speaking for 179 American bishops, urged that the section dealing with membership in the church indicate that the people of God comprises not only all nations, but all "races" as well. In view of the present racial struggle the church must not equivocate in the slightest way on this point.

After a few interventions I proceeded to Bar-jonah, in line with my new conviction that more is happening off the Council floor these days than on. The place was a real rumor factory, but the rumors did not yet have much substance. Apparently no clear answer emerged last night to the question, "Who's in charge here?" Two theories, however, were reported from several quarters: (a) That the moderators *have* gained the right to ask the "four questions," and (b) that the logjam in the Theological Commission is serious enough so that the matter will soon make its way on to the Council floor.

Neither of these hunches got any confirmation or denial back in the *aula,* but Cardinal Doepfner shortly asked for cloture on further discussion of the laity, which he got easily. He then announced that the question of the location of the treatment of Mary would be resolved as follows: There would be speeches by two members of the Theological Commission, Cardinal Santos of the Philippines, arguing for a separate *schema,* and Cardinal Koenig of Vienna, arguing for inclusion of the material within *De Ecclesia.* The fathers will weigh the arguments and vote next Tuesday.

No man to let grass grow under his feet, Cardinal Doepfner then called upon Santos and Koenig to give their speeches. Both were models of brevity and clarity, each man marshaling his arguments without shifty logic or excessively emotional appeals. This procedure, indeed, should commend itself to the Council fathers on other controversial issues.

Santos urged a number of reasons for a separate *schema:* (1) Because of her special dignity, Mary deserves a special *schema.* (2) Alteration of the present plan for a separate *schema* is bound to be interpreted as a diminution of concern for Mary on the part of the Council fathers. (3) Her special role in the church cannot be sufficiently clarified in

a single chapter of a *schema*, nor (4) can the distinction between her powers and those of hierarchy and laity be ad-
equately differentiated in such a context. (5) While Mary is
in the church as its first and chief member, she is in some
ways above the church and cannot therefore be properly
dealt with in a *schema* on the church. (6) The full treatment
of Mary that is demanded by a conciliar statement is difficult to summarize in a single chapter. (7) The present
structure of *De Ecclesia* makes inclusion of the Marian material difficult to achieve. Furthermore, to make this change
now would take precious time that the Council should be
devoting to other matters.

Cardinal Koenig mentioned that in a vote on October 9
the majority of the Theological Commission requested inclusion of the Marian material in *De Ecclesia*. He suggested
four reasons for this decision: (1) *Theological reasons:*
Since the church is the theme of the present Council, it
should emphasize the relation of Mary to the church rather
than putting a dividing wall between doctrines about Mary
and other doctrines. Since Mary is the most eminent member
of the church, her role within it would be enhanced, rather
than diminished, by considering her in the context of the
church. (2) *Historical reasons:* Recent considerations of
Mary in Catholic life and thought such as the Litany of Lo-
reto, the recent Marian Congress at Lourdes, and Pope Paul's
speech on October 11, have been stressing her connection
with the church. (3) *Pastoral reasons:* Popular devotion
should be guided, and the faithful instructed, to understand
Marian teaching not as something independent, but as
something intimately related to the life of the entire church.
(4) *Ecumenical reasons:* Location of the material on Mary
within *De Ecclesia*, particularly if the chapter is amended to
have a foundation in Scripture and early tradition, will foster
rather than hinder the relationship with non-Catholics in
both East and West.

Koenig is one of the strong men of the Council. It is he
who wrote an introduction to Hans Küng's first book on the

Council, and it is he who has Karl Rahner here as his own *peritus* — this despite the strong opposition to both Küng and Rahner that is manifested by the conservatives. I had the privilege of talking with him this evening and when I thanked him for his inclusion of "ecumenical reasons" (even though I wish he had had time to develop them at greater length) he replied, "Ah, that is to me the most important point of all."

There was applause after both speeches. Is it wishful thinking to believe there was more after Koenig's than after Santos'?

Friday, October 25

Things are happening. A few days ago six large booths appeared in one of the side aisles. Translation booths? Apparently. Six booths, therefore, equally apparently, six languages. And this morning a man appeared in our tribune with a headset, listening to someone who was obviously broadcasting from a translation booth. So, although not a word has been said officially, it is apparent that simultaneous translation is on the way. There is no denying that hundreds of bishops haven't a clue about what goes on at the sessions. And for every one who openly acknowledges this fact, there must be another two or three who won't admit it. Few have the honesty of Cardinal Cushing, who simply went home after two weeks because he said he couldn't understand the Latin. ("All I can do in St. Peter's is to pray for the Council, and I can do that just as well in Boston.") Cushing has offered again and again to underwrite the expense of getting simultaneous translation installed. Query: Will he return once it is in operation?

I discussed the appearance of the headphones with one bishop who shall remain nameless, and he envisaged the possibilities of turning the dial and getting French or German . . . or English . . . or Greek. After contemplating these possibilities for a minute or two he said rather wistfully, "I hope there is one channel you can dial and just get music."

I foresee one problem for the bishops worse than not getting music and that is the initial agonizing decision, "Do I wear a headset or not?" Not wearing a headset will surely become an ecclesiastical status symbol. Shows you still know Latin.

Felici may not have said anything about translation booths, but he announced other interesting facts: (1) Since next Monday is the fifth anniversary of Pope John's election, there will be a special session of the Council. Pope Paul will say mass (sensation in the *aula*) after which Cardinal Suenens will give a speech about Pope John. (2) On Tuesday there will be a vote on the location of the Mariological material. (3) There will be no meetings of the Council on next Friday or Monday since this is All Saints' weekend.

Although cloture was voted yesterday on Chapter Three, a number of the fathers availed themselves of the privilege of speaking after cloture. They did not add anything new to the discussion although two of them were rather moving.

Bishop Boillon of France returned to the theme so constantly in the minds of the north European and missionary bishops, the identification of the church with the poor. Not only must the church speak to and for the poor, but it must adopt the garb of poverty itself. (As Fr. Weigel pointed out in the course of translating this for us, *pauperes* does not mean merely those "without money," but also those of the "lower class," who are discriminated against because of their status in society. It is with *these* that the church must identify.)

Archbishop Baraniak of Poland asked that the *schema* discuss those laymen within the church who are in difficult positions. There must be a section on the apostolate of suffering and martyrdom, for the sake of those whose faith gets them into difficulty with the state. They must be empowered to pardon their persecutors and pray for them, to learn that though errors must be condemned, those who are guilty of error must be loved.

Considering the situation out of which this intervention came, and the degree to which its words have been written in blood, it was not surprising that the fathers applauded when Baraniak had finished.

*　　*　　*

I have found myself more and more involved in the question debated yesterday about the location of the Marian material. It will be ecumenically disastrous, I feel, to retain the separate *schema,* and it can be ecumenically creative to incorporate a statement about Mary in *De Ecclesia* that has a strong Biblical basis. Abbot Butler, the head of the English Benedictines, has prepared such a statement and he has said that other statements (one by the French theologian Fr. Laurentin, and another by a group of Chilean bishops) make the same emphasis. These authors will combine forces to produce a single alternate document rather than letting three or four be offered in apparent competition with one another.

Somewhat to my surprise I have found myself campaigning vigorously with all the bishops and *periti* I can find, pointing out the ecumenical implications of the Tuesday vote. Translated into the vernacular my campaign speech goes, "Get your precinct workers out over the weekend and bring in that vote on Tuesday morning."

*　　*　　*

The discussion finally turned to Chapter Four of *De Ecclesia,* which deals with the call to holiness and also the life of those engaged in the special vocation of the "religious," i.e. those who are members of religious orders, and not regular priests or laymen. One of the real strengths of this chapter, as I see it, is that it gets rid of a certain distortion of Christian teaching of which the church has frequently been guilty in the past. This is the belief that there are really two levels of Christian living, one for the "religious," which involves withdrawal from the world and a following of the counsels of perfection (poverty, chastity, and obedience), and the other a kind of second-rate existence for the ordinary mortals who stay in the world. The point of Chapter Four is to insist that *all* are called to holiness, and that the decision the Christian faces is whether he shall strive for holiness in terms of the commandments that are incumbent upon all, or whether he shall strive for holiness in terms of the counsels of perfection, which are incumbent only on those who take special vows. We must discuss this at our next "briefing session."

There was time for only a few interventions. Bishop Silva Henriquez of Chile, one of the most creative voices in South America, approved treating the general calling to holiness and the particular calling of the "religious" in the same chapter. These must not be separated from each other as though they were two entirely different things.

Bishop Charue of Belgium, a Biblical scholar, spoke to the point of my own comment above. The call to holiness is first of all to holiness *within the world* and only then to holiness within a "religious" vocation. The "religious" are the *avant-garde* of the church, not to produce more members for the "religious" so much as to attract people to a life of holiness whatever their station in life. The Reformers, he went on, tried to destroy the gap that medieval Christendom had created between the "religious" and the rest of mankind by stressing that holiness was a possibility for all, whereas Catholic teaching has given the impression that holiness is only for those within a religious order. It is this misunderstanding which must be corrected by the present Council. The notion must be dispelled that those who do not become "religious" are somehow second-rate Christians. The *universal* call to holiness is therefore primary, and the life of the "religious" is important mainly as a way of emphasizing the call addressed to everyone.

Shades of the Reformation! How thrilling to hear this kind of thing in a Vatican Council. I am not suggesting that Charue is coming to the Reformation four hundred years late, but simply that he is articulating in his context what the Reformers articulated in theirs, and is illustrating the fact that all of us, whether Catholic or Protestant, share a common heritage that, when we explore it, can only draw us closer together.

Sunday, October 27

Today is "Reformation Sunday," and it gives me a chance to draw together some reflections on the Council thus far, in the light of my Protestant heritage.

As I was riding into Rome from the Fiumicino Airport a little over a month ago, I fell into conversation with two English priests who were coming to do further study at the English College. One of them told me to keep watching up ahead because at a certain point I would get a clear view of the dome of St. Peter's, after which it would be lost to sight for several more miles. "There was the beginning of the whole trouble," he mused, recalling that one of the contributing factors to the Protestant Reformation was the indignation of the Germans at the way their own church funds were being siphoned down to Italy to pay for the construction of St. Peter's.

With this in mind we continued to watch for the dome. The miles ticked off, but no dome appeared. "Perhaps," the other priest finally suggested, "they've torn it down as an ecumenical gesture."

A turn in the road shortly thereafter reassured us that the dome was still there, that ecumenical gestures in the present era are being dedicated to creative rather than destructive impulses, and that upbuilding rather than demolition is to be the basic concern of what goes on under that dome in Vatican Council II.

It is true, of course, of every movement for reform, that some things must be torn down in order that other things can be built up, and I am sure this will be true of Roman Catholicism in the twentieth century, just as it was true of European Christendom in the sixteenth century. And as I spend Reformation Sunday in Rome (the Sunday closest to the anniversary of Luther's nailing the Ninety-Five Theses to the chapel door at Wittenberg on All Saints' Eve) it seems to me that without trying to make Protestants out of Catholics it is fair to assert that the spirit of reform must increasingly become the spirit of the Council.

That the very word can be used here so frequently is in itself significant. "Reformation" has had such unfortunate psychological and historical connotations for Roman Catholics that until quite recently they have shied away from using it at all. It was a "Protestant" notion, and therefore A Bad Thing. For the Catholic Church, which exists without spot or wrinkle, to acknowledge the need for reformation in her own life would have been a grave disservice to the truth and a cause of scandal to the faithful. I hastily acknowledge that there are some here who still adopt this view, and who look with grave alarm on speeches and tendencies that imply that not everything in the past is *per se* good and to be conserved without change. I am even learning from whom to expect such speeches. But the future, I am persuaded, is not with them, and I am so persuaded because I believe in the Holy Ghost and believe that He is stirring the Roman air and introducing fresh currents. I wish sometimes He would stir the air a little more vigorously, and I find that at this point I can make common cause with many bishops. But even though some in the Council will resist the Spirit, and do so with considerable adroitness, they will find Him in the end to be more nimble than they.

Lest the main burden of these remarks seem too euphoric, let me make perfectly clear that I believe the Reformation still has a long way to go. As I write this, for example, the Council fathers even on the procedural level are, to use a euphemism, bogged down. They are apparently beginning a struggle to find ways to expedite their business so that the air may be cleared of vain repetitions and time-consuming oratory. Better procedures, of course, do not guarantee better speeches or better results, but after four weeks of meetings, most people here are firmly wedded to the notion that better procedures might help! The appearance of simultaneous translation will also be a godsend not only in speeding Council procedures, but in upping the comprehension of Council fathers whose Latin isn't what it once was. This may even mean that the coffee bar won't be so crowded.

No one can yet tell, of course, to what degree some of the vigorous and truly reforming speeches on the Council floor will make their way into the new draft of the *schema* on the church that must be prepared after the current discussion has been completed. The assumption that because ideas are in the air they will surely get into the documents is an assumption that had better not be made too prematurely.

Even so, and being as "realistic" as possible, I would find it very hard to believe that the Spirit will abandon this Council. (If on a few occasions I have been tempted to that heresy, I find that such moments pass, usually when the voice of the Spirit is heard through a Suenens or a Koenig or a Bea or a Philbin or a McGrath.) There will surely not be as much reform and renewal as one could desire, whether one assesses what is "desirable" from a Protestant or a Catholic standpoint, but there will be an impetus given to fresh beginnings. The thing that is essential to remember about the spirit of reform is that it does not come to an end; there is no time when reformation has been completed. *Ecclesia semper reformanda* means the church always to be reformed, always in process of undergoing a reforming of her true self. And this is the only valid concept of reformation, a fact that Catholic theologians are now pointing out with as much vigor as Protestants.

To be more specific, what things at the Council indicate the possibility of reform, not as though the Catholic Church were to begin to look "more Protestant," but as though she were to become more truly catholic, more faithful to the fullness of the gospel God has bequeathed to Christians to share with all mankind?

The first thing to be cited must surely be a series of decisive actions taken by the pope before the Council actually got underway. The now famous speech about the reform of the Curia was an indication that the new pope intends to act vigorously. The Curia, he said, needs to be brought up to date and it needs to be internationalized. When one reflects that there is probably only one group of Catholics on earth who would not welcome this news — namely, the Curia itself — it is noteworthy that the speech was addressed precisely to that group. While it is not yet clear how fast such reform will proceed, a symbol of the new direction is the appointment of Cardinal Bea to the Holy Office. Cardinal Bea is a Biblical scholar, an ecumenical leader, and a German, and these are three graces that can scarcely be said to have dominated the Holy Office in the past. The appointment of Cardinals Suenens, Docpfner, Lercaro, and Agaganian to act as moderators of the Council was another important step by the pope, for these men, pre-eminently the first three, represent forward-looking movements within the church. In all candor it must be reported that up to the time of present writing, lines of authority within the Council have not been clarified, and the moderators have not yet had the impact upon the Council that they hopefully will have in the future.

A second reason for hope that "reform" has become a concept increasingly congenial to the Council mentality is the tenor of many speeches in the *aula* itself. There is always the danger (to which, perhaps, a Protestant observer is peculiarly suspect) of hearing what one wants to hear. But I am impressed, even while trying to keep my reactions sober and tempered, by the degree to which bishop after bishop engages, for the church, in continuous soul-searching. Some of the most impressive instances of this have come from the missionary bishops. They decry, in ringing terms, the church's identification with the rich, with the upper classes, with the external trappings of wealth and pomp and power. They call for the church to humble herself, and to identify herself not with the affluent but with the needy, to become a servant even as her Lord was a servant.

Others insist that the role of the laity will not have been sufficiently established simply by urging the layman to be on hand to help the priest with "church work." Rather, the apostolate of the laity must be an apostolate to the world, concerned to rebuild the structures of society, particularly of a society that has been cruel to so many of its members. From Ireland and Washington and Panama and France and India and South America and, let it also be said, on occasion from Spain, have come statements of a concept of the laity that hold great hope for a radical rethinking of the relation of the church to the modern world, and the place of the laity in that rethinking.

A third area where possibilities of reform exist is in the theological understanding of the church – and I must stress this again, even though I have noted it before. It is a well-known fact that Vatican I defined the teaching authority of the church in almost exclusively papalist terms. It is a less well-known but not less important fact that subsequently the Roman Catholic Church has recognized that the definition of Vatican I is incomplete. It is not wrong, the Catholic would say, since it is infallible, but it is incomplete. The *full* truth was not expressed by Vatican I. And the major theological issue with which Vatican II is wrestling is whether or not it can state the truth in a more ample way – a way that will complete what Vatican I began but did not, for a variety of reasons, finish. That is to say, can a way be found to define the authority of the other bishops along with the authority of the bishop of Rome in such a way that the latter's power is not diminished but is no longer unilateral? This is, if I may say so, quite an assignment, and the way Vatican I hangs over the discussions at Vatican II is at least challenging, if not oppressive.

Many Catholics will not want to speak of such doctrinal problems as matters of "reform," but rather as attempts at development or completion. But to the Protestant, at least, the new concern with collegiality is an example of reform. For it is attempting precisely to replace a less adequate view with a more adequate one. This does not mean that the result is going to be congenial to Protestant theology. But it does mean — and this is the important point — that such moves create greater rather than less possibilities for the ecumenical dialogue to continue at new depth.

One further example of reform within the church is the gradual approval, chapter by chapter, of the *schema* on the liturgy. It is possible that this *schema* may be promulgated during the present session. Even though it may not go as far as some liturgical experts would wish, it opens doors of a sort that could not have been contemplated a decade ago. Further extension of the vernacular in the mass and other sacraments, occasions for concelebration, situations in which the faithful can receive under both species, new attention to Scripture and sermon, reform of the breviary — these things may not seem spectacular on the surface, but they hold promise of great things to come. And when such reforms actually become a possibility within a given diocese, we will have a chance to see whether the bishops will be as forward-looking individually at home as they have been collectively at Rome.

That the Roman Catholic Church will never be the same again, simply because the Council has met, is already clear. But whether the spirit of reform will be translated into actual and specific reforms remains to be seen. Tangibly, all there is to point to so far is progress on the liturgy *schema*. Consequently, many questions still remain open: Will the fathers find a way to break through procedural impasses that threaten to stifle the Council's voice? Will laymen be given a significant role in the church of the future? Will laymen, for that matter, be permitted to speak on the floor of the Council? Will the Council be able to acknowledge that God works through Protestant "churches" and not just through baptized individuals who happen to be non-Catholics? Will a strong statement on religious liberty emerge and be adopted by an overwhelming majority? Will the place of Mary be treated in such a way that ecumenical dialogue is fostered rather than frustrated? Will the Council be able to move beyond glittering generalities when it finally gets to the famous "Schema Seventeen," on the church in the modern world? Can the Council openly and honestly acknowledge the degree to which sin exists within the church as well as outside the church?

The questions are endless. The hopes and the apprehensions therefore remain endless.

Whatever leads to reform or renewal is ecumenically significant, since reform and renewal are significant not in and of themselves but because they are paths toward greater fidelity to the Christian gospel. Their purpose is not so much to exalt the church as to make the church a more fit vehicle through which to exalt the gospel. I saw this symbolically portrayed last week at St. Peter's. During one of the Latin speeches my eyes (and perhaps my attention) wandered from our observer's tribune to one of the gigantic statues in the transept wall across from us. It is a statue of a saint holding a large crucifix. In one of those little tricks of light that lasts only a few moments, a beam of sunlight came in from the opposite window and was focused on the crucifix, illumining the figure of Christ so brilliantly that the saint could hardly be seen in the relative darkness.

This is a parable of the Council, of the Reformation, and of all impetus to reform and renewal today: So to illumine Christ, that it is He, and not ourselves, that the world sees, so that seeing Him, not us, the world may believe.

The Fifth Week
(October 28 – 31)

Commemoration of Pope John – the vote on Mary – the "four questions" finally appear as five – a victory for collegiality – significance of the two votes – the boom is lowered

Monday, October 28

Today there were no announcements by Felici, no distributions of emendations, no votes, no Latin interventions, not even any trips to the coffee bar. For this was the fifth anniversary of Pope John's election to the papacy and Pope Paul set aside the day for special commemoration of this fact. Our tribune was taken over by diplomats, for this was an "open session," and so once again we were in the very front, closer than anyone else to what was going on.

The cynical view of today's proceedings is that the pope realized people were getting tired and gave them the equivalent of a day off. But I have been around Rome too long now to adopt such simplistic views. I have learned to see hidden meanings in everything, and I am discovering that things are done here by subtlety and indirection. Hints, rather than outright statements, are the mode of communication, and there were hints today subtle and not so subtle that the Council fathers are expected to take to heart.

The pope himself said mass and since it was a dialogue mass we all had a chance to participate with him in a common act of worship. He endeared himself to every bishop in the place by fumbling his opening lines and thereby displaying a human ability to err which, even if it does not extend to *ex cathedra* statements, is comforting to behold. (Actually there was reason for the slip. When the pope was archbishop of Milan, he celebrated mass according to the Ambrosian rite, which is slightly different from the one employed in Rome.)

After mass that valiant leader of the progressives, Cardinal Suenens, gave an address about Pope John. Suenens spoke slowly and clearly — in French, which is a significant departure from normal protocol on such occasions — so that it was easy to follow him. It was a moving address, partly because the warm humanity of John came through so clearly, and partly because it made clear how strong is the continuity between the things John initiated and the things Paul will implement. It is significant that reference was made to John's famous statement about the "prophets of doom who are always forecasting disaster" — the Curia men around him who didn't want a Council — and John's dismissal of their lack of vision was reitcrated once again by Suenens. The address was constructed on the basis of the prologue to the Fourth Gospel, "There was a man sent from God whose name was John," and one really felt that what had been true about the apostle was also true of this contemporary descendant of the apostles.

When Suenens had finished, he went up to the papal throne to kneel before the pope, as is customary, and when he had arisen, Pope Paul arose and warmly embraced Suenens twice, as if to give his seal of approval to everything Suenens had said.

There was a touching moment during the recessional. As the pope went by us he unexpectedly left the papal procession, much to the discomfiture of Bishop Dante, the master of ceremonies, and it seemed for a moment as though he were going to claim the Anglicans and accept the validity of their orders. But he went through the Anglicans, and lifting up his hand to the tribune behind us, shook hands warmly with two old men sitting in the front row. A *peritus* whispered to me that these were two of Pope John's brothers who had come down from their peasant village for the day as special guests of Pope Paul. It was a lovely conclusion to the morning.

I feel that today was a very important day in the Council. I feel this because none of it needed to happen; the fact that it did happen indicates that it was meant to convey something. There need not have been any commemoration of the day at all — and yet there was. The pope need not have come to the Council on this day — and yet he did, the only session of the Council he has thus far attended. He need not have picked so obviously a "progressive" voice as Suenens to praise Pope John — and yet he did. Suenens' speech need not have stressed so strongly the continuity between John and Paul — and yet it did. The pope need not have embraced Suenens when the speech was completed — and yet he did, as though to leave no doubt in anybody's mind about his personal *imprimatur* to all that had been said. The voice was the voice of Suenens, but the thoughts were the thoughts of Suenens *and Paul.*

Since it is no secret that the Council has been bogged down in the last couple of weeks, I take today as the pope's way of indicating very gently but very clearly what the direction of the Council is to be from now on: It is to follow in the spirit of Pope John and bring to completion that which he began.

❖　　❖　　❖

I have had a number of occasions — Friday night with a group of *periti,* Sunday night with *periti* and a few bishops, and this noon at a lunch with a number of bishops — to voice my concerns about the Mary vote that is coming up tomorrow. I am somewhat surprised at the number of people who had not seen anything particularly crucial in the decision, and I have thus had an opportunity to make the "ecumenical pitch" for inclusion of Marian material in *De Ecclesia.* Apparently there has been furious politicking over the weekend, particularly by the "friends of Mary" who are trying to suggest that anyone who wants to deny her a separate *schema* is doing her dishonor.

The town is full of rumors — more than I have heard at any other time. Many of them center around the fate of the "four questions" about which we have yet heard nothing, and others focus on the need to reconstitute the commissions so that they will truly reflect the thinking of the Council. There is a danger, as one listens to such rumors, of reducing the Council to the dimensions of a TV melodrama, in which there are two groups of people, the good guys and the bad guys. The good guys are the people you agree with (in this case the "progressives") and the bad guys are the people you don't agree with (in this case the "conservatives"). Some people, for example, see a nefarious plot being hatched every time Ottaviani goes out for a cup of coffee.

Although I try to avoid this sort of thing, I find it harder and harder to avoid feeling that a great majority of the fathers are in danger of being thwarted by a small group of conservatives who have power and influence all out of proportion to their numbers. The one significant disadvantage we suffer as observers is that we rarely meet the conservatives. Thus we tend to share our ideas with that group in the Council most predisposed to take us seriously and listen to us, and while this enhances our hopes for the future of Catholic ecumenism, it also tends to make us even more indignant when "our" side appears to be taking a beating.

* * *

That nobody likes to take a beating was borne in on me by the conclusion of a conversation I had with some American bishops on the way out of St. Peter's:

Bishop: Where did you say you teach?

Brown: At Stanford University.

Bishop: Stanford, eh? Listen, your football team just clobbered Notre Dame. What kind of an ecumenical gesture is that?

Tuesday, October 29

Big things have happened today, even though it is not yet clear what they all mean. . . .

The morning got off to an auspicious start with mass in the

"Byzantine-Ukrainian rite, according to the liturgy of St. John Chrysostom." This is the most impressive liturgy we have yet seen, partly because of the wonderful music, full, deep, strong, and very Russian, which was sung by a choir in constant dialogue with the celebrants, and partly because the chief celebrant was Archbishop Slipyj of Russia, a magnificent figure with a white beard, who has only recently been released from seventeen years in a Siberian prison for his religious convictions.

Churchmen in the West argue and argue about whether certain things should be permitted or not — concelebration (a number of priests celebrating together), communion in both kinds (both bread and wine for the laity), the use of the vernacular, greater prominence to Scripture — while these and many other things have simply been taken for granted in the Eastern liturgies for centuries. Western churchmen cannot help but lose some of their parochialism as they are exposed to these strong and vigorous liturgies.

After mass, Felici had his usual announcements, but several were far from routine: (1) There would be a vote on Chapter Five of the liturgy *schema*. (There was, and it passed easily.) (2) There would be votes on emendations to Chapter Seven of the liturgy *schema*. (There were, and they passed easily.) (3) There would be a vote on whether to maintain a separate *schema* on Mary or to include material on Mary as the last chapter of *De Ecclesia*. (There was, and of this more later.) (4) There would be a distribution of five "propositions" which the fathers were to study and on which they would vote tomorrow. (Sensation in the *aula*.)

Sensation indeed! For the "five propositions" turned out to be an augmented version of the mysterious "four questions." Their appearance indicates that the moderators have been vindicated in the furious tug of war behind the scenes. This is one of the most important facts about the Council thus far — not as important, perhaps, as the *outcome* of tomorrow's vote, but very important as an indication that the Council can emerge from procedural stalemates. The procedure thus established can be a very useful means of arriving at some "sense of the meeting," so that the various commissions will know what direction to take in their revised documents.

❋   ❋   ❋

Yesterday, in what now emerges as a masterpiece of understatement, I suggested that "apparently there has been furious politicking" about the location of the material on Mary. The word "apparently" can be excised. I don't know what the proponents of inclusion of the Marian material in *De Ecclesia* have been doing, but those desiring a separate *schema* have indeed been working at a furious rate. These have been some of the arguments and tactics: (a) To deny Mary a separate *schema* is to downgrade her. (b) Alternate proposals, such as Abbot Butler's, deny the doctrines of the Immaculate Conception and the Assumption of the Virgin into Heaven (an untruth, incidentally). (c) The ecumenical situation will be harmed unless there is a separate *schema* — this being the argument of a leaflet distributed this morning on the steps of St. Peter's by five Eastern fathers who purported (wrongly) to be speaking for all the bishops of the East. (d) The *true* mind of the church favors a separate *schema* — this theme suggested in booklets printed on the Vatican Press in a format similar to official *schemata*, even to the inclusion of the words *sub secreto* on the cover.

The observers have received copies of a pamphlet that argues as follows: The two most significant facts of the past half century have been the rise in Marian devotion and the rise of the ecumenical movement. Clearly the latter is the result of the former and therefore ecumenical advance is dependent upon heightened Marian devotion.

The logic of this argument has not been coercive in its impact upon the observers.

The actual vote on the location of the Marian material was taken shortly after the announcements had been made, but the result was not announced until the very end of the morning. Even after he had given the tally, Felici failed to indicate which position had won. The proposal to include Marian material with *De Ecclesia* was responded to as follows: *placet*, 1114; *non placet*, 1074; null, 5.

It must have been five minutes before we were sure what the figures meant. It was so close that if 51 per cent had been needed (as Felici's original announcement had said), then the move to incorporate the material on Mary in *De Ecclesia* would not have carried. But if a simple majority (50 per cent plus one) was sufficient (as Agagianian had announced) then the vote had carried. The latter, of course, was the correct parliamentary ruling. It means that the more ecumenical decision has been made, but the closeness of the vote certainly makes it impossible to claim any smashing ecumenical victories. Twenty-one fathers, shifting their votes, could have changed the outcome.

The immediate impression one has is of a Council in deadlock, but I think this is a superficial view. There were too many extra factors involved in the vote, many of them emotional, to make it an authentic reflection of the mind of the Council. We will have to wait and see what happens tomorrow on the "four questions" (now five) if we are going to get an accurate gauge of the direction this Council is going to go.

*　　*　　*

There were interventions this morning as well. We had time for six cardinals and a bishop, and the bishop was the best of all. Cardinals Caregeira, Barros Camara, and Gilroy all gave general approval to Chapter Four of *De Ecclesia*. Ruffini gave a fairly mild talk, urging stress on the different kinds of holiness rather than emphasizing that all Christians partake of the same holiness. He also decried the emphasis on "mystery," since the church is a perfect society with a visible juridical structure all can see.

Cardinal Doepfner, speaking for eighty-one German and Scandinavian bishops, expressed approval of the stress that *all* are called to holiness rather than just those who take vows as "religious." He wanted more stress on holiness as dependent on God's grace, and a revision of the material to avoid an overly moralistic treatment. There should also be greater attention to the way in which Christ, through Scripture, Word, and Sacrament, gives content to holiness. Significantly enough, this echoed many of the emphases of the preceding speaker, Cardinal Quiroga of Spain.

All this was highly encouraging, but Bishop Vuccino of France was little short of amazing. He urged greater ecumenical emphasis in the chapter, and referred to Skydsgaard's speech to the pope asking for greater Biblical orientation in Catholic theology. Vuccino therefore tried to give a *Biblical* statement of the meaning of holiness and it came out . . . justification by faith! God is the source of all human righteousness and holiness; God gives faith, and man is justified only by this faith which is God's gift, and through which alone he can become holy.

Even though these themes were overshadowed by the other events of the morning, I find seeds of great hope in the interventions of Vuccino, Doepfner, and Quiroga. When Biblical and Christological emphases are taken this seriously by Roman Catholics, the ecumenical future is bright.

✿   ✿   ✿

After these speeches I re-examined the remarks I had prepared over the weekend for our "briefing session" on "the call to holiness." I am encouraged by the fact that the criticism I offered from a Protestant perspective could be met so fully by the comments of the morning. My concern was cast in the following terms:

In the *schema's* very proper concern with sanctification, it seems to neglect sufficient treatment of justification. I have no wish to polarize those terms. In fact, my concern is that the present *schema* bring them into close relationship. As it now stands, there is so much attention to the achieving of sanctity, and to the "states of perfection," that there is by consequence too little attention to the degree to which all of this is sheer gift, to the way in which the whole life of sanctity is one of *response* rather than one of initiative. That we are justified by faith, that salvation is by grace alone, is surely the Biblical foundation for the conviction that we can grow in holiness — and on this foundation the *schema* is not clearly enough built.

The same concern can be put another way. Protestantism does not have a monopoly on the insight that, in the life of sanctity, sin persists — though Protestantism may have pushed that point rather hard in times past. This recognition, that the life of the redeemed is not a sinless life but a life of the redeemed *sinner*, that in the face of divine holiness all our righteousness is as filthy rags, that grace comes constantly afresh to *sinful* man — this, I think, needs greater stress in contrast to a static notion like "the state of perfection," which is both difficult to understand, and misleading when understood.

The mystery of the interrelatedness of sin and grace, of redeemed man who in the midst of his *sin* is redeemed man, and who in the midst of his *redemption* is sinful man, whose growth in sanctity is one in which sin is always present (particularly when he makes too confident claims about his growth in sanctity) — these things, if acknowledged more clearly, would make the *schema* more Biblical, more evangelical, and more honest.

I even have a Latin phrase to suggest for inclusion in the *schema*, although I doubt that the ecumenical situation is sufficiently advanced to make its use possible. The phrase is Luther's *simul justus et peccator* (both justified and a sinner). This suggests the emphasis that must be present whenever we begin to make claims about the life of holiness.

I do not think any of this is contrary to the true articulation of Roman Catholic faith. And I think the *schema* would represent a more totally adequate articulation of Roman Catholic faith, and also help the ecumenical dialogue considerably, if this dimension could be highlighted with greater boldness.

Wednesday, October 30

One of the newspapers today had the somewhat misleading headline about yesterday's vote, "Council Fathers Vote Mary Into Church." One of the American bishops told me in the coffee bar that as he was coming up to St. Peter's this morning a woman approached him and said, "Father, how grand that you've voted Mary back into the church. What was the trouble? Was it a matter of regularizing her marriage, or had she failed to do her Easter duty?"

If yesterday's vote suggested a Council in deadlock, any such notion disappeared today in the vote on the "five questions." Not only has the authority of the moderators been vindicated, thereby ensuring that the Council will not drift, but the vote on all five questions was decisive — between 75 and 80 per cent in each case — indicating an impressive consensus in favor of a doctrine of collegiality, and by implication a check on what would otherwise have been an increasing triumphalist papalism.

The "five questions" asked whether it pleased the fathers that *De Ecclesia* be revised so that certain things be affirmed. The *first* asked whether the episcopate is to be considered the highest grade in the sacrament of orders. The *second* asked whether *all* bishops are to be considered members of the body of bishops (i.e., whether their authority is sacramental or jurisdictional). The *third*, which was crucial, asked whether the body "or college" of bishops succeeds the apostolic college, and possesses (along with the pope, who is its head, and not without him) full and supreme power over the universal church. The *fourth*, which was also crucial, asked whether the powers of the episcopal college were given by divine right. (The alternative would be that the powers are given by human consent, and that the college would thus exist merely at the whim of the pope.) The *fifth* asked whether the diaconate should be a permanent rank in the sacred ministry, according to the needs of the church in different areas. (No reference was made to a married diaconate in the wording of the fifth question.)

The vote means that a clear mandate has been given to the Theological Commission and that it must rewrite the *schema* so that the above emphases are present within it. A real corner has been turned by the Council and a one-sided nineteenth-century version of papalism has been successfully countered. This is beyond doubt the most important day in Roman Catholic history since 1870.

*   *   *

One has to shift gears rapidly at Council sessions, and even with all the attention to the "five questions" there was still time for thirteen interventions on "The Call to Holiness."

Cardinal Leger was grateful that the *schema* had finally broken through the traditional view that only the monastics can achieve true holiness. But the *schema* must give guidance for achieving holiness in political and economic life, as well as married life. There must be a theology of the laity developed by lay theologians who should be teaching on seminary faculties.

Cardinal Urbani of Venice wanted more stress on the holiness of the church, which more than compensates for whatever may be the defects in the holiness of those within it. Cardinal Bea, however, took the opposite tack. Whoever reads church history, he said, will realize that the church is full of sinners. If the church had been purer in the sixteenth century, the Reformation would not have been needed. As the New Testament reminds us, the Kingdom of God is like a net that catches both good and bad fish, like a field in which both wheat and tares grow until the harvest. Consequently, the *schema* must be much more cautious in using words like "perfection" to describe the life of the Christian or the Christian community.

This theme was picked up later in the morning by Bishop Russell of Richmond, Virginia. When one sees how easily churches accept patterns of racial discrimination, he pointed out, it is clear that terms like "holiness" and perfection had better not be used indiscriminately. Indeed, only Christ and Mary lived "perfect" lives; the most one can say of others is that they *seek after* perfection.

Bishop Buyghe of France pointed out that stress on the three counsels of perfection (poverty, chastity, and obedience) represents an inadequate approach. Not only does Christ not talk about obedience to religious superiors, but the entire Sermon on the Mount should be the guide to holiness, rather than a few isolated precepts.

The final speaker, Abbot Reetz of the German Benedictines, asked for the continued exemption of the "religious" from local episcopal control, so that members of religious orders could be used wherever they are needed in the world. He got a laugh after his comment that there are something like 8000 religious orders, and "the number of their members is so vast that not even the Sacred Congregation can count them."

Sensing that the discussion was moving beyond Chapter Four, Cardinal Lercaro, moderator of the day, asked the fathers if they desired to close discussion. The fathers did indeed. To a man.

✩   ✩   ✩

These last two days have been the most important days of the Council thus far. I have therefore tried to pull together my thoughts on the implications of these two crucial votes.

For a long time it has seemed that little was "happening" on the floor of Vatican Council II. Speeches were being given, routine votes were being taken, but little direction or movement was discernible. Talk of a "ten-year Council" could be

heard, and the faces of those who talked of it were not
wreathed with smiles.

But the votes yesterday and today give some real indication of where the Council is going. The first vote was more
spectacular, more emotion-ridden, and more difficult to interpret. It was also less important. The second vote (really a
series of five votes) was less spectacular, less emotion-ridden,
and less difficult to interpret. It was also more important.
Each vote has significance not only for the inner life of Roman Catholicism but also for the ecumenical posture of Roman Catholicism *vis-a-vis* the rest of Christendom.

The issue facing the Council fathers in the Mary vote
seemed a simple and largely procedural one: Should the presently existing *schema* on the Virgin Mary be retained as a
separate *schema,* or should it be incorporated into *De Ecclesia?* To many of the fathers, the question at first seemed
unimportant: What difference should it make *where* Mary
was treated, just so she got her due? But it soon transpired
that more was at stake than that, and that the impending
decision loomed as a crucial indication of the ecumenical
temper of the Council. If the fathers voted to make their
statement about Mary in the form of a *separate schema,* this
could encourage further excesses of Mariological devotion,
further doctrinal developments proceeding independently of
the rest of Catholic theology, and would thus widen the
cleavage between Catholics and Protestants. If, however, the
Council fathers voted to include their statement about Mary
within *De Ecclesia,* this would indicate that they were eager
to understand Mary in relation to the church, and as a part
of the church, rather than independently.

Perhaps the difference could be put this way: Was Mary
to be seen in the context of the church (so that there could be
safeguards against excesses of Marian emphasis) or was the
church finally to be seen in the context of Mary (as the independent development of Marian dogma in the last hundred years has seemed to suggest)? If the latter choice were

made, then the onward march of Marian dogma toward core-demptrix would be encouraged.

The vote was so disturbingly close that one is a bit uneasy to observe the Holy Ghost triumphing by so narrow a margin. Certainly the vote itself does not indicate a surging triumph of ecumenical concern. It is important to remember that, where Mary is concerned, Roman Catholics have as much piety and emotion, perhaps, as they do theology. The average Catholic feels as strongly *for* Mary (sometimes for good and sometimes for bad reasons), as the average Protestant usually feels strongly *against* Mary (also for good and for bad reasons). Many of the fathers genuinely felt that to deny to Mary a *schema* of her own was somehow to degrade, or at least downgrade, her. Many felt that such an action would appear as a repudiation of Mary, which would cause confusion among the faithful for whom Mary is a very active part of daily devotional life. Others felt that the action would appear to be a retreat from certain already defined, and therefore irreformable, dogmas. Others felt that the shift was simply designed to appease non-Catholics.

Reasons for voting to include Mary in *De Ecclesia* were likewise mixed. For some it was surely a matter of providing a context for bringing Marian excesses into some kind of control. (One South American bishop explicitly said this on the floor of the Council.) For others it seemed only proper theology to discuss Mary in a treatment of the church of which her Son is the head. For others, it was a matter of ecumenical emphasis, to demonstrate to the "separated brethren" that the *church* is basic for Catholic theology, rather than Mary, and that while Mary is important she is not at the center.

Close as the vote was and difficult to interpret as it is, the Council fathers have nevertheless taken a step which has the possibility of being ecumenically creative rather than ecumenically divisive. Whether it is one or the other will depend, of course, on the *content* of the statement that is finally made, and not simply on its *context*. It is clear that those who have ecumenical interests in this matter wish the revised statement about Mary to be as Biblically oriented as possible. While it will not "withdraw" anything about Mary that has been formally defined (as no Catholic statement could), it will emphasize as much as possible what the New Testament tells us about Mary.

If this happens, it seems to me that we Protestants have an important task on our hands. We do not and cannot accept the Mariological dogmas of the Immaculate Conception and the Bodily Assumption into Heaven. Because we do not accept them, we have tended to dismiss all things Marian from our minds, usually with an emotionally charged polemic. If, however, our Roman Catholic brethren are willing, partly out of concern for us, to deal with Mary as much as possible on the basis of our commonly shared Biblical revelation, then we have an obligation to open up our minds once again to the question of *the Biblical evidence* about Mary. We have paid too little attention to this in the past, partly because of our emotional bias against Catholic treatments of Mary and where they have led. But if we do indeed take the Scriptures seriously as the fountain and source of our faith, then we must examine afresh what the Scriptures tell us in this neglected area of our own theology.

Did yesterday's vote, then, really reveal an ecumenical concern at the Council? By itself, no. But today's vote had some clear ecumenical overtones, particularly the response as to questions three and four.

To question three, the bishops strongly affirmed the principle of the "collegiality" of bishops, and to question four they affirmed that this collegial power is "by divine right" and not just by human consent.

It may clear the air to point out what the alternatives would have been. A *denial* of collegiality would have been an affirmation of the supreme and sole power of the pope. But the *affirmation* of collegiality meant that the Council fathers were insisting that Christ had given power not just to Peter but to *all* the apostles; in terms of Catholic history this means that power in the church is not vested solely in the one Catholics believe to be Peter's successor, i.e., the pope, but also in those who are believed to be the apostles' successors, i.e., the bishops, meeting as a body or "college." Similarly, a *denial* that collegiality is "by divine right" would have meant that the power of the bishops is something that is bestowed by the pope and can therefore be taken away by the pope. But the *affirmation* that collegiality is "by divine right" means that the bishops share, along with the pope, in the rule of the church, and that this sharing of power is ordained by God rather than conceded by the pope.

I see two ecumenical implications in this decision about collegiality, one that will help the ecumenical climate immediately, and one that will raise later problems for it.

1. Positively, the decision means that Roman Catholicism is now completing the one-sided view of church authority promulgated by Vatican Council I, which gave the impression of the church as a kind of monarchy in which the monarch's power was unlimited and infallible. It was a picture uncongenial to Protestants, and (as events are now showing) one also uncongenial to many Roman Catholics. It would be false, however, to say that Vatican II is "retreating from" Vatican I; it would be truer to say that Vatican II is "advancing beyond" Vatican I. An incomplete definition, which dealt only with the power of the bishop of Rome, is now being completed by relating his power to the power of the other bishops. All of this will be helpful on the ecumenical scene, for it will dispel the notion that Roman Catholicism means extreme papal monarchical government. This is a clear gain over the past.

2. But the ecumenical problem that is thereby raised must not be overlooked. All Protestants will be happy if the idea of "papal imperialism" recedes into the background, but many Protestants will be less than happy at the notion that the office of bishop is by divine right and that the bishops alone are seen as the successors of the apostles.

Many Protestants who do not stand in an episcopal tradition can affirm at least the following about the episcopate:

(a) There were bishops in the church from a very early time; (b) bishops, for many branches of Christendom, have served as a symbol of the continuity of the church down through the centuries; (c) the appointment of men to oversee the life of various areas of the church is a useful way to have things done "decently and in order." On those terms, many non-episcopal Protestants could be persuaded to "accept episcopacy" as one of the terms of reunion with other Protestant bodies. This would constitute a recognition of bishops by human consent.

But today's vote goes far beyond that. It insists that bishops receive their power by divine right and that they are thus an essential part of the pattern of the church as God wills it. While many Episcopalians can accept this, most other non-Roman Catholics would have considerable difficulty with it. Thus the action of the Council must be seen on two levels. On one level it must be welcomed as a safeguard against extreme papalism, an indication of genuine reform within Roman Catholicism. But on another level it accentuates the difference between Catholics and most Protestants over what they mean when they think of "episcopacy" or propose to define the church in episcopal terms.

Does this mean that the impasse between us becomes greater? I do not think so. I am sure that the step toward collegiality is a reforming step, and that it will be creative of new life and vigor in the Roman Catholic Church. It will help the Roman Catholic Church become more truly *catholic* in the sense of being faithful to the fullness of the gospel — a gospel that was bequeathed not just to Peter but to others as well. If such renewal creates some new problems, we must be willing to meet them with courage and hope, believing that in His own way, the Spirit is leading us into all truth.

Thursday, October 31

Today will go down in history as The Day Doepfner Lowered The Boom. The atmosphere could not have been more changed. Now that the moderators have won their struggle for real power (as evidenced by the producing of the "five questions"), and now that it is clear that they were using that power to implement the will of the majority (as evidenced by the decisive nature of yesterday's vote), they seem ready for the first time to wield their power for the good of the Council.

Cardinal Doepfner, today's moderator, took giant strides to cut through the senseless repetition that has characterized the whole first month's debate. He began by pointing out that there were seven minor emendations to Chapters Six and Eight of *De Sacra Liturgia*. Rather than voting seven times he suggested that the fathers vote *en bloc* for all seven.

Did the fathers resent this rough treatment? The fathers applauded.

Then Doepfner made quite a speech. He said that full freedom of expression should be maintained, but that the pace of the Council was far too slow. He said that cloture had been voted yesterday on Chapter Four, but that twenty-five fathers had nevertheless asked for permission to speak beyond cloture. He said that he had no choice but to let them speak. But he warned them not to repeat what had already been said. He warned them that the moderator was the sole judge of whether or not a speech should continue. He warned them that the time limit would be cut from ten minutes to eight. He warned them that no matter how unhappy a speaker might be, his microphone would be cut off at the end of eight minutes.

Did the fathers resent this rough treatment? The fathers applauded.

Cardinal Arriba y Castro of Spain began by promising to speak briefly, a comment that was received with prolonged, if somewhat nervous, laughter in the *aula*. He spoke about worldliness, atheism, and divorce, but did not continue long enough to test the ire of the moderator. Bishop Emmanuel wanted the *schema* to make clear that married people could become saints.

Before announcing the third speaker, Doepfner announced that three of the twenty-five speakers for the morning had already sent word to scratch their names from the list. Applause.

A South American bishop stated that priests should show charity toward their people. Doepfner stirred uneasily. Another father wanted stress on the fostering of holiness. Doepfner commented that his remarks added nothing whatever to the discussion.

The next speaker was interrupted for straying from the point.

By this time, attention began to shift from the speeches to the reactions of the moderator. After a man had spoken two or three minutes, Doepfner would get edgy, or move up and down in his chair, or reach for his microphone, or press the warning bell, or confer with Suenens about whether to stop the man or not. He got us through twenty-two interventions, which is certainly a Council record.

At the end of the morning he announced that a number of fathers still wanted to speak on Chapter Four when the Council reconvened next Tuesday after the long weekend. He ordered them to submit their speeches before the weekend, so that the moderators could go over them to be sure they contained new material. Any material that was not new must be excised before presentation to the Council.

All of this may sound heavy-handed. But the fathers were with Doepfner all the way. And, as a matter of fact, nothing new *was* said all morning long.

Interlude: The Delicate Art of Observermanship

The four-day break in the Council, over this long but not lost weekend (November 1–4), provides an opportunity to shift gears and ponder the observer's role from a more relaxed perspective.

Here we are — thirty or forty of us non-Roman Catholic observers, allowed to remain in St. Peter's when the ominous *Exeunt omnes* has been uttered, granted copies of the *sub secreto* documents that the fathers are debating, so close to the center of things that we could reach over and tickle the ear of Archbishop Pericle Felici, the secretary-general of the Council, if any of us felt so inclined. How are we to behave in this privileged position? How are we to practice The Delicate Art Of Observermanship?

Observermanship we can define as The Art Of Giving The Impression That You Are With It Even Though You Don't Know Latin Very Well. Many of the observers do, of course, know Latin, and know it very well indeed. But others like myself bade farewell to Cicero after the New York State Regents' Examinations, and even a self-imposed refresher course with Scanlon and Scanlon, *Latin Grammar*, designed for priests "making a late vocation," hasn't given us a nonchalant attitude toward anything we hear beyond the *Venerabiles Patres* with which every speech on the floor begins.

It is true, of course, that we are provided with simultaneous translation by linguistically and theologically adept priests who give us a running account of the speeches and proceedings. Indeed, at this point we are far ahead of the bishops themselves, more than one of whose Latin isn't what it once was, and who are dependent on a *peritus* to cue them in each day after lunch about what happened at the morning session.

But even though we observers have had translators all along, it is important not to appear too dependent upon them, as this might betray lack of facility with the tongue of Mother Church. The only solution is to break away on occasion from the group surrounding a given translator, and *sit alone,* several feet from anyone else, listening with rapt attention to the torrent of Latin being amplified to the far corners of St. Peter's. During this time of studied emancipation, frequent head noddings of approbation are necessary, along with occasional slight clucking noises of disapproval. Most important is the sudden dive for the notebook to write down what has obviously been the gist, the real gist, of the last ten minutes of Latin oratory. Such a phrase as "Rem lv lndry prtr" has a kind of Latin look about it if scribbled carelessly, and can also serve as a prod after the morning session to remember to leave laundry with the porter.

The other way to create an impression of facility with Latin is by the collection and memorization of a select group of Latin terms which, in one's day to day jostlings with bishops and *periti,* can be made to roll so trippingly off the tongue that one's linguistic ability simply has to be taken for granted. (Note, for example, the correct use in the preceding sentence of the plural of *peritus,* itself used in the singular two paragraphs back. *That* sort of thing. . . .) Certain types of speaking that must be mastered are the following: (1) Never refer to the Council hall. It is always the *aula.* (2) Never talk about "the observers." They are always *observatores.* (3) For special effect, refer to the "separated brethren" (the usual term used by Catholics of non-Catholics) as the *fratres seiuncti.* (4) All "Council jokes" based on Latin puns are better than ordinary "Council jokes." If they can be drawn from that part of the Latin liturgy that is still in Greek, so much the better. For example, when it is rumored that Bishop So-and-So is in trouble with the Curia, one reports him saying at mass not *kyrie eleison* (Lord, have

mercy) but *Curia eleison* (Curia, have mercy). (5) The
term *schema* may be used to refer to the printed texts, but it
is preferable to refer to "a series of *schemata*," since Latin
plural terms that are not easily assimilable to English cog-
nates are more impressive. (6) The *schemata* (n.b.) should
always be referred to by their Latin titles. Never, for example, should an observer refer to "On the Sacred Liturgy," but
always to *De Sacra Liturgia*. (7) The *schemata* are not
printed in "pamphlet form," but in *fascicules*. (8) Reference
is never to be made to affirmative or negative votes, but always to *placets* or *non placets*.

Quite apart from Latin, there is a Council lingo that must
be adopted. A bishop never, for example, never "gives a
speech," he "makes an intervention." One does not get into
St. Peter's each morning with his Council "pass," but with
his "passport." One must distinguish carefully between
"Cardinal-moderators" and "Cardinal-presidents" (four of
the former who run the sessions, and twelve of the latter
whose role is not too clear). *Observatores* do not sit in a section or stand, but in a "tribune."

If a handy list of Latin terms and Council lingo is relatively
easy to acquire, how much more difficult and complex is the
whole branch of Observervermanship related to the press photographer. Flashbulbs pop around the Vatican Council in
ways that make a Democratic National Convention on TV
seem like a World War II blackout. There are, it is now established, three ways in which an Observer can get himself
photographed. He must (a) be Orthodox, or (b) have a
beard, or (c) Muscle His Way Up Front. The first two types
are by definition going to be photographed automatically,
so they need do nothing about it. They can even retire to the
fringes, sure that the photographer will seek them out, since
large purple hats or imposing beards make much more interesting and exciting pictures than simple little Anglo-Saxon
types in coats and ties. The simple little Anglo-Saxon types
in coats and ties are, as a matter of fact, the rarest species
of all in St. Peter's during a Council, but they are a dime a

dozen in the photographer's life elsewhere, and they just don't seem worth that extra flashbulb.

There have been some splendid examples of adroit footwork at this Council when the word "photographer" was mentioned. The surest ploy is to make one's way immediately to the side of the most prominent person in the room — be he monsignor, bishop, archbishop, cardinal, or pope — and engage him in conversation until, say, four flashbulbs have popped. (The number "four" ensures coverage by the main international press services.) On the other hand there is real balm for the person who Got There Second and gets cropped out of the finished print, for he can always refer to the "ecclesiastical pride" of the one who Got There First. In fact, *not* appearing in pictures could become a device to earn points for humility.

Casual Name-Dropping is the next most useful weapon in the arsenal of the observer. Who of us has not written, to someone back home, "As Cardinal Suenens said to me, in talking about the late Pope John . . ."? The folks back home do not realize that while Cardinal Suenens did in fact say it to you, he also said it to 4000 other people who were jammed into St. Peter's at the very same moment, let alone the millions who saw him on Italian TV. Another name-dropping device is possible because of the number of receptions in Rome to which the observers, along with the bishops (2300 of them), get invited. Indeed, often two names can be dropped in one sentence: "As Cardinal Koenig said to me at Prince Colonna's party. . . ." But this device is subject to the law of diminishing returns if pressed too far. The effect is undoubtedly lost when the line goes, "As Cardinal Koenig said to Oscar Cullmann and myself while we were talking with Cardinal Doepfner in the garden of the Palazzo Colonna. . . ."

Another string in the observerman's bow is knowledgeability about rumors. It is not enough to be the recipient of rumors. One must also disseminate them. One never says, however, "It occurs to me that perhaps the pope. . . ." He says, "I have it from a source close to the Vatican that the pope. . . ." He need not, however, divulge that the "source close to the Vatican" is the chestnut vendor who sets up his portable stove every evening near the Santa Anna Gate.

Parties are the best places to engage in the type of midwifery that brings rumors to birth. The system goes like this. The observer turns to the person on his left, who may be (and usually is) Father Weigel, and says, "Father Weigel, have you heard that the pope is going to appoint a fifth cardinal-moderator?" After a couple of minutes of exploring this possibility the observer turns to the person on his right and says, "Father Weigel has just heard that the pope is going to appoint a fifth cardinal-moderator." He then goes off to get himself another sandwich. By the time he returns, the oral tradition has grown to more intimate and therefore more authoritative form at the far side of the room, *viz:* "Gus got it straight from Lercaro; they'll announce the new moderator's name tomorrow."

The fact that "Gus" subsequently denies all connection with the rumor only lends more credence to it, since who would want to be accused of breaking conciliar secrecy in such a flagrant way? As the evening wears along the rumor is well on its way to maturity as a Verified Rumor if it can be associated with the names of people who are Really On The In — "Frank Murphy," perhaps, or "Malachy Martin," or (since it is Very Good Form to be able to refer to a Right Reverend Monsignor by his first name) "George Higgins." And the observer knows that his rumor has really caught hold if he picks up *Time* magazine the next week and finds his rumor mentioned in the Religion section after a paragraph that begins, "Rumors fluttered up and down the Via della Concilazione last week like butterflies moving across a windswept field."

One further dimension of Observermanship must be itemized. It is essential to say, once a week or so, "I had a most illuminating chat in the coffee bar with the man who is reputed to be Xavier Rynne." The response will come, "You mean Father ——— ?" To which the observer must be able to reply, "No, no, it's pretty clear now that he's just a cover for the real Xavier Rynne. And I have reason to believe that the real Xavier Rynne is the auxiliary bishop of ———." (Or, for the sake of variety, ". . . that *peritus* from France," or ". . . one of the seminarians who works with the computors.")

If the observer has talked to enough people in the course of five three-hour sessions each week for nine and a half weeks, the mathematical chances of his having, whether knowingly or not, talked to "Xavier Rynne" are pleasantly high. And if pressed as to which of these hundreds of people really *is* Xavier Rynne, the observer is always entitled to reply kindly, "I'm not at liberty to say," or, less kindly, but in a perfect example of Observermanship, "Sorry, *sub secreto.*"

The Sixth Week
(November 5 – 8)

A new *schema* sails into rough waters – bishops *vs.* Curia – Curia *vs.* bishops – significance of the vote on the "five questions" – the Frings-Ottaviani exchange

Tuesday, November 5

The long weekend has produced a new Council story. The mystery of the one bishop who always votes *placet juxta modum* (acceptance with modifications) is a mystery that may never be cleared up. But now, so it is reported, there is a bishop *so* cautious that when he signs his attendance card *adsum* (I am present) each morning he writes across it *Adsum juxta modum.*

The moderators, at any rate, are growing less cautious and more assertive. Suenens continued the Doepfner tradition by announcing that the seventeen remaining interventions on Chapter Four of *De Ecclesia* had been reviewed by the moderators. None of the interventions had contained anything new or significant, therefore none of them would be given.

So we have a new week, a new situation, a new moderatorial policy, and a new *schema*. The latter is entitled *De Episcopis ac de Diœcesium Regimine* (On Bishops and the Government of Dioceses). This sounds tame on the surface, but it contains potential fireworks, particularly the first chapter dealing with the relationship of the bishops and the Curia. I was told last night that, if the smouldering feeling about the Curia is ever going to erupt at the Council, this is the place to expect it. The second chapter deals with the government of dioceses and the relations between bishops, coadjutor bishops, and auxiliary bishops. The third chapter (which will also bring forth differences of opinion) deals with the "national conferences" of bishops, and the powers such conferences should have: Is a bishop the absolute ruler in his diocese, or can a national conference of bishops enact legislation that is binding upon him even if he disagrees with it? The fourth chapter deals with the boundaries of dioceses and ecclesiastical provinces.

The first speaker after the *relatio* was that wonderful man Cardinal Lienart of Lille, whom to watch during mass is to learn what prayer really is. He is tall, with a finely etched face, perhaps the most "holy" face I have ever seen, kindly but with real strength and power behind the kindness, and absolutely snow-white hair. While he gave general approval to the *schema*, he made clear that it needs drastic revision, particularly to bring it into line with last week's vote on collegiality. He referred to the pope's speech, calling for reform of the Curia, and insisted that if the bishops are to collaborate with one another and with the pope, the Curia must not stand in their way. Therefore there must be a new chapter dealing directly with the relationship of the bishops and the pope, and clarifying the fact that bishops do not rule only in their own dioceses but have rule in the entire church.

Cardinal McIntyre of Los Angeles took up a different problem. He was worried that the episcopal conferences, described in Chapter Three, might achieve juridical power, and thereby challenge the authority of the bishop in his own diocese. Such a change would be so radical as to threaten the very church itself.

Cardinal Gracias was critical of the *schema* as a whole, claiming that it was too narrow, that it was written from the point of view of old-style Canon Law, and that it did not make sufficient provision for widespread reform of the Curia.

Cardinal Richaud of Bordeaux, a member of the commission preparing the *schema*, was even more blunt. He said that the text had been tampered with between the time the commission last saw it and the time it was distributed to the Council fathers. Bishop Gargitter of Bressanone also charged that the text was not the one the members of the commission had drawn up, but had been changed in order to emphasize in a one-sided way "the rights and the central organs of the Roman Curia." Leon of Columbia said that Council rules had been broken in presenting it, since half of the members of the commission had never had a chance to discuss the present text.

The same critique continued relentlessly all morning. Rupp of Monaco felt that every suggestion in the *schema* had a loophole through which escape from change was possible. Jubany of Barcelona found it fuzzy and confused. Bazelaire of France felt it was too juridical. Garonne of France did not like the order of the chapters. Marty of France wanted it rewritten on the basis of the collegiality vote. Baudoux of Canada felt that it downgraded the bishops for the sake of upgrading the Curia.

Summary of the morning's discussion: *De Episcopis* sailed into rough waters. Every speech was critical. The criticisms are on two main fronts: (a) The content, which exalts the Curia at the expense of the bishops, and (b) the mode of its composition, which makes clear that it exalts the Curia because the Curia members of the commission rewrote it to suit their own point of view.

* * *

While wandering around Bar-jonah this morning, I was casually informed by one of the *periti* that he was looking forward to my intervention tomorrow on "A Protestant View of Religious Liberty." Taking this as a good-natured leg-pull I informed him that I couldn't appear on the Council floor until Wednesday since the Latin translation wasn't completed yet. I then discovered that I am, in fact, scheduled to address the American *periti* tomorrow afternoon on "A Protestant View of Religious Liberty." By dint of rushing around I got a copy of the Council's as yet unreleased statement on religious liberty; by dint of friendly pressuring I strong-

armed Father Weigel into translating it for me, and by dint
of some evening work I was able to prepare a few comments.
A kindly providence had seen to it that I had on hand some
World Council materials on religious liberty, picked up at
Geneva on the way to Rome.

Anyone who thinks Roman Catholicism is an efficient,
monolithic structure, in which orders come from above and
everything follows thereafter like clockwork, need only
spend a few weeks in the Eternal City to learn otherwise. I'm
just glad I found out about my assignment *this* morning and
not tomorrow.

                    *   *   *

At our "briefing session" this afternoon we lingered with
Chapter Four of *De Ecclesia* on "The Call to Holiness," feeling that *De Episcopis* is a bit beyond our bailiwick. An
interesting thing happened. After I had given my Presbyte-
rian-tinged-with-Niebuhr comments, the gist of which I
recorded in last Tuesday's entry, Professor Skydsgaard, a
Lutheran, and Professor Miguez-Bonino, a Methodist, likewise gave reactions to the chapter. Hébert Roux, the French
Reformed pastor, pointed out afterward that the three of us,
coming from three different traditions of the Reformation —
Calvinist, Lutheran, and Methodist — had all offered substan-
tially the same critique. Even more significant, perhaps, was
the fact that the Catholics who responded to our comments
felt that everything we had mentioned could be said in a
Catholic framework and hence incorporated within the
schema.

I must say a word about Skydsgaard's comments at all of
these sessions. He is particularly impressive because he is so
genuinely humble and so genuinely searching for the truth
of the gospel rather than for a platform on which to score
points against the Catholics. When he criticizes, one feels
that it costs him real pain to do so. His difficulty with Chapter Four was that it lacked a Christological and Biblical

foundation. The approach was too moralistic and lacked the sovereign freedom and real joy of the New Testament, where a man is a radically new creature because his sin is forgiven. The call to sanctity can only be a call to despair unless it is grounded in the sanctity that is a pure gift from God. Since this is lacking in the *schema,* its tone resembles an uplifted forefinger of warning rather than a beckoning to joy.

To hear this put so simply and directly is to realize that one has been exposed to something basic and authentic, common to both Catholicism and Protestantism at their best.

Wednesday, November 6

De Episcopis got rough treatment yesterday, but that was nothing compared to what it sustained today. Seldom have I heard a document exposed to such a sustained battering. With the predictable exception of Cardinals Ruffini and Browne, seventeen speakers declared war in no uncertain terms. The main point, reiterated with all the delicacy of a battering ram, centers on the need to clip the Curia's wings. Put more positively, there is a concern to develop the practical implications of collegiality so that the bishops may exercise the powers that are rightfully theirs.

The list of cardinals announced to speak is always a good tip-off on how the discussion will go, and the lineup this morning was unambiguous: Ruffini, Koenig, Alfrink, Bea, and Browne — three of the strongest progressive voices flanked on either side by the strongest conservative voices.

Cardinal Ruffini, doughty defender of things past, argued that last week's vote does *not* establish the principle of collegiality. The fathers must realize that it would be particularly dangerous to use that vote as a basis for giving power to episcopal conferences. The latter will make laws and thereby force the hand of the pope so that his absolute power will be weakened. The church must therefore move very slowly and cautiously in dealing with a principle such as collegiality.

Cardinal Koenig, however, insisted that the *schema* must be rewritten to incorporate the principle of collegiality. What is needed, indeed, is an international college of bishops that can meet regularly in Rome and assist the pope. This is eminently feasible in the era of swift transportation, and would be a specific and practical way of implementing collegiality, so that bishops and pope can genuinely share in the rule of the church.

Cardinal Alfrink of Utrecht pushed Koenig's recommendation further and gave the most important speech of the debate thus far. Since last week's vote has made clear that collegiality is *de jure divino* (by divine right) and not merely by human consent, there must be a central organ established through which the bishops can assist the pope in Rome. The present situation is not representative, for the pope's assistants (the Curia) are not sent to Rome by the bishops and cannot speak for them. The Curia must not be an instrument of authority *over* the bishops, as it tends to be now, but must become an instrument *of* the bishops, subordinate to them. The order must no longer be pope, under whom is the Curia, under whom are the bishops; the order must become pope and bishops together, under whom is the Curia.

It is hard to see how it could have been more directly put, and when Alfrink had concluded there was a burst of applause from the rear of the *aula* (where the younger bishops sit) that made its way clear up to the front.

Cardinal Bea made the point that bishops not only have responsibility in their own dioceses, but must also act together for the good of the whole church. This means that they must work more directly with the bishop of Rome than the *schema* now indicates. The Catholic Church is often accused of a desire to dominate, and its excessive centralism gives some cause for the accusation. To establish a way for bishops from all over the world to give assistance to the pope would help to neutralize these charges and be a boon in the ecumenical encounter.

There was so much applause this time that Suenens,

moderator of the day, was forced to remind the fathers that applause is forbidden.

With considerable emotion, Cardinal Browne, vice-chairman of the Theological Commission, reminded the fathers that collegiality had not yet been clearly enough defined to make it a suitable basis for the present *schema*. Some of the speakers, he noted, seemed to feel that an episcopal college would have clearly defined power and structure. But the fathers should remember that all of this is idle speculation until the Theological Commission had ruled on the validity of the principle of collegiality.

The intervention did not last five minutes, but it neatly posed the problem of the last five weeks: Does the Theological Commission act in defiance of the expressed conviction of the Council, or does the Theological Commission merely state what the Council has already decided? Put more bluntly: Is the Theological Commission the master of the Council or its servant? If either of the initial alternatives is correct, the fathers might as well pack up and go home.

The *schema* may have found some defenders among the cardinals this morning, but it found none among the bishops. The first two interventions were particularly strong. Veuillot of France simply stated that since the *schema* doesn't reflect a doctrine of collegiality there is little point in discussing it until it is rewritten. Gomes dos Santos of Brazil, speaking for sixty Brazilian bishops, was even more blunt. The *schema* must be completely redone. The Curia must be reconstituted to become the arm of the pope *and the bishops*, and national conferences of bishops must be able to deal with regional problems without having to appeal every time to Rome for a ruling.

This was the tenor of the rest of the morning. The text must be completely redone (Bandiera de Mella of Brazil); the text is too juridical (Olalia of the Philippines); the text is out of touch with the modern world (Simons of India); the text is too cut and dried (Ruotolo of Italy); the text must reflect a doctrine of collegiality (Hodges of Wheeling, West Vir-

ginia, and Hermaniuk of Winnipeg); the text is not ecumenical and lacks reference to the patriarchs (Gonzalez of
Spain); there must be a new text prepared by a new commission (Cooray of Ceylon).

Toward the end of this procession, Cardinal Suenens asked
for cloture and got it without difficulty. This was followed
by a vote on the acceptability of the *schema* as a basis for
detailed discussion. The only options were *placet* or *non placet*. The result: *placet,* 1610; *non placet,* 477; *placet juxta
modum* (and therefore null), 2.

I see two implications in this vote. First, it does not mean
that a majority of the fathers approve the text and that the
speeches have merely reflected a dissident but vocal minority. Many bishops have commented in the coffee bar that,
although they dislike the text, they will vote to accept it *as
a basis for discussion,* since it can be modified, changed, and
rewritten as drastically as they please. To vote for outright
rejection would mean starting from scratch and this might
take years of work. The wiser course, therefore, is to accept
the present text for discussion, and then make perfectly clear
in discussion which way the revisions must go.

The second implication of the vote is that a real revolution
is underway: the bishop who votes *placet juxta modum* has
made his first convert.

❋　　❋　　❋

The first speaker on Chapter One, the relation of the
bishops to the Curia, was that venerable and formidable
patriarch of Antioch, Maximos IV, and he made clear that
criticism has not been stifled by the vote to accept the *schema*
for detailed discussion. Indeed, the theme of the bishops and
the Curia is a natural for Maximos, who is always inveighing
against the extreme Latinization of the church. He felt that
the *schema* was much too timid. It left too much power in the
hands of the Curia. More use must be made of the bishops,
and if there is to be a senate to assist the pope it must include

patriarchs as well. The need for such a permanent senate is clear, but it must be over the Curia rather than subordinate to it.

It is this kind of sentiment that has led to another Council story. Since Bea and Maximos present the greatest challenge to the entrenched conservatives, it is reported that instead of confessing *Mea culpa, mea culpa, mea maxima culpa* at mass each morning, the conservatives beat their breasts and exclaim, *Bea culpa, bea culpa, bea maximos culpa.*

     *   *   *

What has happened to plans for simultaneous translation? We had thought it would be introduced yesterday. But apparently a new technical problem has arisen. Since the translations will be broadcast over short wave, it would be possible to pick them up outside St. Peter's with a sensitive set. Ways must be found to circumvent this possibility (though with the full press coverage being given I can't quite see why). But there are all sorts of melodramatic possibilities. I envisage somebody inadvertently kicking over the portable stove of a chestnut vendor on the Via della Concilazione and discovering that it is really a high-powered short-wave set being operated not by a chestnut vendor but by Louis Cassels of United Press, out to scoop the world. And I can see groups of evil-minded progressives and conservatives working out plans to "jam" the interventions of the Ottavianis and the Doepfners.

     *   *   *

This evening Lukas Vischer, of the World Council of Churches, and I spoke to about sixty American *periti* on the religious liberty question. Since there will be other occasions to present this material in Rome, I shall polish up my hastily constructed notes and include them later (see Sunday, November 17). I was much heartened by the response. With one possible exception, the *periti* were fully "with us," con-

cerned to affirm all the things Protestants want to hear the
Catholic church affirm, and sharing with us a measure of
perplexity about how to define the "limits" of religious liberty
so that it does not become license.

The evening ended over a meal with two Jesuit friends,
neither of whom expressed the slightest interest in marrying
my daughter.

Thursday, November 7

Today for the first time I was late for mass, due to a frustrated attempt to buy some stamps beforehand at the Vatican Post Office. (Whatever charism of grace descends on
bishops at ordination has no visible effect on the way they
conduct themselves in a crowded post office.) As I was rushing down the side aisle of St. Peter's during the *Gloria*, trying
to find my place in the missal, I was stopped by one of the
periti who was eager to pursue a couple of matters arising
out of my comments last night on religious liberty. It has
surprised me that many of the fathers can adopt such a casual
attitude to what is going on at the altar. Clerks are always
bustling about during the prayers, little clusters of people are
frequently conferring with one another, photographers always run wild, and there is even an occasional flashbulb out
of the bishop's section.

This seems to be what can happen when one has an
"objective" view of what is taking place at the altar, when
the bread and wine become the body and blood of Christ
regardless of how people "feel" during the sacramental acts
themselves. The same point came out last night in my discussion with the Jesuits. I mentioned how much the mass
yesterday had meant to me because it was said slowly, and
while they agreed with me, they also said that a group of the
fathers had criticized the celebrant for being so emotional
and "subjective." I think Protestants and Catholics have over-
reacted against one another at this point, Catholics caricaturing a Protestant view of the sacraments as "mere

subjectivity," and Protestants caricaturing a Catholic view of the sacraments as "sheer magic."

Some of us in the observers' tribune have come to refer to Archbishop Pericle Felici, the secretary-general of the Council, as "Uncle Pericles," because of the way he lectures the fathers during his announcements. Today, however, he was in good form: Announcing that one of the bishops would be 101 years old next Saturday, Felici said that he had sent him a telegram on behalf of the Council, wishing him "good health and a long life."

* * *

The moderators seem determined that things shall move at a quicker pace. Agagianian interrupted many speakers this morning, either to call them back to the point or to inform them that their time had run out. I hope this represents the new pattern, for if so there will be time not only to discuss *De Oecumenismo,* but also the supplementary chapters on the Jews and religious liberty.

After two days of relentless attack on the Curia, we had a bit of return fire. Following the course of discussion was like watching a tennis match in which the ball goes rapidly from one court to the other. The point of difference in relation to the present *schema* is clear, and it is a crucial point not only for the future of the Council, but for the future of the church. The *progressives* argue: Since we have already given overwhelming support to the notion of collegiality, the present *schema,* written before that vote, must be drastically overhauled in order to bring it into line. The *conservatives* argue: No decision has been made about collegiality. A straw vote does not bind the Theological Commission, and we must wait and see what the commission decides about collegiality before we talk about a new doctrine that seriously threatens the supreme authority of the pope.

The fact that this issue continues to be debated indicates how crucial the vote last Wednesday really was. Without that vote, the Council would be floundering badly, devoid of any criteria by which to test its own mind. But with that vote, the mind of the fathers has been made so clear that it is obvious that the principle of collegiality must be reflected in everything further the Council says and does. That the Theological Commission could disregard the import of the "five questions" in redrafting *De Ecclesia* is conceivable; that the fathers would accept such a draft is not. That the chairman and vice-chairman of the commission may nevertheless try to thwart the majority seems well within the realm of possibility. This is why the complaint is increasingly voiced that the crux of Vatican Council II lies in the Theological Commission, whose officers seem unwilling to accept a clear mandate.

*   *   *

Cardinal Ritter applied the collegiality principle to the complex interrelationship between pope, Curia, and bishops. Since the bishops have their power by divine right (the fourth of the "five questions"), it is clear that they do not receive their *power* from the pope, but only the privilege of *exercising* their power. Thus the bishops are not "the pope's men" in the same sense in which Curia officials are, but share with him in the governing of the church. The relationship of bishop to pope is the crucial one rather than (as the *schema* suggests) the relationship of bishop to Curia. Furthermore, the *schema* errs in implying that bishops could be given "new" powers; the proper way to put it would be to indicate that "old" powers (absorbed in actual practice by the Curia) are to be returned to them.

The tennis ball of conciliar debate went immediately to the furthest extreme when Peter XVI, patriarch of Cilicia, arose on the other side of the nave and gave a strong papalist speech, in the course of which he defended the Curia, which has done its job well and served the church faithfully. An organization can always be improved, but the attacks on the

Curia in recent days have been unwarranted, and will cause great scandal to the faithful. One should never forget the great services the Curia has rendered to the church.

Archbishop Florit of Florence agreed that there could be a central group of bishops above the Curia, thereby placating the left, but he went on to dismiss the importance of the vote on the "five questions," thereby placating the right. Last Wednesday's action, he said, should be taken *cum grano salis*—a phrase even I can get now without benefit of translator.

Souto of Spain defended the Curia, strongly insisting that the powers of the bishops are conferred by the pope and not "by divine right." But the ball went back to the other side of the net as Gouyon of France insisted that bishops be actively involved with power, in decisions made at Rome. Bishop del Pino, contrariwise, has had relations with the Curia for thirty years and has discovered that the Curia moves with wisdom and holiness. Indeed, divine providence is at work within it.

My discussions in the coffee bar now tend to center on the religious liberty question. Most men that I talk to couldn't agree more about the things that need to be said and the importance of saying them now. The fear is that the chapter on religious liberty, which the fathers have not yet received, may be held up indefinitely in the Theological Commission, and that by a series of delaying procedures it may be prevented from reaching the Council floor in time to be acted on. I keep pointing out how unfortunate this would be for ecumenical understanding, and keep being reassured that all pressures are being exerted that can be exerted. I am encouraged by the degree to which the Americans at the Council profess no interest in a culture in which religion and nationality are intertwined. We have seen how unfortunate this can be for both church and state, whether in Spain or Scandinavia. Since cultural pluralism is here to stay, rather than harking back nostalgically to the thirteenth century (or the sixteenth) it is better to come to terms with the present situation and find ways of dealing with it creatively.

The interventions for the rest of the morning continued to be critical of the *schema* and its elaborate defense of the Curia. There is increasing support for the idea of some kind of senate of bishops that would be independent of the Curia and would work directly with the pope. Indeed, Bishop Van der Burgt of Indonesia went so far as to suggest that such a senate should be established even before the Council adjourns.

I can imagine members of the Curia who hear this kind of thing wondering what evil quirk of fate ever brought the Council into being in the first place. Things the Curia has done for decades, even centuries, are for the first time being openly called into question and subjected to a devastating critique. It is too soon to know how much of the discussion we have heard can be legislated into a conciliar document and promulgated into church law. But it is clear that the genie is out of the bottle, and nobody is ever going to be able to get it back in.

Friday, November 8

Mark this down as a day long to be remembered. During the course of the morning the dome of St. Peter's was blown sky-high, and in just what form it will come down and be reassembled, nobody knows.

The session started easily enough. Felici announced that the 101-year-old bishop was in the *aula*. Applause. He wanted to convey his thanks for the fathers' telegram and wish them good health in return, and "an even longer life" than his. Appreciative chuckles. Felici also gave the welcome word that the long-awaited statement on the Jews would be distributed as Chapter Four of *De Oecumenismo*, the *schema* to be considered next. He then announced the speakers for the morning. The cardinals alone represented all shades of the ecclesiastical spectrum: Barros Camara, Frings, Lercaro, Rugambwa, Ottaviani, and Browne.

Barros Camara spoke in the name of 110 Brazilian bishops who want the regional conferences of bishops given power to change laws in their own territories without having to appeal each change to Rome, since the Curia has no way of knowing what is needed in Brazil. The Brazilian bishops also support the idea of a senate of bishops in Rome working with the pope.

Then Cardinal Frings of Cologne got up to speak. He is elderly, frail, and almost blind, but he is also strong, clear, and direct. In a matter-of-fact, unemotional tone of voice he delivered the most telling indictment of the Curia to date. He began very mildly, announcing that he wanted to make three points. The first had to do with collegiality. The voto of October 30 had been perfectly clear, even though only indicative, and he had been astonished to hear Cardinal Browne, vice-chairman of the Theological Commission, not only question its significance, but assert that it would be up to the Theological Commission to determine the truth or falsity of the doctrine of collegiality. The commission's only job, Frings continued, is to execute and obey the Council's wishes; its only reason for existence is to follow the expressed will of the Council. Certain speeches have seemed to suggest that the commission has sources of truth at its disposal that are denied to the rest of the fathers.

Secondly, a distinction must be made between the administrative and judicial procedures of the Curia, and this must include the Holy Office as well. The Holy Office does not fit the needs of our times. It does great harm to the faithful and is a cause of scandal throughout the world.

At the words "a cause of scandal," the Council fathers broke into applause, both loud and sustained. That Frings was applauded is significant, but what is even more significant is that his intervention was *interrupted* by applause. This is the first time such a thing has happened all fall and nobody in the tribune could remember it happening all last year.

Frings, however, had not finished. He went on to spell out the reasons for the scandal. The Holy Office should not be able to condemn a man without giving him an opportunity to answer the charges leveled against him. Nor should it be able to condemn books and give no reason for the condemnation. Even though many men have served it faithfully, its entire structure must be revamped.

Frings' third point was that there should be a drastic reduction in the number of bishops working in the Curia. Bishops should be ordained to care for souls, rather than to have status as administrative assistants. Much of the work in the Curia could be done just as well by laymen.

Although Agagianian announced the next speaker's name the moment Frings concluded, he could not forestall a second round of applause. In some inexplicable and unforeseen way, Frings' speech was the right speech at the right time by the right man. Alfrink said much the same thing two days ago, and many bishops have spoken in the same vein, but it was Frings who brought the Council to a moment of piercing clarity.

Cardinals Lercaro of Bologna and Rugambwa of Tanganyika strongly supported the creation of an episcopal senate to collaborate directly with the pope. It must not be within the Curia, but independent of the Curia. Since the pope had asked for such help, the fathers must respond. A new committee should draft plans for such an organ, and make specific suggestions as soon as possible.

Both of these speeches were delivered quietly, but as one of the observers commented, "You don't need to speak loudly to drop dynamite."

While Rugambwa was speaking, Ottaviani, the head of the Holy Office, came down to the other microphone and from the moment he began to speak it was obvious that he was very angry. Before commenting on Chapter One, he began, he wanted to make the highest possible protest against what had been said about the Holy Office, whose real head is the pope himself. (Applause, but not much, coming from the front of the *aula*.) The criticisms that have just been made are misunderstandings of the procedures of the Holy Office. The Holy Office always examines cases carefully, and always calls in acknowledged experts before it makes a judgment on any man's writing. Since the Holy Office is under the pope, any criticism of the Holy Office is a criticism of the pope himself.

Ottaviani then went on to discuss collegiality. From some of the speeches in the *aula,* he said, one would think that collegiality had already been defined. It has not. The vote on the "five questions" was not a definition. Only the Theological Commission can decide such matters. Furthermore, why had the moderators framed the questions? They should have referred the matter to the Theological Commission, which alone is competent to do such things, and which, if consulted, could have provided a more adequate way of posing the issue. The questions framed by the moderators were based on a vicious circle. The existence of an apostolic college in the New Testament was simply assumed, in order that a modern episcopal college could be based on it. But there are no arguments whatever to support the notion of an apostolic college in the New Testament. Finally, those who are defending collegiality say that it does not diminish papal power. But it would indeed diminish papal power. Full authority was given only to Peter and to Peter's successor, the pope. The sheep are not to lead Peter; Peter is to lead the sheep.

There was no applause at the conclusion of this speech. Ottaviani was followed immediately by Cardinal Browne, vice-chairman of the Theological Commission, who again reiterated the conservative theme that collegiality is a threat to papal power and contrary to the teaching of Vatican I. Shaking his hand dramatically at the fathers, Browne concluded *Venerabiles patres, caveamus, caveamus!* (Venerable fathers, beware, beware!)

✳   ✳   ✳

By this time I was emotionally drained and sought refuge in the coffee bar. So did practically everyone else, all of us assuming that the rest of the morning could only be an anticlimax. It wasn't, as Bishop D'Souza's later intervention made clear. Most of the crowd I hobnob with at the bar felt a great sense of relief: "Thank goodness the whole thing is finally out in the open." Ottaviani's notion that an attack on the Holy Office is an attack on the Holy Father was not taken seriously by anyone; all were quoting Pope Paul's words to the Curia in September, "We must welcome the criticisms which surround us."

But another matter cannot be so lightly dismissed. This is the continued unwillingness of the minority group to accept the reality of last Wednesday's vote on collegiality. We have just heard the two top men of the Theological Commission say that the vote had no meaning, and that what it affirmed was erroneous. How can such men represent the mind of the Council in redrafting the present text? This is the point that came out in the later intervention of the brilliant young Bishop D'Souza of India. He had heard it said that the fathers were unclear about collegiality and that the vote of October 30 had no meaning. But it is a derision of the Council to say this, when 80 per cent of the fathers responded with utter clarity to a question that was equally clear, particularly when their response was totally consistent with Pope Paul's opening allocution. Decentralization is no threat to unity — bishops are not that dangerous! The needed reforms should be instituted now. For if a handful of men on a commission can thwart the will of 2300 bishops assembled in Rome, what will happen to proposed reforms when the bishops have gone home?

This was strong meat. But the fathers were ready for it. Once again, disregarding the rules, they applauded.

At the end of the morning, discussion began on Chapter Two of *De Episcopis*, which deals with the relationship of bishops, coadjutors, and auxiliaries, and touches on touchy things like a retirement age for bishops. Ruffini, as usual, spoke first, and the main burden of his intervention was a strong protest against compulsory retirement. Leo XIII died at the age of ninety-three, and John XXIII was almost eighty when he became pope; under a compulsory retirement rule the church would have been deprived of the most fruitful years of both of these popes. He concluded with a story about Leo XIII, who, as a very old man, had urged an elderly bishop to retire. The bishop responded with the words, "Holy Father, we are both old." The laughter this elicited provided a safety valve for pent-up emotions, and Ruffini sat down, beaming broadly and hugely enjoying himself.

*   *   *

Today's press conference was jammed, and members of the panel gave significant documentation to the charge that the Holy Office condemns Catholic theologians without a hearing, suppresses their books without giving reasons, and orders theologians not to publish on certain subjects. But it was also made clear that some men outlive the charges leveled against them. A signal example is Père Congar, whose book *True and False Reform in the Church* (published in 1950) was condemned by the Holy Office, which withdrew the book from circulation and circumscribed Congar's teaching and writing activities for many years. Today, however, Congar is one of the official *periti* at the Council, and at a recent audience with the French ambassador, the pope remarked that Congar is the theologian who has had most influence on him.

We were also given a definitive answer to the question, "What is the difference between an auxiliary bishop [who has no right of succession when his superior dies] and a coadjutor bishop [who succeeds on the death of his superior]?" When an auxiliary greets his superior in the morning he says, "Well, what shall we do today?" But when a coadjutor greets his superior he asks, "How are you feeling this morning?"

*   *   *

The Paulist Fathers gave a reception this afternoon for the American bishops, the *periti,* and the observers. This was a splendid occasion since all of the observers were introduced individually and we had a chance to talk afterward with many bishops and *periti* whom we have hitherto known only by name. Professor Albert Outler, an American Methodist observer, spoke on our behalf. He could not have been better. He pointed out that, although it might surprise the bishops, the observers want the Roman Catholic Church to become more, rather than less, catholic. There has been such an ecumenical miracle in the last five years that we can hope for more miracles in the years ahead. The course of the present Council suggests that the Roman Catholic Church has just finished the chapter of its history entitled "The Counter-Reformation," and that it now appears to be working on the first chapter of a new *schema* that will be called "Reformation and Renewal."

During the informal period afterward I talked with a number of American Catholics I have known from previous occasions, and also made three new acquaintances: Cardinal Spellman, Cardinal McIntyre, and Msgr. Fenton.

The Seventh Week
(*November 11 – 17*)

An abundance of rumors – will there be an appeal to the pope? – getting ready for *De Oecumenismo* – the *schema* on "Instruments of Social Communication" – the importance of the chapter on religious liberty

Monday, November 11

After last Friday's fireworks I see possibilities in a Broadway musical based on the Council's transcripts. It would be entitled *A Funny Thing Happened On The Way To The Curia* and the theme song would begin, "I was acquitted."

Over the weekend we heard rumblings and rumors everywhere about a Big Move in the offing, but the morning couldn't have been quieter. It was The Feast of St. Martin ("Theirs, not yours," as I commented to a Lutheran observer), and after a very straightforward mass we moved into a very straightforward morning. It is probably a good thing that there was a two-day break in the sessions, and it would be possible to describe today as The Day We All Catch Our Breath.

The topic today was the relation of bishops to their coadjutors and auxiliaries, and as the discussion proceeded it became clear that the problems being treated could have been virtual verbatim transcripts of similar discussion held by every Protestant denomination within the last quarter century: Should church leaders (supply "bishops" or "denominational executives" as appropriate) be required to retire? If so, at what age? What can be done with them after they retire?

Should retirement be left voluntary? What about a pension plan?

These were the burning issues of the morning and I don't feel impelled to report on them in detail.

Cardinal Doepfner, however, introduced into his otherwise straightforward intervention about auxiliary bishops an opinion on behalf of the moderators about the status of the "four questions." He pointed out that the "competent [i.e., properly appointed] leaders of the Council," the moderators, had after long examination submitted questions to the fathers, and that the questions had been taken from the Theological Commission's own draft of *De Ecclesia*. While the questions did not "impose" anything on the commission, they did make clear what the mind of the Council was, and the commission's task would be to reflect that mind in its redrafting.

Since there are matters that excite me more than the retirement age of bishops, I spent a large part of the morning in Bar-Jonah. Numerous *periti* reported assurances that time would be left for a thorough discussion of *De Oecumenismo*, and that this would include Chapter Four on the Jews and probably a fifth chapter, comprising the religious liberty material. I think it is most important that the latter be discussed openly in order to determine the mind of the Council. I got encouraging reassurance that the American hierarchy is ready to support a strong statement on religious liberty, and that it will take the initiative when the matter comes up for discussion on the Council floor.

Professor Skydsgaard reported that the Lutheran Center for Ecumenical Studies that he has been planting and watering up in Copenhagen will shortly be transferred to Strasbourg, where, hopefully, God will give the increase. Having heard the marvelous interventions of Bishops Weber and Elchinger of Strasbourg, I can't think of a better place to foster ecumenical dialogue.

I pursued these happy themes at lunch in an open-air restaurant with Fr. Quinn of the Paulists. We're living on borrowed time, however. The rains are already eleven days late.

Tuesday, November 12

Rome is a city of rumors this week. Those begun over the weekend continue to build up each day. The persistent one that keeps cropping up at meals, in the coffee bars, in the press, and among those who know a "source close to the Vatican," is that an appeal to the pope is going to be made on the Council floor, asking him to establish a senate that would oversee the Council's work, carry on between sessions, provide a permanent link between pope and bishops, and thus (whether stated or not) bypass the Curia. The name most persistently linked with this appeal is Cardinal Silva Henriquez of Chile, and we hear that there are already four hundred signatures affixed to his speech. It will be better if the impetus comes from the Council rather than from the pope, so that this can be a genuine exercise of collegiality "from the bottom up," rather than an instance of papal fiat imposed "from the top down."

There was more discussion today about the retirement age of bishops, the relation of auxiliaries and coadjutors, and so forth. Cardinal Suenens gave a vigorous plea for a compulsory retirement age. The basic question, he said, is not "How do we honor these men?" but "What does the welfare of souls require?" It is hard for one of advanced years to help the welfare of souls when he is out of touch with the modern world. A glance at any diocese where the bishop is senile indicates the harm that can be done. In other professions retirement usually precedes the age of seventy-five, and although a bishop is given supernatural powers, he is not exempted thereby from the laws of psychology and physiology. Thus a clear law, and not an appeal to persuasion, is demanded.

After hearing the changes rung on this theme a number of times, I sought the coffee bar and learned one very important piece of information: The religious liberty statement is finally coming out of hiding. It has been buried in the Theological Commission all fall, but there was finally enough pressure exerted to get a subcommission appointed to examine it. This subcommission, under the leadership of Cardinal Leger, approved the statement and brought it back to the full commission for acceptance. Last night the full commission accepted it by a vote of 18 – 5, which indicates that the commission as a whole has a very different attitude from that of its chairman and vice-chairman. (Somebody asked over a cup of coffee, "I wonder who cast the other three negative votes?") This means that the text will be printed and given to the fathers for examination as Chapter Five of *De Oecumenismo*. The optimists are predicting (after only one or two cups of strong Italian coffee) that at the rate debate is proceeding on the retirement age of bishops we may get to ecumenism by early next week.

Indeed, I got back to the tribune just as cloture was voted on Chapter Two and discussion turned to Chapter Three on the more explosive issue of "episcopal conferences." Bishop Carli of Italy introduced the chapter, which suggests that episcopal conferences must have some juridical status (i.e., when bishops meet together regionally, the decisions they make should be binding within the individual dioceses). Bishops must be united in more than charity; they must also have the possibility of corporate action.

No clear mind of the Council emerged in reaction to this proposal.

Cardinal McIntyre of Los Angeles was unequivocally against giving the regional conferences any power. Voluntary meetings were helpful, but they should not have binding authority over individual bishops. Indeed, the establishment of episcopal conferences with juridical power is really an attack on the Curia, since this results in taking power away from the Curia. An attack on the Curia, which is an instrument of the pope, therefore is an attack on the pope. And an attack on the pope is an attack on the doctrine of infallibility, defined in 1870 by Vatican I. If the pope has confidence in the Curia, why shouldn't the Council fathers also have confidence in it?

Cardinal Gracias of Bombay, arguing from very different premises, came to a somewhat similar conclusion: The power of the episcopal conferences should be moral but not necessarily juridical. The powers should be determined by the conferences themselves, depending on the needs of the area. Cardinals Meyer of Chicago and Ritter of St. Louis took slightly different positions, Meyer feeling that juridical obligation should be imposed by the conference only when absolutely necessary and that when so imposed it should have the approval of the pope, while Ritter felt each conference should be free to make its own laws. Cardinal Landazuri of Peru made the valid point that it would be better not to refer to "national" episcopal conferences, since in some regions the nation might not be the best unit for organization.

It is clear that everybody agrees that episcopal conferences are A Good Thing, but that many fathers fear that the conferences might usurp power from the bishops themselves in their own dioceses.

*   *   *

At the observers' "briefing session" we decided that our best contribution to Vatican II would come not from debating the retirement age of bishops, but from beginning a discussion of *De Oecumenismo*, which is surely going to be on the Council floor by the beginning of next week.

Canon Thils of Louvain gave an introduction to the text and described its evolution, after which the floor was ours.

Here are the types of Protestant reactions that are beginning to emerge:

(1) All are agreed that *De Oecumenismo* is an historic document and ecumenical event of unparalleled proportions. The very fact that it has been written, and will shortly be presented to the fathers, heralds the advent of a new day in Protestant-Catholic relations.

(2) Among the Protestants, certainly, the greatest difficulty with the present text centers on the distinction that is employed between the "churches" of the East (the Ortho-

dox), and the "communities" of the West (the Protestants).
This point was touched upon in the discussion of Chapter
One of *De Ecclesia,* and it does not take much of a prophet
to realize that we will hear a lot more about it before the
second session adjourns. Bluntly put, the distinction seems
to Western Protestants to be an invidious one, particularly
when the Catholic Church grants that by baptism all Protestants are, in some sense, already within the church. If
it is acknowledged that grace comes *through* our Protestant "communities," however imperfectly, and not simply *to*
them, then a designation which acknowledges their "ecclesial" (i.e., churchly) reality would seem more fitting.

(3) In the document are traces of an attitude toward non-
Catholics known technically as *vestigia ecclesiae,* that there
are "vestiges," traces, of the church within them. The difficulty with this notion is not so much, I think, in its initial assertion, as in the implications frequently drawn from it. For
if the Catholic Church has all truth, and we non-Catholics
have only some "vestiges" of truth, then the obvious thing
for us to do is to "return" to the Catholic Church. This always seems to imply a static and passive attitude on the part
of Catholicism, whose role is simply to "wait" receptively
until the rest of us have seen the light. I do not think this
reflects the attitude of the Secretariat for Christian Unity,
but the problem is commented upon by enough observers
to be worth recording. Ecumenism must be a path on which
both partners are trying to move toward one another.

(4) The great difficulty between Protestants and Catholics, of course, centers on what constitutes the true source of
unity. Crudely put, Protestants say Christ is the source of
unity, while Catholics say Peter is the source of unity. This
is crude, for to Catholics, of course, Christ is found through
Peter, i.e., in the church where Peter and his successors, the
popes, are acknowledged as the divinely appointed means
for fulfilling Christ's will. But since this claim is accepted by
only a part of Christendom (Roman Catholicism, but not
Orthodoxy or Protestantism), many observers argue that its

reiteration actually fosters the perpetuation of division. If true catholicity is found only where Peter (or his successor) is found, then departure from Peter is departure from true catholicity. But, as Pastor Roux of the French Reformed Church asked, was this the criterion of true catholicity in the controversies in the early church? Surely the issue there was not fidelity to the see of Peter but fidelity to Jesus Christ.

The Catholic response, of course, is that it is through fidelity to the see of Peter that fidelity to Jesus Christ is expressed, and here, I imagine, is the ultimate source of division between us.

(5) Another question relating to the *schema* itself was raised. Does the chapter on the Jews, added to the original document, belong here, or elsewhere? We had both views presented this afternoon: (a) Since ecumenism deals with relations of Christian bodies, the material on the Jews is out of place, and if it is included, material on other non-Christian religions must be included as well. (b) The problem of Israel is part of the problem of ecumenism, since Israel stands in a *unique* relationship to Christianity, as the religion out of which Christianity sprang, and the religion to which it is therefore inextricably tied.

*   *   *

I had an interesting discussion at supper with a number of Catholic scholars, at least one of whom has been under the ban of the Holy Office, and all of whom have friends who have been in trouble. I could not help asking, "What does it do to one's *psyche* to be informed by the church that he must not publish in the area where he feels he can genuinely contribute to the renewal of the church? Is one so conditioned that he simply accepts this, even when he has reason to doubt the omniscience of those men in Rome who have ordered the ban?"

Some very interesting reactions were voiced: (1) If possible, one tries to ignore the order, e.g., to assume that what one continues to publish will be "acceptable." In nine cases out of ten nothing further happens. (2) When the ban seems particularly unjust, and represents merely the triumph of one theological position at the expense of another, one sometimes "wonders if he is in the wrong outfit," but (3) this entirely human reaction is usually followed swiftly by the self-searching question, "Can I be so sure *I* am right, when the church feels I am not?" (4) The latter question is buttressed by a life of obedience to the church and by years of accepting her collective wisdom as greater than the individual wisdom of her children. (5) One takes comfort in the fact that if his position *is* right, the church in time will come to see this and accept it. (6) If one feels sure he has been wronged, he may try to get his friends to intercede for him, though this may lead to guilt by association, and one is therefore chary about requesting it.

After such a conversation I see more clearly why Cardinal Frings was applauded last friday.

Wednesday, November 13

As Al Outler and I were dodging cars and busses across St. Peter's Square this morning, I asked him if he thought that being run down by some cardinal's Mercedes-Benz would constitute a valid martyrdom. He replied that, while he had never given the matter previous thought, he was inclined to respond *non placet,* and that anyhow as he made his way toward the *aula* each morning he wasn't about to let a cardinal precipitate him prematurely into the *aula aeternitatis.*

We got a slight preview of the *aula aeternitatis* (which might roughly be translated "heaven") at mass this morning. We had the Liturgy of St. John Chrysostom, celebrated in the Byzantium-Russian rite, and the music, sung by members of the Russian Pontifical College, was magnificent. The liturgy includes much that is not found in the Latin rite, such as the Great Entrance of the bread and wine, the kiss of peace, the use of the vernacular, communion under both species, and

concelebration (i.e., a number of priests celebrating together). I think the difference between the Russian music
we heard this morning and the Gregorian music we usually
hear is that one *listens* to the Gregorian music, enthralled
and uplifted, whereas one wants to *sing with* the Russian
settings. Happily, there is room for both reactions whether
in the present *aula* or in the *aula aeternitatis.*

We are assured a fairly full discussion of *De Oecumenismo,*
for Cardinal Doepfner announced that it will be the next
schema for consideration, and that bishops who wish to comment on it should hand in their names. This leaves time for
a full airing of the first three chapters, and with any kind of
leadership exerted by the moderators it should be possible
to discuss Chapters Four and Five as well before the Council
recesses.

The general thrust of today's discussion was that episcopal
conferences must not have too much power. I do not know
whether this generally prevailing sentiment represents a
backing away from the practical implications of collegiality,
or whether it represents a realistic recognition that power
exerted close at hand is more difficult to cope with than
power exerted far away.

*   *   *

Because of the repetitive nature of the interventions this
morning the bar was terribly overcrowded. The main topic
of discussion was not "How do you stand on juridical power
for episcopal conferences?" or "Who should provide the
funds for retired bishops?" The main question was, "When
are we going to get that intervention asking the pope to reconstitute the commissions and establish a senate of bishops?" Since nobody knows, the answers are varied and
colorful.

As I contemplate these masses of celibate bishops packed
into this tiny coffee bar with their flowing garments and intricate lace finery, all smoking at a furious rate to the in-

finite peril of their flowing garments and intricate lace finery,
and as I contemplate the comparatively fireproof raiment of
the married observers who have no lace flapping from their
sleeves, and as I further contemplate what would happen if
a fire broke out here, I am led to a new appreciation of St.
Paul's statement that it is better to marry than to burn.

Thursday, November 14

A good many people have been sustained through this very
dull week of debate by the expectation each morning that
perhaps *this* was the day when the intervention would be
given asking the pope to establish a senate of bishops
and/or reconstitute the commissions so that they would not
be dominated by the minority. As I commented on Tuesday,
it is expected that the speech will be given by Cardinal Silva
Henriquez, and some of the European newspapers have even
carried outlines of the speech, which has been circulating
for moro signatures. The result is that tension mounts each
morning. Today seemed to be the day. The four seats of the
cardinal-moderators were conspicuously, even startlingly,
empty during mass. "This," I thought, "is It. Last-minute
arrangements are being completed for the intervention that
will change the course of Catholic history." But the morning came and went with no hint whatever that anything was
in the air.

What is going on? It betrays no confidence to report that
there *is* such a speech, that it *does* appear over Silva
Henriquez' name, and that it *does* contain the supporting
signatures of many hundreds of bishops. It builds on the
pope's desire to reform the Curia, and on his invitation to the
fathers (in his opening allocution) to help him in the task
of bearing rule in the church. It informs the pope of the
fathers' desire to help him in whatever way can be most useful, and expresses their willingness to respond to his suggestions during the present session.

This seems an admirable way to do things, granted the
nature of the Roman Catholic structure: (1) the pope ex-

presses a desire for help; (2) the fathers respond by expressing willingness to help; (3) the pope tells them how they
can help best; (4) the fathers start helping. But there seems
to be a division of opinion over whether the matter should
come to a head on the Council floor, or whether the communication should simply be sent to the pope. My own feeling is that the more openly things can be done, the better.
But thus far my opinion has not been solicited.

The other thing that is somewhat mysterious is the where-
abouts of the chapter on religious liberty. We know that it
was approved, 18 – 5, by the Theological Commission last
Monday and that it is to be presented as Chapter Five of
De Oecumenismo. But the text has not yet been released.
Having had a chance to see it last week, I am very eager to
hear the bishop's reactions to it. If there is leg-dragging
going on here, I hope those who need to push for its release
are pushing for all they are worth.

Fortunately Chapter Four, on the Jews, has been made
available. Indeed, it has been the subject of so much informal
discussion that there is talk of setting up another coffee bar
along with Bar-jonah and Barrabas. This one would be
called Bar-mitzvah.

❖   ❖   ❖

The floor debate today continued a discussion of the
power of episcopal conferences, after which discussion
moved to the final chapter, dealing with the size of dioceses
and their boundaries. I think it is a fair description of the
morning to report that the fathers have attained a genuine
consensus on this matter, summarized in the following gem-
like affirmation: *Dioceses should be neither too large nor too
small.*

The last speaker of the morning recognized that everyone was weary; instead of beginning with the salutation
Venerabiles patres (Venerable fathers), he began *Patientis-
sime patres* (Most patient fathers).

The *schema De Instrumentis Communicationis Socialis* (On Instruments of Social Communication), which was approved in principle last year with the suggestion that it be condensed, was presented for approval. From something like forty-six pages it has now been reduced to nine. Votes were taken to accept its two separate chapters and they passed without difficulty — only 92 *non placets* on Chapter One and 103 *non placets* on Chapter Two. Within the next few days there will be a vote to accept the *schema* as a whole so that it can be promulgated by the pope on the final day of the Council.

* * *

I have just gotten around to reading the *schema* "On Instruments of Social Communication," which I had totally neglected in my concern for *De Oecumenismo*. I cannot escape the feeling that many of the fathers who voted for it must likewise have neglected to read it. I am disturbed by its contents, and I cannot escape the feeling that its adoption by the Council would be a tragic mistake. By an extreme gesture of good will I can muster up a feeling that the *schema* is banal and innocuous, unoriginal and obvious. I cannot feel that it is a document worthy of a church Council, particularly as the culmination of two years of work. The world, reading it, is going to say, "This is *aggiornamento?* This is bringing the church up to date? If so, we've placed our expectations far too high."

But that is not the end of the matter. If the *schema* were merely platitudinous, that could be tolerated, perhaps. But it also contains many statements that are susceptible to quite devastating interpretations. Not all people will read it with "an extreme gesture of good will." They will read it at face value and will find lurking just beneath the surface, and sometimes right on the surface, the kind of implications with which anti-Catholics can have a field day.

Consequently my feeling is that a resounding *non placet*

vote on the *schema* as a whole would represent the Council's finest hour to date. Such an action would say to the world, "We prefer not to speak at all unless we can speak well. We prefer to wait rather than to be premature. We prefer to think more rather than to speak hastily."

As I read and reread the text I cannot avoid finding the following implications just waiting to be drawn from it:

a. *All* people who use instruments of mass communications must meet the church's stand as to what a "correct conscience" is (whether they are Catholics or not), or fear the consequences.

b. News can be censored if it does not edify, and art can be suppressed if it does not teach.

c. Novels or plays that do not at all times teach a particular and precise kind of moral rectitude are inadmissible.

d. The opinion of competent authorities must be sought by those who read, watch, and hear, lest they read, watch, and hear the wrong things — a notion that implies the rights of censorship, boycott, and reprisals.

e. The task of the church is to protect and insulate youth from all possible contamination in the area of mass media, rather than to help youth develop criteria for making their own discriminating judgments.

f. Reporting of news about the church must not be critical.

g. Civil authorities must legislate widely in the field of the morals of mass communications.

h. Catholics should be encouraged to develop a cultural ghetto of Catholic press, Catholic radio, Catholic television, and so forth rather than making it their primary task to raise the general level of all the mass communications media.

i. All that Catholics do in the field of mass communications should be under the strict supervision of church authorities.

Not many people are going to read the long liturgy *schema* in its entirety, since it *is* long and since it is concerned with the inner life of the Catholic Church. But many people are going to read the Communications *schema*, since it *is* short and since it is concerned with the relation of the church to the whole of secular culture. I am very much afraid that if it is adopted it will undo much of the good the Council is doing elsewhere.

Friday, November 15

We are juggling many balls these days: interest in ecumenism, concern for the religious liberty chapter (which has still not been distributed), anticipation of the as yet undelivered intervention on a senate of bishops, and dismay over the possibility that the Communications *schema* may be adopted. There is an important meeting tonight of the moderators, the presidents, the coordinating commission, and the pope. Perhaps some of these items will be on the agenda.

Once again it looked as though the intervention on the senate of bishops was going to be delivered. When Felici announced the speakers' names, the first three were Cardinals Lefevre, *Silva Henriquez,* and Pereira. The moment had come. But when the moderator, Cardinal Suenens, announced the first speaker (*Loquatur nunc . . .*) it was Lefevre, and when he announced the second speaker (*et accedat ad microphoniam . . .*) it was not Silva but Pereira. So the speech will not be given today. My guess is that it will now not be given at all, but will simply be sent directly to the pope. If it *is* sent to the pope, it will be interesting (to employ careful understatement) to see what he does about it.

The whole morning, therefore, was devoted to the size of dioceses, after some leftover speeches on episcopal conferences. When it became clear that this was to be the tenor of the morning, I forsook the observers' tribune and spent over two hours in Bar-jonah, quite frankly lobbying against the Communications *schema.* I buttonholed every *peritus* I could find, and even a few bishops (which takes more courage), and put my case to them, along the lines I recorded yesterday.

I found no one prepared to defend the *schema*. All agree that it is unfortunate. All feel that it was treated by the fathers much as it was treated by the observers, i.e., nobody paid much attention to it. Those who read it carefully voted against it. The rest assumed that, since it was approved in principle last year, it was at least inoffensive. The French bishops, however, seem to have been much distressed by it, and the lateness of the moderators yesterday morning may have been due to last-minute attempts by a group of bishops to forestall the vote. Those who are really unhappy about the *schema* are encouraged by the fact that no date has yet been announced for the final vote. This means there might be time to muster support for a whole rash of *non placets*. Admittedly, this is a stiff undertaking since it would need nearly 800 negative votes to kill the *schema*.

My pitch throughout the morning has been two-fold: It would be unfortunate to accept the *schema* since (a) on the one hand it is mediocre, bland, and unworthy of a church Council, and (b) where it is not innocuous it is positively harmful and will give the lie to the notion that the church really wants to relate itself to the modern world.

The only resistance I encountered to this line of reasoning was from a couple of *periti* who said that the document can be ignored, or explained, or at least engulfed by later and better conciliar documents. But if the document can be justified only on those terms, why promulgate it at all, and then be forced to assert that the Holy Spirit was actively at work guiding the fathers to produce it?

❊ ❊ ❊

I am a little amazed at my own forwardness in this matter. Is this what "observers" are supposed to be doing? A month ago I wouldn't have thought so and I would have given two reasons: (1) I was invited here to "observe," not to "par-

ticipate"; (2) anyhow, it's not *my* council, it's a Roman
Catholic Council.

I find these arguments less and less compelling. We *have*
been urged to participate, even though we may not do so
directly on the Council floor. We have been asked from the
very beginning to offer our honest reactions both orally and
in writing. All fall it has therefore seemed quite in line with
my function to respond to the question, "What is your reaction to how things are going?" Now that I know a number of
periti and bishops fairly well, I am simply answering the
question before they ask it.

As for this being a Council of the Roman Catholic Church
rather than of all Christians, that is certainly true, and we
have no right to expect it to produce statements that would
get the *imprimatur* of the World Council of Churches. Nevertheless, all Christendom has a stake in what happens here in
St. Peter's. If what happens is creative, the whole of Christendom benefits. If what happens here is unfortunate, the
whole of Christendom suffers. Therefore, simply as a Christian I have a stake in seeing that the Council does the most
creative job it can. And enough understanding and trust has
been built up during these past weeks so that I can freely express not only gratitude for the good things, but dismay at the
bad things. My Catholic counterparts may not accept my assessment of what is "good" and what is "bad," but at least
they display a remarkable willingness to hear me out. I learn
every day how important is Professor Cullmann's distinction
between *unity* in Christ and *solidarity* in Christ; Catholics
and Protestants do not yet have the former, but to an ever-in-
creasing degree we have the latter. For this we can only respond, "Thanks be to God." Or, as we say around here,
Deo gratias.

Sunday, November 17

Information about the Friday-night meeting of moderators, presidents, coordinating commission, and pope is
mighty hard to come by. If there was a discussion of recon-

stituting the commissions or establishing a senate of bishops, nobody is doing much talking. The most I could discover in the course of an entire Sunday evening with *periti* and bishops is that somebody saw someone who was at the meeting, and all that someone would say to somebody was, "Pray hard for us!" I continue discussing the Communications *schema* with all who will listen, and there really seems to be a head of steam developing. Three Catholic laymen in Rome, Robert Kaiser of *Time*, Michael Novak of the *New Republic*, and John Cogley of the Fund for the Republic, have been circulating a statement indicating very persuasively why the *schema* is unsatisfactory. Reaction to this will provide a good test of whether or not the fathers are yet prepared to listen to laymen in an area where the latter can claim to have both knowledge and experience.

The morning was spent at the Canadian Theological College, where, thanks to Fr. Gregory Baum, of the Secretariat for Christian Unity, Canon Pawley of the Church of England, Al Outler of the Methodist Church, and I had a chance to speak to the Canadian bishops on various aspects of *De Oecumenismo*. I will include a draft of my comments on Chapter Five as an example of what I have now given several times in Rome before Catholic groups.

The Importance of the Chapter on "Religious Liberty" in *De Oecumenismo*

My thesis this morning is a simple and direct one: I do not think there is a single thing the Council can do that will have more *immediate* effect in bettering Catholic-Protestant relations than a forthright and unambiguous statement favoring full religious liberty for all. There may be many other things that will have more important long-range implications (and surely the *schema De Ecclesia* is the most serious task the Council faces), but in terms of the present and immediate future, the chapter on religious liberty leads all the rest.

Before dealing with reasons why this is true in the arena of Catholic-Protestant relations, let me make a basic point that underlies all the rest. The *basic* reason for a statement on religious liberty is not to "please the Protestants," or "make friends with the secular world," but simply because such a declaration is a clear part of the gospel, and the church has now reached the stage where she can clarify her own thinking on the matter. There has been enough writing and thinking in this area by Catholic theologians for the past quarter of a century to make clear that the time is "ripe" for such a statement, and that the church has thought the position through to maturity. Those, of course, are the reasons why *you* must be concerned with the matter. It is not, however, my task to deal with this basic point, but, as a Protestant, to deal with the by-product flowing from this basic point, namely, the impact that such a statement will have in the Protestant, and indeed the whole non-Catholic, world.

The reason a statement on religious liberty is so important, therefore, is because (to put it bluntly for the sake of time and not pause over ecumenical niceties) the Catholic Church is not fully trusted on this point. Whether rightly or wrongly, non-Catholics do not believe the Catholic Church has yet made up her mind about religious liberty, and they are fearful that the church may still espouse a position of intolerance, persecution, and penalty for the exercise of a faith not Roman Catholic.

What are the reasons for this fear on the part of non-Catholics? I think they can be reduced to three main ones.

1. There is the past history of the Catholic Church, in which there have been notable instances of persecution by the Church, particularly when it was in positions of political power. It is unnecessary to detail this, for we are all familiar with it. And it must be reported that the images conjured up by a word like "Inquisition" still linger in many non-Catholic hearts to give cause for feeling that this represents the "real" position of the church, even though for reasons of expediency, it may not be openly espoused at the present time.

2. In addition to past Catholic history, present Catholic practice in certain parts of the world lends credibility to the notion that the Church does not really believe in religious liberty. It is perhaps unfortunate always to use Spain and Colombia as whipping boys here, but the fact is that in present times in these and other countries, non-Catholics have serious penalties and liabilities visited upon them because of their espousal of a different faith. The fact that religious oppression appears to be condoned in areas where Roman Catholicism is in the heavy majority, and is not condoned in areas where Roman Catholicism is in the mi-

nority, sometimes makes it appear that the attitude of the church on this matter is not consistent, is not based on a conviction of faith, but is simply a matter of expediency.

3. The final reason for this fear — and the reason that makes passage of a conciliar statement so crucial — is the relative lack of *authoritative* utterances by the church on the subject of religious liberty. There are, to be sure, many fine statements by individual Catholic theologians that say all the non-Catholic wants to hear and more, and a wealth of such material is available in the booklet published by the World Council of Churches, Carillo de Albornoz, *Roman Catholicism and Religious Liberty.* There are a few, though not very many, statements by members of the hierarchy, the best being a pamphlet by Cardinal Lercaro. But I discover, every time I speak to a Protestant group and try to introduce such evidence, that I am immediately confronted by the reaction, "For whom do these people speak? They don't speak for the whole church; they speak only for themselves. If the Catholic Church really believes in religious liberty, why doesn't it say so, plainly and unambiguously?" And when one tries to answer this charge by citing "official" and authoritative utterances, what are the resources available? The resources thus far are pretty slim: Pius XII's speech to the Italian jurists of June 6, 1953, paragraph 104 of *Mystici Corporis,* a couple of sentences in *Pacem in Terris,* and that is about all. And the relative dearth of such authoritative statements in the face of past Catholic history and present Catholic practice (points 1 and 2 above) does not exactly assuage the fearful heart.

It is for these reasons, then, that a formal and authoritative conciliar utterance, promulgated by the pope with all of his authority, is so important. For it would lay to rest, once and for all, the fears non-Catholics have had — fears that have a certain degree of justification until such an utterance has become a part of the church's formal teaching. Not only would the issue of where the church actually stands be cleared up, but there would then be a standard that could be invoked in areas where the principle of religious liberty was still being abrogated by certain segments of the church. No Protestant would expect that every violation of the principle would be eliminated overnight, but every Protestant could believe that such violations were now acts *contrary to* the clearly defined teaching of the church, and could expect the church to act promptly to set such situations right. If, therefore, the church speaks without equivocation on this burning issue, it will be making one of its most important contributions to the establishing of better relations among men. At the risk of overemphasis, I must stress the immediate impact of such action once more: When I return home and begin to speak to Protestant groups about the Council, no matter how eloquent I may wax over the "collegiality" debate or the liturgical reforms, the first question I will get in the discussion period will be, "What did they do about religious liberty?" I want to be able to report that an excellent statement was approved for discussion and that it received significant support on the floor of the Council.

I have had a chance to look at the proposed chapter, and I think I can report that it says *all* the things that a non-Catholic wants to hear the Catholic Church say on this matter. We might say them a bit differently — and have indeed done so in World Council statements — but I do not think we can complain that any important point in a declaration about religious liberty has been overlooked. I think the statement itself is an important ecumenical achievement. Its adoption will be an even more important one.

It is, of course, likely that there will be some serious opposition to the chapter in the *aula,* and that certain bishops will want to get rid of this or that emphasis within it. I do not know to what degree the chapter can get through unscathed, but I would hope very much that the Council fathers can hold the line at each of the following six points. All of these are present within the *schema,* and the disappearance of any of them would be unfortunate from the point of view of the impact of the *schema* upon non-Catholics:

1. The solid foundation of the nature of religious liberty as based on the very nature of the act of faith. Faith is a gift given by God, and it cannot be imposed on man by any other than God. For an individual, or a church, to try to force faith is to engage in an act of idolatry, to be usurping a prerogative that belongs to God alone. It is from this fact that the sovereign rights of conscience flow. Also, such a foundation makes clear that religious liberty is not being offered as a matter of expediency, but is being guaranteed as a matter of principle.

2. The clear denial of the propriety of any form of coercion in this matter.

3. The distinction between the abstract proposition that "error has no rights" and the truth that "persons in error have rights that must not be denied them." Here, I think, is the point at which the chapter guards against the charge that belief in religious liberty leads to indifferentism. One is not asked to surrender the sovereignty of truth; he is asked only to recognize that he cannot impose the truth upon another, and that he must love, not punish, the other even in his error.

4. The stress on the right to give *external expression* to one's faith. This is very important. Many people will grant that an individual has a right to his own inner conviction of conscience, but balk at the notion that he must be allowed the right to express that conviction outwardly to others. But unless declaration on religious liberty explicitly guarantees the right to preach, witness, testify, evangelize, and so forth, it is a hollow statement.

5. The stress on the right to engage in *corporate expression* of one's faith. Religious conviction is never an affair simply between God and an individual; it always involves God and the individual and the neighbor. The right to religious liberty, then, involves the right not only to witness to the neighbor (point 4 above) but also the right to engage with the neighbor in corporate acts of worship, corporate life together in a community of faith, and corporate witness and evangelization to others.

6. The stress on the fact that civic penalties cannot be attached to the exercise of one's religious convictions. Unless this is present, it is possible for a church to let a state do the actual job of suppressing religious liberty. As long as there is legislation penalizing a citizen for his religious convictions, true religious liberty has not been achieved.

I say that all of these emphases are present, in one form or another, within the present chapter, and we must hope that all of them will be retained. To the degree that you accept them as valid conditions of religious liberty, I hope that you will be able to resist attempts to remove any of them from the final document.

The atmosphere to be achieved can perhaps be further distinguished by making a distinction between "toleration" and "religious liberty." The former seems to me essentially a negative notion, while the latter is positive. "Toleration" seems to imply the granting of a privilege that is not deserved, and which could therefore be revoked, while "religious liberty" implies the acknowledgment of a right that is intrinsic, and therefore cannot be revoked.

Beyond that, there is a major problem raised in any discussion of religious liberty. This is the question of *limitations* of the exercise of religious liberty. Liberty cannot be allowed to become license. One cannot do "whatever he wants" in the name of some private religious revelation, so-called. What are these limitations to be? The *schema* suggests the criterion of "the common good." This is a difficult criterion, since it allows so much latitude. Who determines what is the common good? Public consensus (very hard to arrive at)? The church, as the guardian of faith and morals? The state, as the preserver of law and order? There are difficulties with each answer. Furthermore, who enforces the decision? I do not know a clear answer to this complex set of problems, and I take small comfort from the fact that I don't believe anyone else does either. I think Fr. John Courtney Murray's suggestion at this point is a good one, that a criterion like "public *order*" is at least better than "the common good," since it does not give quite so much leeway either to an authoritarian state or an authoritarian church that wishes to tyrannize in the name of "protecting the common good." In its dealings with this question, the World Council of Churches has not gone too much further. Statements of the limits of religious liberty offer such criteria as the following: ". . . such limitations, prescribed by law, as are necessary to protect order and welfare, morals and the rights and freedoms of others . . ." (Amsterdam 1948) and ". . . those which are necessary for the defense of morals and public order . . ." (Buenos Aires, 1949). On the basis of all this, I think the thing to avoid in the *schema* is any suggestion that the church is to be the watchdog of these limits in ways that will give the church the opportunity to use the principle of limitation as a means of short-circuiting the principle of religious liberty.

I offer a final comment in the form of a suggestion for an emphasis not now present within the chapter. Perhaps it is presumptuous of me to suggest it as a non-Catholic, but I do so in the hope that the chapter will be as *fully* Catholic as possible, and make the best possible impact on the Catholic and non-Catholic world. I think it would give the entire chapter deeper integrity if the Church could say, somewhere within it, that although these are the principles of religious liberty that the church espouses, the church acknowledges in penitence that there have been times when she has sinned against them. Not only is this the fact, but the honest admission of the fact would be further indication of the genuineness of the church's present unequivocal stand. The fact that in his opening allocution Paul VI could say this kind of thing about the whole disruption of Christendom, asking forgiveness for wrongs the Catholic Church has inflicted on others, leads me to think that there would be nothing "un-Catholic" about a similar statement here. I make this suggestion in full knowledge of the grievous Protestant sins in this area as well, and would hope that as we enter into the increasingly fruitful period of dialogue that lies ahead, we would realize in all areas, religious liberty included, that the bases of mutual confession and mutual forgiveness are the bases on which a strong structure of integrity and love can be built.

The Eighth Week
(*November 18 – 22*)

De Oecumenismo is launched in rough seas but weathers the storm – introduction to chapters on the Jews and religious liberty – clouds on the conciliar horizon – varying reactions to ecumenism – reconstitution of the commissions – acceptance of Chapters One, Two, and Three of *De Oecumenismo* – adoption of *De Sacra Liturgia* for promulgation – the intrusion of Dallas

Monday, November 18

Today is a historic day in Roman Catholic history, and indeed in ecumenical history. This morning, for the first time in four hundred years, the Roman Catholic Church has initiated formal discussion of its relation to divided Christendom. Père Congar's comment before mass was significant: "This is the day for which we have been waiting for many decades." He should know, better than most, for it was his pioneering book on ecumenism, suppressed by the Holy Office, that began to focus Catholic attention on the problem.

Today is also the feast of the dedication of St. Peter's, so TV cameras were admitted for the mass and all the bright spotlights were on. When the lighting was reduced to its normal wattage, we were left in relative darkness – not a very appropriate symbol for the initiation of ecumenical discussion.

Although the text of *De Oecumenismo* is still *sub secreto*, enough can be said about it to indicate that it, at least, is an excellent initiation to ecumenical discussion. Chapter One, "Principles of Catholic Ecumenism," indicates how, through baptism, brethren who believe in Christ have within their churches and communities a real life of grace, even though they do not enjoy full unity with the Catholic Church. The chapter calls on Catholics to engage in inner renewal, to cultivate charity, to see the Holy Spirit at work in the separated brethren, and to work toward the removing of obstacles. Chapter Two, "The Practice of Ecumenism," counsels Catholics to inner renewal, conversion of heart, holiness of life, continuing prayer for unity, acquaintance with the separated brethren, ecumenical training, clear statements of Catholic doctrine, and cooperation on social issues with the separated brethren. Chapter Three, "On Christians Separated from the Catholic Church," first describes the Oriental churches and the close bonds they have with Catholicism, and secondly the "Communities That Have Arisen from the Sixteenth Century Onwards." Chapter Four, "The Relationship of Catholics to Non-Catholics and Especially to the Jews," states the continuity that exists between Jew and Christian and gives special attention to the need for the Christian church to purge itself of anti-Semitism. The themes of Chapter Five, "Religious Liberty," are described in yesterday's entry. It was announced that the text of the latter chapter would be distributed tomorrow.

This morning we had introductions to the *schema* as a whole and to Chapters One, Two, and Three. Tomorrow the introductions to Chapters Four and Five will be presented.

During these introductions (which are printed and distributed in advance), I made my round of the coffee bars so that I would be back when the actual speeches began. There was a general feeling that we must not anticipate anything "dramatic" between now and the end of the Council—no papal intervention establishing a senate and no drastic reconstitution of the conciliar commissions. But the situation on the Communications *schema* sounds hopeful. More and more bishops are reading it carefully and commenting, "I hadn't realized what was in it." A few are voicing the hope that there will be no vote or that the material will be recast for inclusion in "Schema Seventeen," on The Church and the Modern World. The vote, if it comes, apparently won't be for several days.

Archbishop Martin's introduction to Chapters One and Two of *De Oecumenismo* was applauded, as was his departure from the prepared text to refer to Cardinal Bea, architect of the *schema*.

It would be unwise, however, to infer that such sentiments were universal. The first three interventions were very negative, and the fourth only a bit less. For once Ruffini didn't lead off, since Cardinal Tappouni of Antioch, who outranks him, chose this occasion for his first intervention of the Council. Tappouni is afraid that the *schema* will not be understood and that it will confuse the faithful. Strike One.

Ruffini found himself full of doubts and anxieties. The word "ecumenism" should not be used, since this has so many different meanings. It must be made clear that Catholicism is the one true faith and that the Catholic Church expects non-Catholics to return to Rome and accept the pope. While the Orthodox share a great deal with Catholics, the separated communities of the West preserve very little of Catholic faith and life, being divided into almost three hundred different sects. The norms for dialogue are not adequate; only outstanding Catholics should engage in it, and then only with the permission of proper authorities. Strike Two.

Cardinal Arriba y Castro of Spain felt that the ecumenical dialogue was dangerous: Catholics may get involved in it and find themselves unable to cope with arguments offered by the "sects." As a condition of dialogue, the separated brethren must agree to cease all proselytism. Catholics can pray that the separated brethren will discover that true authority was given to the Roman Catholic Church and to no other, but the suggestions of the *schema* are not helpful, and so the *schema* should not be accepted for discussion by the Council. *In genere non placet.* Strike Three.

But not Out. At least not quite. For a new tone began to enter the discussion. Cardinal Monreal of Spain pronounced the more welcome words *in genere placet,* though he wanted various changes made, and felt that the *schema* should be rewritten in more cautious language. The next two speakers, however, gave ringing defenses of the *schema*.

Cardinal Ritter of St. Louis, speaking for a number of American bishops, began, *In genere nobis placet*. The *schema* brings out practically the consequences of *aggiornamento* and signifies the end of the Counter-Reformation mentality of theological polemics. Since an unequivocal affirmation of religious liberty for all is the absolute prerequisite of ecumenical encounter, the fifth chapter should precede all the others. At a number of points, the *schema* can be improved. More attention should be given to the liturgy as a factor in ecumenical understanding, and the *schema* should be examined carefully to be sure that it does not cause unnecessary offense to the separated brethren. Why, for example, should their corporate life of faith be described only by the neutral and nontheological term "community," rather than by the term "church"?

If this was exciting, the next intervention by Cardinal Quintero of Venezuela was equally exciting. Interior reform by the Catholic Church is basic for ecumenical outreach. Not all the mistakes of the past can simply be blamed on "history." Many of them were due to inner defects of Catholicism. The lives of bishops in the sixteenth century were a scandal. Catholics put many wrinkles in the seamless robe of Christ and must be willing to acknowledge their own guilt. The church must not be like the Pharisee who proudly denied his own sin, but like the publican who beat his breast in contrition. The *schema* must state that the Catholic Church asks pardon from God and the separated brethren for its responsibility for the divided state of Christendom.

Could one have predicted five years ago that such a speech would be given by a cardinal? Could one have predicted it five months ago? Could one have predicted that such a speech would be given by a member of the Latin American hierachy? When I ask these questions – and answer them – I am convinced that the Holy Spirit is hovering pretty close to the *aula,* and I can imagine a special radiance of joy emanating from that corner of heaven where John XXIII is cheering the Council on.

In opposition to Ruffini, who wanted no mention of Jews in the *schema,* Cardinal Doi of Japan suggested that the *schema* must be even more inclusive and deal with the relation of Catholics to other non-Christian groups, since this is the particular ecumenical problem of the missionary churches.

The morning ended with interventions by two of the patriarchs who, characteristic of those strong-willed individuals, vigorously disagreed with one another. His Beatitude Stephen I of Alexandria found the *schema* inadequate, since it played down the primacy of Peter and the indefectibility of the church, whereas Maximos IV of Antioch supported the *schema* strongly, feeling that it lifted the church out of a sterile period of polemics, that it reflected the spirit of John XXIII, and that it would open more doors to the Orthodox. The two men agreed on one point, however: The chapter on the Jews, while important, should be transferred to some other location in the conciliar documents.

It is clear that we have not yet heard the last word on the location of Chapters Four and Five. But the ecumenical ball is finally rolling.

Tuesday, November 19

How much is it really possible to appreciate the significance of events in which one is sharing? Yesterday was a milestone in Christian history. So was today. When before in its history has the Catholic Church concerned itself so sensitively with the "mystery of Israel" as it does in the fourth chapter of *De Oecumenismo,* introduced today by Cardinal Bea? When before in its history has the Catholic Church concerned itself so openly with religious liberty as it does in the fifth chapter, introduced today by Bishop DeSmedt of Bruges? In spite of all attempts to suppress the latter chapter — and that in itself is a nice little ecclesiastical

horror story that some future historian with access to all the
facts must tell — it has now been printed and delivered to
2300 bishops. Even though there will be heated dispute
about both of these chapters, they are at last out on the floor
before the fathers.

Cardinal Bea emphasized that the chapter on the Jews
does not deal with the political entity of modern Israel but
is exclusively concerned with the religious dimension of
Judaism. Since the preparation for redemption and the development of the church began in the Old Testament, the
Christian community can never be separated from Israel.
The church is a *continuation* of the people of Israel. Romans
9 – 11 makes clear that God does not reject the Jews; indeed,
the New Testament promise is that all Israel will finally be
saved. The attitude of the church toward the Jews must therefore be like that of Paul, who was willing to be accursed
for the sake of his brethren. This must be said today because
the church has sometimes succumbed to anti-Semitism and
must explicitly disavow it.

When one considers the history of Jewish persecution, and
the shameful rôle the church has played in it, one wonders
how any Christian could oppose the text Bea introduced.
And when one considers the complicity of the church in Nazi
ideology, one realizes how appropriate it is that this disavowal of anti-Semitism came from the lips of a German.

Bea's strong speech, which was strongly applauded, was
immediately followed by an introduction to Chapter Five on
religious liberty, by that champion of things ecumenical,
Bishop Emile DeSmedt of Bruges, one of the most effective
speakers of the Council. The speech was long and complex,
but it held the fathers by its sheer brilliance and momentum,
and by the passion with which it was delivered. When
DeSmedt finished there was not only applause, but thunderous applause — by all odds the greatest single outburst of the
entire Council. Even when it began to die away it lingered
on in the back of the *aula* where the younger bishops sit.
I count this speech, together with its reception, the most

thrilling moment of the Council to date. (This speech, too important to summarize briefly, is given in full as Appendix B below.)

The day's interventions represented almost a flood tide of ecumenical approval, indicating that "friends of ecumenism" can be vigorous, articulate, and persuasive.

Cardinal Leger spoke first. After citing Pope John and Pope Paul, he reminded the fathers that one of the aims in calling the Council had been ecumenical. The prayer of Christ *ut omnes unum sint* (that all may be one) has never been heard more clearly than in our day, and it is obvious that the Holy Spirit has thrust this prayer to the forefront of the church's life, so that the church can no longer be equivocal about ecumenism.

With this background, Leger spoke the words we can now recognize without benefit of translator, *Schema de Oecumenismo mihi placet* (I am pleased by the *schema* on ecumenism). It offers a bold but prudent way of reaching out to other Christians; it establishes principles for this venture; it gives latitude to bishops for working out the best ways to pursue ecumenism in their own dioceses. Leger's reservations: Chapters Three, Four, and Five, all matters with which the Council must deal, can better be dealt with in other *schemata*.

Cardinal Koenig of Vienna, after affirming that the text corresponds to the scope and purpose of Vatican II, supplemented Cardinal Ritter's feeling that the distinction in Chapter Three between the "churches" of the East and the "communities" of the West was an unfortunate one. The latter have ecclesial elements within them which the *schema* must recognize, since men receive truth *through* these communities and not merely *in* them. A better term would therefore be *communitates ecclesialis* (ecclesial communities).

Cardinal Rugambwa of Tanganyika, speaking for a group of African bishops, also reported *Schema nobis placet* (We are pleased by the *schema*). He congratulated the Secretariat for Christian Unity on its work and emphasized that the attitude toward the separated brethren must be characterized by humility and love. Those working in non-Christian countries, however, would like more emphasis on ways in which Catholic and non-Catholic Christians could share their common concerns about non-Christians.

During my sojourn in Bar-jonah I had the good fortune to meet Bishop Mendez of Mexico, one of those creative Latin American bishops who is exerting real leadership in the Council, and I also had a conversation with an American auxiliary bishop. As we found ourselves extolling Bishop DeSmedt's *relatio*, a certain *peritus* came along who is rumored to have had a hand in its composition. The following exchange occurred:

Auxiliary bishop (to *peritus*): I understand you wrote most of DeSmedt's intervention.

Peritus: I had nothing to do with it.

Auxiliary bishop: I don't believe you.

Brown: Neither do I.

Peritus: That's my story and I'm sticking to it.

While I was puzzling this one out, I encountered one of the Canadian bishops who was present at my talk last Sunday and who shared my joy over Bishop DeSmedt's presentation. But he also reported a strong undercurrent of feeling against endorsement of the religious liberty chapter on the part of bishops in areas where the Catholic Church is in the majority; these bishops look upon acceptance of the *principle* of religious liberty as tantamount to endorsing atheism. Hopes for immediate action must therefore not be placed too high.

Gori of Jerusalem wanted no mention of non-Christian groups (the Jews) unless all were covered (Moslems, Hindus, Buddhists, and so forth), and Peter XVI of Cilicia found the *schema* unacceptable since it does not come out clearly enough for papal authority. But Bishop Garonne of France emphasized the fact that ecumenical concern comes not from indifferentism but from firm faith; courageous charity rather than vague benevolence is the basis of fruitful ecumenical encounter.

The speech of the morning, however, was delivered by Bishop Elchinger of Strasbourg, and I must report it more fully since it seems to me one of the high points in the Council, which already makes two "high points" in a single morning.

The *schema*, he said, is a special favor and grace of God for our times. The first ecumenical task of the Catholic Church is to engage in sincere and profound reformation of its ways of investigating the truth. As Leo XIII said, in opening the Vatican archives to scholars, we must recognize and confess historical truth, even if it is bitter. We believe that the church is holy, as it is one, catholic, and apostolic. But God has given His gifts in earthen vessels, i.e., He has entrusted them to sinful men. Consequently Catholics must not refuse to confess their sins, as Pope Paul said in his opening allocution and in his talk to the non-Catholic observers. This must not be done in general terms, but in terms of particular times and places where we have erred, and/or where divinely revealed truth has been honored more fervently by the separated brethren than by us. For example, the Reformation was not first of all an attack on the church and its unity, but a desire to clarify certain aspects of the faith that had been thrust into the background. Today, Catholics who try to engage in ecumenical dialogue have found themselves under attack, and much greater initiative has been exercised by the separated brethren. Likewise, non-Catholics have shown greater confidence in their Biblical scholars than Catholics have, as is clear from the difficulties that beset Père Lagrange and the Biblical School of Jerusalem.

Today, rather than rejecting the doctrines of the separated brethren outright, as we have tended to do in the past, we must recognize the partial and often deep truth professed by the separated brethren and profess along with them as much as we can. Catholics have too often examined Protestant theology only to discover those things that "deny" some aspect of Catholic faith, rather than recognizing the positive truth in their stress on Scripture, for example, or the liberty of the Holy Spirit. Catholics have been too passive and static in their understanding of divine truth, and must be more open and outgoing in seeking it. The separated brethren have a right to better Catholic treatment of the differences that divide us than we have yet provided. None of this leads to doctrinal relativism but simply to the recognition that human words and personal ideas can never exhaustively contain God's word, which always transcends the power of the mind of man. *Dixi.*

Such an intervention is worth a whole Vatican Council.

❋   ❋   ❋

Exhilaration continued through lunch and the early afternoon. A group of us had lunch with a group of bishops, and met with them afterward to discuss *De oecumenismo.* I was nearly bowled over by the question one of them asked. "Is there anything you observers want said on the Council floor about *De Oecumenismo?*" We spoke of the matters that have caused us concern, growing out of last week's "briefing session," and also raised questions about the description of the Protestant "communities" in Chapter Three. The result was that a few of us were asked to submit what we would consider a more adequate description, out of which some of the bishops will draft a written intervention incorporating as much of our material as they can conscientiously use. If ever there was need for evidence of the *genuineness* of Catholic desire for dialogue, this meeting provided it.

❋   ❋   ❋

The rest of the afternoon was devoted to our regular Tuesday "briefing session." I am surprised by the degree to which certain observers resist the inclusion of a chapter on the Jews. These observers, who tend to come from predominantly Arab areas, feel that the Jewish question inevitably has political overtones. Others feel that a chapter on the Jews makes necessary the inclusion of chapters on the rest of the non-

Christian religions. The chapter title and first paragraph lay themselves open to this complaint, but the bulk of the chapter is a splendid exposition of the really important point, which is that Jews and Christians are bound together in such an inextricable fashion that one cannot understand the New Covenant apart from the Old. I am, therefore, strongly in favor of its inclusion.

Occasional fears are voiced that Catholic ecumenism is really only a way of providing for a less painful "return" of the wandering sheep; there must be assurance that the manual of suggestions for ecumenical activity that the Secretariat is to prepare does not turn out to be a "Manual On How to Receive Converts."

The other emphasis in our discussions is a stress on the provisional character of the *schema*. The ecumenical situation is fluid; hopefully it will be very different in a decade. It would therefore be unfortunate to bind the church too rigorously today to patterns of ecumenical activity that may soon be "dated."

❋   ❋   ❋

The good mood produced by the morning's interventions and the afternoon's sessions with the bishops was a bit chastened by an evening of discussion with both Catholics and Protestants. Everyone, of course, is pleased that ecumenism is now before the house, and that the chapters on the Jews and on religious liberty are finally on the agenda. But underneath this pleasure is a certain current of dismay, even of apprehension. It is hard to put one's finger on the reason for this. Part of it can be traced to a growing fear that, after all the talk about collegiality, perhaps nothing specific will really come of it. Part of it grows out of a feeling that the shaky Italian political situation is intruding into the life of the Council. Some of the Italian newspapers, for example, are arguing that if the Curia is publicly rebuked (by the establishment of a senate of bishops or clear papal support

for collegiality) this will undermine the authority of the
Curia's consistent denunciations of communism, and give the
Communist Party a good chance of taking over Italy. Another
argument goes as follows: The religious liberty chapter is
based on *Pacem in Terris,* Pope John's last encyclical. This
encyclical gave great encouragement to Italian Communists.
Therefore, approval of religious liberty, which is tantamount
to endorsing atheism, will further strengthen the communist
cause in Italy.

I do not know how much weight, if any, such arguments
carry within the Vatican. But it is clear that such arguments
are being voiced in high places. More and more in the past
few days, when I have expressed some irritation at the slow-
ness of change, I have been met not only with the stock response, "The church moves slowly," but also with a new
response, "Well, yes, but you've got to understand Italian
politics. . . ." If I reply, "Why should Italian politics have
anything to do with it?" the reluctant response is usually,
"Well, it shouldn't, but it does."

However widespread or minimal this sort of thinking is,
it must be reported to counteract the euphoria that follows
an intervention by a Bishop Elchinger.

Wednesday, November 20

Today we had (1) further significant interventions on *De
Oecumenismo,* (2) one moment of drama, and (3) one moment of genuine comic relief.

Cardinal Meyer of Chicago spoke approvingly of Chapters
One through Three, but also urged the acceptance of Chapters Four and Five, both of which belong in the *schema.*
Cardinal Bacci of Italy, however, claimed that Chapters Four
and Five have nothing to do with ecumenism. The *schema*
as a whole tends to support the notion of collegiality, and
this is a dangerous notion which undermines the primacy
of the pope. Furthermore — and here Bacci indulged in a
"parenthesis," i.e., a comment not directly related to the subject under discussion — on the morning of the vote on the "five

questions," Bacci had asked permission to make an important comment on the "five questions" and had been denied permission to speak. In good conscience he had felt compelled to protest to the pope that the matter had been pushed through too fast.

End of parenthesis. End of speech. But not, as we discover day after day, end of the controversy over the "five questions."

Bishop Jelmini, speaking for a group of Swiss bishops, emphasized that all who believe in Christ in some sense already belong to the church. A unity that is sheer uniformity must not be demanded, and the beginning of ecumenism on the part of Catholics must stress the inner renewal of the church.

Bishop Morcillo of Spain, who "warmly welcomed" the *schema*, put the ecumenical dilemma clearly: non-Catholics insist that ecumenism cannot just mean "return," whereas Catholics believe that their church has the fullness of the truth. Nevertheless, genuine dialogue is possible if both groups try to be faithful to the truth and recognize that it does not belong to them but to Christ. As though to supplement this point, Archbishop Baudoux of Canada stressed the fact that ecumenical encounter can be promoted by reciprocal forgiveness, friendship, and confidence in one another. The hopeful thing about the *schema* is that it is not condescending, but acknowledges the degree to which the separated brethren are incorporated into Christ through baptism and through confession of His name. Such a viewpoint is an expression of, rather than a betrayal of, Catholic theology.

Archbishop Heenan, speaking in the name of the hierarchy of England and Wales, was clear and forthright. His earlier intervention, some weeks ago, had left the impression that ecumenism was only a preliminary step to make conversion of the non-Catholic easier. Today he gave warm support to the *schema*, and lamented that there had been so little dialogue between British non-Catholics and British Catholics. Nevertheless, the *schema* must distinguish more clearly between the immediate and ultimate objectives of ecumenism.

The immediate objective is mutual understanding and love. The ultimate objective is the visible union of all Christians within the one true Church of Jesus Christ.

Heenan's intervention, which was greeted with applause, admirably poses the problems of ecumenical dialogue. *Can* it be, for the Catholic, any more than a preliminary step toward drawing separated Christians back into the Roman Catholic Church (since there is no doubt *which* church a Catholic means by "the one true Church of Jesus Christ")? My response would be that there is one recognition that can avert an impasse, and that is the recognition, growing on both sides, that each side ventures out *toward* the other, neither one denying its own essential nature, but each acknowledging that in the process of the ensuing dialogue something *new* enters the situation and that, under the mysterious alchemy of the Holy Spirit, we do not yet see exactly what this new thing is. The most we can know is that the new thing will not simply be our old existence, unchanged by the encounter. We engage in dialogue, in other words, at risk that something will happen to both of us, but we do so in trust, for we know that what emerges will have the hand of God upon it.

A new note was struck by the interventions of Bishops Weber, Chopard-Lallier, and Jacq. Each insisted that there must be more possibility for common worship together than the present text allows, particularly in such family events as baptisms, weddings, and funerals. When non-Catholic worship is sincere and true, there is no reason why Catholics should not be allowed to participate in it, and some degree of common participation in worship will be a great help to the cause of unity.

Bishop Mendez of Mexico, whom I met yesterday in the coffee bar, ranged over the various emphases of the *schema* and gave it strong endorsement. Christ, he said, has given us many gifts, and in our day one of His gifts is the new ecumenical situation. The *schema*, however, should give more explicit attention to the pentecostal groups, since they also are a part of the stirrings of the Spirits. Liturgy as a resource of inner renewal should also be emphasized. Not only is the religious liberty chapter important, but it should be the first chapter, since it is the basis of ecumenical encounter rather than a corollary of it.

It makes a tremendous difference, I am discovering, if one knows the speaker, even if only casually, and I find that, when I can visualize the man, I usually derive much more benefit from his speech. The moral: Get acquainted with as many bishops as possible. The problem: There are 2200 bishops at the Council.

*   *   *

I found a good many people in the coffee bar wondering whether or not the moderators would respond to Cardinal Bacci's charge that, in bluntest terms, they had railroaded the "five questions" through the Council without allowing Bacci a chance to make his crucial point. The moment of drama came when Cardinal Agagianian, moderator of the day, rose to the question. All bustle in the *aula* ceased as Agagianian reported that Bacci had indeed come to the moderator's desk on the morning of the vote with a request that *jus primatiale* be changed to read *jus primatus*, since the former was vague and ambiguous. The moderators, however, had agreed that since the reference was clear and unambiguous there was no need to postpone the vote further simply to allow debate on a matter of grammatical construction.

The announcement was greeted with loud applause — a good indication that the fathers approve of the new firmness being exerted by the moderators.

Tension was relaxed by the last speaker, who announced that the definitions of ecumenism thus far had been too narrow. So, he went on, "I will speak about the ecumenism of God, the ecumenism of Jesus, the ecumenism of Mary, the ecumenism of the apostles, the ecumenism of the bishops, the ecumenism of the laity . . ." at which point Agagianian interrupted, "Venerable father, please confine yourself to the ecumenism *of the schema*." This brought down the house, as did the bishop's response that the *schema* was confused. Then, realizing that he was under pressure, he began to talk at a faster and faster pace. Each sentence was delivered at a speed more breathtaking than the last. Agagianian was about to interrupt him again, but realizing that no human being could stop such an unquenchable torrent of words, he finally smiled, shrugged his shoulders, and let the speaker continue. Bishops all over the *aula* stood up to catch sight of this amazing performer. Those who couldn't were engaging in the ecclesiastical equivalent of rolling in the aisles. When the speaker finally came to the word *Conclusio*, the fathers were ready, and the word *Dixi* was no sooner pronounced than there was thunderous applause.

The incident proved two things, neither of which, unfortunately, I can verify: (1) The Holy Ghost *must* have a sense of humor, and (2) the moderator, if he had asked for cloture at that point, could have gotten it without a dissenting vote.

* * *

The evening was a pleasant one arranged by Archbishop McGucken of San Francisco, who invited me to dinner at the Hilton to meet other bishops from the central California area. I discovered, incidentally, how word gets around Rome. There has been no official word at all about the date of the next session of the Council. The pope may not know the date, the cardinals may not know the date, the bishops may not know the date, but the Hilton does; there is a notice in the lobby inviting bishops to make reservations for the third session beginning next September.

Thursday, November 21

Mass this morning was the "simple Latin rite" of the Western church — all done in Paleo-Slavonic. It was possible to follow the sequence perfectly, even though not a single word could be understood. The fathers were in precisely the situation as most of their laymen, who don't understand Latin any better than the average bishop understands Paleo-Slavonic. A more telling argument for wider use of the vernacular could hardly have been devised.

There was great excitement due to a rumor that the pope would appear in the Council this morning. When we got to St. Peter's the papal throne was in place with a backdrop behind it. But no pope appeared. This disappointment led to a new rumor: the pope will appear tomorrow.

But if the pope did not come, a message from the pope did come. To my theological friends I would describe this as a demythologized appearance of the pope. It was, however, more exciting than most demythologized appearances, for the message began: The pope, after receiving a petition from numerous of the Council fathers, has consented, in order to expedite the work of the various conciliar commissions, to make certain changes in their structure.

At this moment, a pin being dropped in St. Peter's would have had the approximate impact of a hydrogen bomb explosion.

The details of the changes were these: Each commission will be increased from twenty-five to thirty members (except for the Commission on the Oriental churches, which already has twenty-seven, and the Secretariat for Christian Unity, which has only eighteen). The fathers will elect four new members to the commission and the pope will choose a fifth. (For the Commission on the Oriental churches, the fathers will elect three; for the Secretariat for Christian Unity, the fathers will elect eight and the pope will choose four.) Nominations must be handed in by Monday, and the vote will be on Thursday, a week from today. When the new commissions meet, they themselves will elect a second vice-chairman and a second secretary.

By the time 10:30 rolled around and the coffee bars were in business, there was no dearth of conversation. Reactions

to the pope's move seemed to cover the following range of
attitudes: (1) The pope has moved creatively in response to
the fathers' request, and this is good. (2) The pope has not
moved as creatively as we hoped he would, and this is not so
good. (3) The pope has moved in a statesmanlike way:
nothing has been taken away, but something important has
been added. (4) The move will make the commissions more
truly representative of the Council. (5) The move fails to
get at the heart of the problem, which is that every chairman
represents the Curia point of view. (7) Even though the
chairmanship is not affected, the increase in members will
offset that fact. (8) The idea of double vice-chairmen and
secretaries will be clumsy and awkward in the commissions
themselves, but may be useful device in subcommission meetings. (9) Having given the bishops a four to one advantage,
the pope cannot be accused of trying to pack the court. (10)
Since the pope has given this much initiative to the bishops,
they had better devote the weekend to drawing up the best
possible slate of candidates.

During the morning there was an important vote on an
emendation of the liturgy *schema*. Many fathers requested
greater use of the vernacular in the sacraments than the
schema originally provided for. This is particularly important
for the missionary bishops. To have part of the sacrament in
the vernacular, and then to switch to Latin for the central
portion (such as the absolution of sin at confession) is to
give the impression of resorting to a magical rite or incanta-
tion from which the pagan convert may only recently have
been delivered. Such bishops, therefore, are eager that
permission be granted to say the central portions in the vernacular as well. The change was approved, 1848 to 335, and
symbolizes an important victory.

❋   ❋   ❋

The interventions plowed over increasingly familiar territory, and the first two were good indications of the ex-

tremes within which the rest ranged. The sentiments of these two were as different as names of the two speakers (Flores and Florit) were similar. Bishop Flores' intervention was significant not only because it supported the *schema*, but because Bishop Flores is from Spain, which has not exactly been the center of Catholic ecumenical creativity. He expressed joy that a Council was finally speaking about ecumenism, and doing so in the spirit of Pope John. He was glad the *schema* was positive and not negative. The doctrine of the church is not complete until the place of the separated brethren within it has been clarified; since they are by baptism incorporated within the church, they also share in some sense in the priesthood of Christ, and Catholics and Protestants can therefore make common cause against evil in the world. They can do so without fighting or quarreling among themselves, and together perform works of missionary zeal. The *schema* is right in stressing that the first step toward ecumenical action is the inner reform of the church, but it must go on to give more freedom to Catholics to participate in non-Catholic religious services.

Spain . . . thus do the walls of stereotype and misunderstanding come tumbling down.

Things were kept in balance, however, by Archbishop Florit of Florence, who found the *schema* too optimistic in asserting that certain elements of the true church can be found within the separated communities. Prayer for unity must be a prayer that non-Catholics will become Catholics. The *schema* is too indiscriminate in its praise of the separated brethren, not all of whom are deserving of such commendation. It should stress those things the separated brethren lack, so that non-Catholics, made aware of their sad lot, will return to the true church. It is questionable whether the church should affirm religious liberty, since to permit diffusion of a false religion is to be guilty of great evil. The only reason to permit such diffusion would be for reasons of expediency.

After more of the same, Cardinal Lercaro, no doubt eyeing this morning's list of thirty-three speakers, asked whether the fathers wished to close discussion on the *schema* in general, and vote on its acceptability as a document for detailed discussion, chapter by chapter. After an affirmative answer to the first question, he announced that there would be a vote on accepting Chapters One through Three for discussion, and that a similar vote on Chapters Four and Five would be taken "in a few days."

This is probably a wise move since there is a certain amount of feeling that the latter chapters belong elsewhere, and it would be unwise to jeopardize the whole *schema* by insisting on a package vote. The fact that all five chapters have been the subject of the general discussion just concluded means that the moderators can ask for a vote on Chapters Four and Five at any time they choose to do so.

The vote on Chapters One through Three was a stunning victory for ecumenism: 1966 *placets* to only 86 *non placets*. (Unanswered mystery: Was the *juxta modum* bishop out having a cup of coffee?) Approval of these chapters is one of the most important things the Council has yet done. Close to two thousand bishops have now gone on record indicating that they believe ecumenism is here to stay.

The interventions on Chapter One indicated, however, that "ecumenism" still means different things to different bishops. Two examples will suffice.

Bishop Volk of Germany insisted that the starting point must be the conviction that division is contrary to the will of God. While presupposing that Roman Catholicism has all that is necessary to the fullness of the church, Catholics must be ready to accept everything in other churches that is truly Christian, and make clear to non-Catholics that whatever portion of truth they have is not being condemned. Unity is not the same thing as uniformity, and just as there is one Christ but four gospels, so there is one church but various manifestations within it of the one faith.

Bishop Carli of Italy gave qualified (*juxta modum*) approval, but he emphasized the *juxta modum* part pretty heavily. The Roman Catholic Church is the one true church, so all must join it. There must be no equivocation in affirming *extra ecclesiam nulla salus* (outside the church is no salvation). There must not be emphasis on the activity of the Holy Ghost among Protestants, since this might suggest that the Holy Ghost has left the Catholic Church. Finally, there must be no suggestion that the church is founded on "the apostles and prophets." The church is founded solely on Peter. To say anything else is to imply a doctrine of collegiality, and the mind of the Council is not yet clear on collegiality.

"The mind of the Council is not yet clear on collegiality. . . ." The significance of an 80 per cent vote on the "five questions" is an almost infallible "litmus paper test" for determining the theological orientation of a bishop. Does 80 per cent approval indicate a consensus or does it not?

*   *   *

It is interesting to note the near total acceptance by the fathers of the term "separated brethren." Only a few years ago the very use of the words would have rendered one suspect. Now it is the common coin of the ecumenical realm. Indeed, as someone has said, so much has the atmosphere changed, that when the bishops go back home they won't dare preach about the devil any more. They'll have to call him "our separated brother."

Friday, November 22

As the lay auditors were kneeling this morning at communion, heads upturned, mouths open, waiting for the priest, it suddenly occurred to me that they looked for all the world like very young baby birds in a nest, straining after the food their mother is bringing to sustain them. The analogy is not bad, even though unaesthetic, for in the Catholic view every child of the church *is* a fledgling whose spiritual nourishment is utterly dependent on the food that Mother Church provides.

The rumor was abroad again that the pope would come to

the Council. Sure enough, just after the enthronement of the gospel, applause started in the back of the *aula,* a sign of the pope's entry. The applause died out and Felici gave a great many announcements — announcements about pamphlets, votes, and speakers, but not about the coming of the pope. Later on in the coffee bar I asked one of the bishops what had happened. "Oh," he responded, "very simple. The choir boys were walking by and we wanted to let them know we had appreciated their singing."

There was little in the speeches that was new. Two bishops argued against the inclusion of a statement about the Jews in a *schema* on ecumenism. One bishop thought that charity was a good foundation for ecumenical activity. Another felt that there were dangers in ecumenism. Bishop Huyghe of France, however, spoke very creatively, advocating Professor Cullmann's proposal that Catholic and Protestant churches take up offerings for the poor of one another's parishes, and urging common pastoral action whenever possible.

The big event of the day was not the speaking, but the climactic vote on *De Sacra Liturgia* as a whole. When the computors had tallied up the voting cards, the results were announced as follows: *Placet,* 2158; *non placet,* 19; and (still doggedly persistent to the end) *placet juxta modum* (therefore null), 1. Announcement of the latter vote brought the usual laughter, and then the import of the total vote sank in and the fathers burst into prolonged applause. The most sweeping reforms in four centuries had just been completed with only nineteen negative votes. The mood was very gay. Cardinal Tisserant, whose total contribution to the Council thus far has consisted in leading the *Adsumus* at the beginning and the *Angelus* at the conclusion of each day, expressed gratitude to the commission for its faithful work, indicated how hard it had labored, and urged the other commissions to go and do likewise. (Laughter in the *aula,* followed by applause.)

This was an appropriate day on which to approve a *schema* on the liturgy, since it is the Feast of St. Cecelia, the patron saint of music. It is also the sixtieth anniversary of Pius X's *motu proprio* "On Sacred Music" which signalized the real beginning of the modern liturgical movement. Do these historic coincidences "just happen"?

*   *   *

No matter what else the Council does or does not do, *De Sacra Liturgia* will stand as a significant achievement. It is too long to summarize, but I must indicate something of the spirit of reform that breathes through it. Each chapter sets out basic principles and then indicates what contemporary changes are necessary to be faithful to the principles. Here, almost at random, are some of the things that delight, and even astonish, a Protestant observer: (1) stress on the active participation of all the faithful in the liturgical actions of the church; (2) emphasis on more significant liturgical instruction for all; (3) considerable authority to local bishops to adapt the liturgy in terms of their own needs (particularly helpful to the missionary bishops); (4) new importance to the place of Scripture, (5) specific portions of the liturgy restored to the people; (6) revision of the rites to eliminate repetitions and encumbrances, so that the direction and meaning of the liturgy will be clearer; (7) inclusion of a sermon as the norm rather than the exception; (8) more extensive use of the vernacular; (9) development of territorial liturgical commissions; (10) greater opportunities for con-celebration; (11) greater opportunities for the faithful to receive communion under both species; (12) new interpretation of the last sacrament, so that it is more fittingly called "the annointing of the sick" and is not to be withheld until the moment of death; (13) simplification and improvement of the breviary and wider permission for reading it in the vernacular; (14) emphasis on Sunday as having priority over multiplication of feast days; (15) greater opportunities for congregational singing; (16) openness to new modes of expression in sacred art; and (17) willingness to discuss with other groups the establishment of a fixed date for Easter.

I can already hear a certain type of reaction: "See how Protestant the Catholic Church is becoming: greater stress on Scripture, congregational singing, emphasis on preaching, use of the vernacular, more participation of the laity — it sounds like the Reformation four hundred years later." I think Protestants must resist this interpretation as much as Catholics will. The thing to be emphasized is that Roman Catholic worship is becoming *more catholic,* more all-embracing of that which is most characteristic of the fullness of the liturgical tradition, and consequently less Western, less parochial, and less Latin.

A glance at the Reformation liturgies makes clear that the Reformers were trying to recapture the authentic elements of worship that they felt had disappeared from late medieval Christendom. They went back to the liturgical patterns of the early Christian community. This, of course, is exactly what the Roman Catholic liturgical revival has done. It, too, rather than "innovating," has tried to recapture the authentic liturgy of the early church and adapt it to the present day. Thus in their concurrent, but separate, liturgical revivals, both Catholicism and Protestantism are going back through their history to the common source that both shared before the division of Christendom. Liturgy, then, is one of the greatest resources for ecumenical endeavor, and all those bishops are profoundly right who have been urging this point on the Council floor.

The task of the church now is to see how rapidly the *schema's* reforms can be incorporated into the actual worship life of the church. One of the leading liturgists at the Council has suggested that, as a way of symbolizing the new liturgical era, there be concelebration at mass on the day the *schema* is formally promulgated, with a number of bishops celebrating together and the rest receiving communion. This would mean that for the first time during Vatican II the Eucharist would unite the fathers around one altar, rather than sending them to 2200 separate altars.

*   *   *

The days are getting very full. Today was only typical of what is gradually happening: 8:15 – 8:45 A.M., worship at the Methodist Church; 9 – 12:15, attend the Council; 1 – 2 P.M., work on revisions of a draft to replace certain paragraphs of Chapter Three of *De Oecumenismo*; 2 – 3 P.M., meet with a group of American bishops; 3 – 4 P.M., more work on revisions of Chapter Three; 4 – 6:30 P.M., speak to the Trappists on a Protestant interpretation of the Council; 7 – 10 P.M., evening at the Canadian Theological College and speak to graduate seminarians about the Council, with special emphasis on the religious liberty statement.

I had a wonderful time with the Trappists. I was picked up in their Volkswagen Microbus and driven to their house of studies at the edge of Rome. (I already have a title for a murder mystery set in Rome: *The Monk in the Microbus.*) I spoke for about forty-five minutes, after which there was a considerable time for questions. I felt genuine rapport with the group, and was reminded of Reinhold Niebuhr's comment that sometimes we discover that the truth we share *in* Christ is more important than the truths we do not share *about* Christ.

At the Canadian Theological College, I had the privilege of eating with Cardinal Leger, one of the really great spokesmen for Catholic ecumenism, after which we discussed the church in a secularized culture. He asked some penetrating questions about American churches in relation to the race issue — tragically relevant, in the light of developments later in the evening.

Since I had been told that many of the theologians I was addressing would be French-speaking, I laboriously wrote out a French introduction pointing out that although bishops had *periti* to put their speeches in Latin, I did not have a *peritus* to put mine in French, and would therefore prefer to continue in English.

Once again we had good questions and discussion. Toward the end of the evening, however, Cardinal Leger came into the room looking absolutely ashen. He whispered to me, "Have you heard the news?" Since I didn't know what he meant, he said to the entire group, "I have very bad news for all of you. The pope has just informed us that President Kennedy has been assassinated." Then, turning to me, the only American in the room, he said, "I extend our sympathy to you and your fellow countrymen." The immensity of the news, without any warning whatsoever, was almost impossible to take in. After one halfhearted attempt at another question, the leader wisely said that the news made any further discussion unimportant if not impossible. He asked us to stand, and we all said the *Pater Noster* together in tribute to President Kennedy. I felt through these painful few minutes an intense sense of being surrounded by bonds of sympathy and Christian charity from "mes chers frères en Jésus-Christ."

This is not the place for extended comments on Kennedy's death, which I still hardly believe. I can only hope that such a thing will rouse our nation to the folly of its ways, and that out of this truly tragic event, some creative good can be wrested. All over Rome tonight, and indeed all over the world, Catholics are saying prayers for John F. Kennedy. And I, who on many occasions in public worship have asked God to bless "thy servant John, President of these United States," feel very much at one with them.

The Ninth Week
(*November 25 – 29*)

The vote on the Communications *schema* – ecumenical pros and cons – conciliar ups and downs – where is the vote on Chapters Four and Five? – elections to the commissions

Monday, November 25

There was high drama on the steps of St. Peter's this morning. I'm not sure, however, whether it more resembled Shakespeare or the Keystone Cops. A group of priests distributed mimeographed sheets, signed by twenty-six bishops, urging the fathers to vote against the Communications *schema* as an ill-conceived document unworthy of the Council. The statement concluded: "If the *schema* is promulgated, the authority of the Council will be called into question." The signatories were from all over the world, indicating that the document did not represent the pique of a clique.

The conservatives took special umbrage at this, even though they had engaged in precisely the same activity on the morning of the Mary vote, and a quick tableau in nine scenes promptly unfolded:

1. One of the priests was accosted by Archbishop Felici.
2. Felici demanded that the petitions be given to him.
3. The priest demurred.
4. Felici went to call the Vatican police.
5. A German bishop appeared and took charge of distributing the petitions.
6. Felici returned and again demanded the surrender of the petitions.
7. The bishop demurred.

8. The archbishop lunged at the bishop, trying to pull the petitions out of his hands.
9. The result was not successful, and, the police wisely deciding not to interfere in episcopal warfare, the distribution continued.

By the time mass was over, Felici was his usual unruffled self again, and proceeded to the announcements, two of which were of considerable importance. First, by decree of the pope, Wednesday, December 4, will be a public session, to vote on and promulgate the *schemata* (plural) completed in this session. Second — and this was news to almost everyone — on Tuesday, December 3, there will be another public session commemorating the four hundredth anniversary of the completion of the Council of Trent, with Cardinal Urbani giving the address.

Both items had a depressing effect on me. The presumption that two *schemata* will be promulgated means that plans are being made to promulgate the Communications *schema* as well as the one on the liturgy. And the sudden decision to make Tuesday a day of commemoration means that a full working day is lost and that there is even less time left for treatment of religious liberty and the Jews.

The immediate prospects, however, were brighter than the long-range ones, for the first three speakers announced were Cardinals Leger, Ritter, and Bea. Who could remain depressed at the thought of hearing them?

Cardinal Leger, who will always be linked in my memory with the news of President Kennedy's death, expressed two main desires for the chapter. (1) It must have a more clearly articulated conception of the unity of the church. In the past the Catholic Church has given the impression of being monolithic, without acknowledging the diversity that is always possible within unity. Missionary priests have especially felt this problem. Since the pope himself has emphasized the need for diversity within unity, the *schema* must reflect this more clearly. (2) More attention must be given to ways of eliminating doctrinal dissension with the separated brethren. In dialogue with them, Catholics must exemplify not only truth and charity, but also humility. The need now is for *intellectual* humility. Catholics must strive for ways to express Catholic truth in forms of thought that are understood by the separated brethren, and not just in the traditional and rather static forms of the past. Schisms are not resolved by authoritarian fiat, but by diverse groups working toward one another in humility. The church, in other words, must be willing to confess her sins. If the church can claim to have all truth, she must also be willing to acknowledge that she fails in her communication of that truth. Revelation is a mystery, and Catholics must not assume that they have an exhaustive grasp of every aspect of that mystery. As the pope said in his talk to the non-Catholic observers, "immobilism" of doctrine is a real sin and no true Catholic can accept it. Through dialogue, not only can the separated brethren be brought closer to the truth, but Roman Catholics can themselves learn more of the truth of the Christian mystery than they now possess.

Perhaps it is because I have so recently seen and conversed with Cardinal Leger that this intervention made such an impact on me, but I think it would have stood out even if he had been only a name to me. At all events, it will remain as one of the most moving utterances I heard in Rome. When Catholics and Protestants can approach the mystery of revelation both acknowledging that they have much to learn, and that in their mutual quest they can learn from each other, the possibilities of what can emerge from such encounter are beyond human imagination to encompass. When I hear negative comments by other bishops, I shall try to hold on to Cardinal Leger's words.

Cardinal Ritter asked for more stress on the pastoral and theological aspects of ecumenism. He reminded the fathers that the unity to be sought must be the unity *Christ* seeks, not just a unity that is advantageous to Roman Catholics. Speaking on behalf of the American bishops, Ritter then thanked all of the fathers for their prayers over the weekend on behalf of President Kennedy. Where there is charity, hatred ceases, and the tragic events of the past few days must remind the Council that its aim is to help charity increase throughout the world.

Cardinal Bea, speaking for the Secretariat for Christian Unity, expressed thanks for the comments that had been made about the *schema*, and commented on certain types of apprehension it seemed to have aroused. He was surprised that some had felt that ecumenism would foster religious indifferentism or false eirenicism, since its purpose is to make the truth clearer; non-Catholics have no desire for the Catholic Church to present a watered-down version of Catholic truth. The local bishop can be the judge of appropriate ecumenical activity, and he will know better how to proceed than members of the Curia who are not acquainted with local situations. Others have been worried that the *schema* does not set forth full Catholic doctrine, but not everything can be said in one *schema*, and accounts of full Catholic doctrine are available elsewhere. Finally, there should be no difficulty about the *schema's* suggestion that Catholics and non-Catholics pray together for unity. This possibility has been permitted ever since the Instruction of the Holy Office of 1949. The intent of corporate prayer for unity is not to impose *our* ideas on the other partner, but to ask for the unity that Christ desires for His church, and to leave to God just how this is to be achieved.

After these interventions, Cardinal Lercaro announced that, before the vote on the full text of the Communications *schema*, Cardinal Tisserant, the French head of the cardinal-presidents, wished to make a comment. Tisserant, with considerable feeling, referred to the petitions that had been distributed on the steps of St. Peter's and said that the presidents and moderators deplored the action, which was unworthy of the bishops who had consented to it.

Two comments: (1) When Tisserant finished this little lecture there was no applause whatever. (2) No similar rebuke was administered to the conservative bishops who did precisely the same thing on the morning of the Mary vote. If I were to quote a proverb (as Cardinal Gracias does so aptly in his interventions) I would choose, "What's sauce for the goose is sauce for the gander."

        *   *   *

The moods in the coffee bar covered the entire spectrum from hope to gloom. I asked one of the *periti* if he had eight hundred votes in his pocket to defeat the Communications *schema*, and with a broad smile he said he thought he did. But there was considerable disappointment that the commemoration of Trent would eliminate a whole working day and thus make consideration of the Jews and religious liberty far less likely. But, as another *peritus* pointed out, since all five chapters of the *schema* have been discussed "in general," all that is needed is that the moderators call for a vote to accept Chapters Four and Five as a basis for detailed discussion. No further discussion of the latter chapters is needed to achieve this. The advantage of such a move is that the texts would then be "frozen" until the next session, whereas if they are *not* approved as a basis for detailed discussion they might be drastically edited and altered in the interval.

Just before voting began, Archbishop Felici, sounding very impassive and neutral, announced that one of the signers of the petition had informed him that his name had been affixed to the document without his approval. The name of this bishop was not revealed by the secretary-general, but the impact of the announcement was to discredit both the petition and the *non placet* vote the petition advocated. Tension is mounting in the *aula*.

Interventions on *De Oecumenismo* proceeded with no new material emerging. The discussion presently shifted to Chapter Two on "The Practice of Ecumenism." Cardinal Monreal of Spain urged that more stress be placed on devotion to Mary, and that Protestants be asked to disavow proselytism, but a number of bishops spoke in much more positive terms.

Just before closing, Felici announced the results of the voting on the Communications schema: *placet,* 1598; *non placet,* 503. This means that despite all the efforts of the past week, the *schema* has passed and will be promulgated. That there was a rise in the *non placet* vote from 103 to 503 indicates that some people have been busy, but not quite busy enough. The fathers were not particularly proud of their achievement. Whereas the announcement of the adoption of *De Sacra Liturgia* was greeted with wild applause, today's announcement brought only a feeble attempt at applause that died out almost immediately. There is an outside chance, of course, that since there were over 500 negative votes the pope will decide not to promulgate the *schema,* but this hope is being entertained only by the visionary.

Tuesday, November 26

It is clear that there will be no simultaneous translation during the present session. Apparently the technical difficulties have not been overcome, for the translation booths are closed up and the little men with headsets no longer wander around the *aula* stopping here and there, lifting their eyes heavenward (in an act of concentration, not meditation) to test the abilities of the transmitters. But simultaneous translation should transform the nature of the third session, about whose dates, incidentally, we are still as much in the dark as ever, since there is no disposition as yet to grant infallibility to the desk clerk at the Hotel Hilton.

Half a dozen bishops wished to speak on Chapter One, beyond the cloture imposed yesterday. While none of the material this morning was new, much of it served as a convenient summing up of the various poles of opinion on "the principles of ecumenism."

Bishop Manek of Indonesia, speaking for thirty bishops, repeated the request for elimination of the distinctions between "churches" of the East and mere "communities" of the West. Bishop Zoa of Cameroun pointed out later in the morning that the ecumenical movement has really come out of the missionary areas, where the separation of Christians is a particular scandal, and where at the very least there must be cooperations between Catholic and non-Catholics in areas of social concern. Bishop Hengsbach of Essen also spoke forcefully about the need for working together on common social problems, citing his work with Protestants in the industrial area of the Ruhr Valley. He suggested that it would be a good idea for Catholics to get as worked up about the threat of poverty and hunger as they do about the threat of communism.

We also had negative speeches. One of the Cistercians underlined the fact that ecumenism can only proceed in the context of Mariology, since Mary is the true source of unity. If a man doesn't go to Christ through Mary, he will never find the whole Christ. Bishop Compagnone of Italy urged much more stress on the fact that the church is founded on *Peter*, even if the other apostles may have been present when this happened.

Even at this late date, we are being told that the collegiality vote was all wrong.

The most rousing intervention of the morning, however, was given by Bishop Leven of San Antonio, defending the propriety of ecumenical concern in the face of the criticisms of certain bishops in southern Europe. It also indicated the willingness of members of the American hierarchy to enter into the fray with uninhibited vigor, and is worth quoting as an example of the forthrightness of conciliar exchange:

Every day it becomes more clear that we need the dialogue, not only with Protestants but also among us bishops.

For there are some Fathers who have already spoken to us frequently in the Council who speak as if the only text in the Holy Bible were Matt. 16, 18 "Thou art Peter and upon this Rock I will build my Church." In every intervention they argue against the collegiality of the Bishops. They preach to us and chastise us as if we were against Peter and his successors or as if we desired to steal away the faith of our flocks and to promote indifferentism.

They speak as if Our Holy Father John XXIII had never cited in our day the expression of St. Augustine "They are our brothers; they will not cease to be our brothers until they cease saying Our Father." They speak as if the whole doctrine of the freedom of conscience due every man, so clearly stated in *Pacem in Terris*, were offensive to pious ears.

Again and again in this *aula* they continue to chastise us as if the Prelate who feels compelled by clear evidence to acknowledge the gifts of the Holy Spirit in persons of other ecclesiastical bodies were denying the Faith and giving grave scandal to the innocent.

They prefer to blame non-Catholics whom perhaps they have never seen, than to instruct the children in their parishes. Otherwise why are they so afraid the effects of Ecumenism would not be good? Why aren't their people better instructed? Why aren't their people visited in their homes? Why isn't there an active and working Confraternity of Christian Doctrine in their parishes?

It seems the dangers arising from Ecumenism may be exaggerated. The Prelates who seek a sincere and fruitful dialogue with non-Catholics are not the ones who show disaffection and disloyalty to the Holy Father. It is not our people who miss Mass on Sunday, refuse the sacraments and vote the Communist ticket.

It is not we who make little of the well known and often repeated (by word and example) desire of Pope Paul VI and John XXIII. And what of the will of God who as St. Paul says (I Tim. 2, 4) "wishes all men to be saved and to come to the knowledge of the truth." Jesus said (Mark 9, 40) "He who is not against you is with you."

Our Catholics are good Catholics, loyal to us Bishops, to Holy Mother Church and to the Holy Father. We have not lost the working class. They are the foundation and the support of the Church.

Venerable Conciliar brothers, I pray you: let us put an end to the scandal of mutual recrimination. Let us proceed in an orderly way with the examination and study of this providential movement called Ecumenism so that with patience and humility we may achieve that unity for which the Lord Christ prayed at the Last Supper. Saint Paul wrote (I Cor. 13, 13) "So there abide faith, hope and charity, there are three; but the greatest of these is charity."

Cardinal Gracias, in his comments on Chapter Two of the *schema,* pressed the point that ecumenism must center on common activity together on behalf of the poor. He cited many facts and figures underlining the desperate situation of poverty and undernourishment in the world and called upon all Christians to face these scandals together. English proverbs, very much to the point, came thick and fast. "The world is too strong for a divided church"; "If we don't hang together we shall hang separately," and so on.

Cardinal Silva Henriquez of Chile reminded the fathers that in approaching the separated brethren Catholics must remember that Protestants today are not just transplanted sixteenth-century men. Many of the religious needs of the people of South America have not been met by Roman Catholicism due to the shortage of clergy, the overly moralistic catechisms, the scandals in the church's life, and so forth; in this situation it has been the Protestant sects that have really been speaking to people's needs. This means that the regional episcopal conferences must have greater power to determine the nature of local ecumenical activity, since the needs and possibilities will be different in different places.

Fortified by the comment of a cardinal from South America, who, instead of attacking the Protestant sects, could acknowledge that they were a judgment on the ineffectiveness of Catholicism, I made my way to Bar-jonah. Everyone is getting tired, and it is hard to discover much enthusiasm about these concluding days. It may also be that we Americans are emotionally drained by the impact of President Kennedy's death, and that this is coloring the assessment of other things as well. The halls and bars were very full this morning, reflecting a general feeling that nothing new is emerging in the discussion, which is proceeding so slowly that it seems less and less likely that much attention can be given to Chapters Four and Five. A vote to accept them as a basis for discussion now seems about all that can be hoped for, and this, of course, can be done at any time the moderators see fit.

There was one forward-looking intervention, however, by Bishop Gay of Guadeloupe, who feels that the whole approach to missionary activity must be rethought in the light of modern ecumenism. It would be best to preach Christ only to those who do not yet know Him at all—in other words, not to try to make Catholics out of those who are already part of another branch of Christendom. The church should be very slow to receive into membership those who come from another Christian body, and should concentrate on those who come from non-Christian religions or from paganism.

Other speakers urged, in considerable numbers, that only qualified Catholics take part in ecumenical dialogue (Gori, Conway, Klapacz); and Farah, a Melchite from Lebanon, repeated the request for new legislation regarding corporate worship and mixed marriages. One bishop requested that the *schema* give more attention to charity—but when nine reasons for being charitable must be offered, one wonders if something hasn't been lost in the process.

* * *

I spent the evening at the North American College, speaking to the American graduate students in theology on the religious liberty question, using the same basic material I've used on several other occasions this fall, with the difference that tonight I felt a greater sense of urgency about the matter than ever before. Behind-the-scenes pressures seem to be building up to avert even a vote on Chapters Four and Five, and my concluding comments were *almost* reducible to the plea, "If you know any bishops, get to work on them."

Wednesday, November 27

Mass this morning was celebrated by Archbishop Gray, of St. Andrew's and Edinburgh, and, bless him, he did not rush, but was slow and clear. The last gospel in particular tends to be treated in perfunctory manner by most of the celebrants, so that what we get is something like this: *"In principio erat Verbum, et VerbumeratapudDeumetDeumerat-Verbumhoceratinprincipiofffzzzfffzzzffffzzzzfffzzzfffffffzzz-zzzzfffzzzzzzzzzzffffzzzz."* But Archbishop Gray made clear that the magnificent affirmation of the prologue to the Fourth Gospel cannot be treated in an offhand manner. As a matter of clinical interest, one of the observers has been timing the celebrants to see how long it takes them to read the last gospel. It can be done, in the *fffzzzfffzzz* manner, in less than one minute. This morning, he reports, it went about one hundred seconds, and I can think of few better ways to use forty seconds.

Forty-three names were on the list to speak this morning, and, in addition to reading them all, Felici gave careful and meticulous instructions to the fathers on how to vote tomorrow on the new members of the commissions: Write clearly . . . print in block letters if possible . . . on and on and on.

The early speeches said nothing new: There should be more opportunities for common worship, there should be more dialogue between Christians, there should be repentance as a precondition of ecumenical involvement, there should be inner renewal, there should be more attention given to Mary our mother.

These drove me to the coffee bar, depressed by the prospect of forty-three speeches of a similarly repetitive nature. I get a more sinking feeling each morning that the Council is not going to tackle the thorny issues of the Jews and religious liberty, and that things are grinding to a slow halt. I would suspect this feeling as being no more than a projection of personal disappointment if it did not appear to be shared by so many other persons whose opinions I respect. The image of a basketball team freezing the ball in the final minutes of the game until the clock runs out is the rather irreverent image that I cannot quite dispel from my mind's eye.

Many of the individuals in Bar-jonah have already come to terms with the possibility that this session of the Council will end indecisively, and are readjusting their sights in the light of this fact. Many times this morning I heard the words, "The church moves slowly." They were no longer said complainingly, but almost defensively. I accept the fact that the church must not move precipitously, but at the same time I want to keep saying that it is dangerous to play the long future off against the genuine needs and necessities of the present. Perhaps my task in these closing days is to keep pointing out that there will be genuine dismay in the non-Catholic world if the fathers are unwilling to take even the very tentative and cautious step of accepting the chapters on the Jews and religious liberty as an adequate basis for detailed discussion.

These gloomy reflections were interrupted by the unmistakable voice of Doepfner over the loudspeaker, and he wasn't saying *"Loquatur nunc . . . et accedat ad microphoniam. . . ."* Could he possibly be calling for cloture on Chapter Two this early in the day? I raced back to the tribune, narrowly avoiding collisions with two archbishops, three bishops, seven *periti,* and one Lutheran, and arrived just in time to see the fathers standing in support of the proposal to begin debate on Chapter Three.

This action produced a real change of mood. A brand new timetable now has to be worked out: Even if the rest of today, all of tomorrow, and (to be generous) a part of Friday are devoted to Chapter Three, the bulk of Friday and all of Monday would be available for interventions on Chapters Four and Five. Since it seems clear that the American hierarchy is pushing hard, particularly on the religious liberty question, it is still possible that the Council can end on a positive instead of an indecisive note.

With the change of chapters, Cardinal Suenens became moderator. The first speaker on Chapter Three, "On Christians Separated from the Catholic Church," was our old friend Cardinal Bacci, who made a completely predictable speech, reminding the fathers that they must never forget Vatican I and the dogma of papal infallibility. Unless this is stated without equivocation, the impression will be fostered that Catholics are ashamed of papal primacy. He then added another "parenthesis," replying to Agagianian's comment on his "parenthesis" last Wednesday. His request to speak on the day of the "five questions" vote had not been a matter of mere linguistics. The linguistic change he proposed had been an important one, since the moderator's phrasing of the question had been equivocal and had departed from the language of antiquity. It was not right that the question should have been phrased ambiguously.

The minute Bacci finished this complaint, Suenens (who had now been moderator for all of eight minutes) replied firmly, "The moderators do not believe there was the slightest equivocation in the wording of the question," and announced the next speaker, another old friend, the French-speaking patriarch, Maximos IV. The word immediately got around that he was speaking, for the front of the *aula* filled up at once with all the bishops and *periti* who had been frequenting the coffee bars. I had difficulty concentrating on his speech since my brain was whirring with higher mathematics ("How many interventions can we have, at ten minutes an intervention, and still get through the entire ecumenism *schema* without limiting debate unfairly?"). Maximos' main point centered on the need to maintain diversity within unity, a theme that represents the particular contribution the patriarchs bring so creatively to a church likely to think of itself in too exclusively Western and Latin terms.

There were eight more interventions, but even though we had moved to a new chapter, the discussion revolved around already familiar themes, particularly the plea for changes in legislation about common worship and mixed marriages. It is interesting and significant that both these themes keep recurring. For years these two matters, particularly the second, have been real ecumenical roadblocks to Protestants on any local scene, but I had not realized to how great a degree Catholics were upset about them also. If the bishops who have spoken represent any significant body of opinion, perhaps we can hope for specific changes at the next session, particularly when the *schema* on matrimony is discussed.

Bishop Dwyer of Leeds made the alliterative point that dialogue should be based on *claritas* as well as *charitas* — which even comes over well in English: "clarity as well as charity." Charity alone is not enough, since Catholics and Protestants disagree on many essentials. Dwyer dropped something of a bombshell by referring to non-Catholic bishops who don't seem to believe in the virgin birth (a clear dig at J. A. T. Robinson, Anglican Bishop of Woolwich) and Quakers who condone premarital sexual relations (a reference to a recent report by some English Quakers on the matter of premarital chastity). Since these opinions exist, Roman Catholics must not assume too lightly that the teaching church is really functioning outside Roman Catholicism. From this rather chilling blast, however, Dwyer went on to urge extension of dialogue between Catholics and non-Catholics, without the precondition that non-Catholics "change" before such dialogue could commence.

Bishop Baraniak of Poland made extensive reference to the observers present in the *aula,* and we were conscious of an eyes-right maneuver by the bishops sitting on our side, and an eyes-left maneuver by those on the far side, as they visually acknowledged our presence.

Thursday, November 28

Any hopes yesterday that we were going to move at a faster pace proved illusory this morning, and today can only be described as the most dismal morning of the Council.

Not to put too fine a point on it, the whole morning gave the appearance of being a sustained filibuster with nobody doing anything to prevent it. I would love to be proven wrong, but it is hard to come to any other conclusion. Even though cloture was voted yesterday on Chapter Two, thirteen bishops requested permission to speak beyond cloture this morning, and during the morning two more names were added to the list.

All that is fair enough, but the last time this happened the moderator was very rigorous with such speakers. He told them in no uncertain terms not to repeat, not to stray from the point, to relinquish their time if their point had been made, and he imposed an eight- rather than a ten-minute time limit. These were the ground rules when the Council still stretched ahead for several weeks. But today, with time running out at a furious rate, no such requests were made, even mildly. No control was exercised over the debate. Nobody was called to order. The function of the moderator was reduced to introducing the speakers. As a result, the discussion rambled on and on, with nothing new being said, and it was not until 11:45 A.M., fifteen minutes before closing time, that we got to the announced order of the morning. The high point of the day came when Bishop D'Souza of India, one of the most progressive voices of the Council, relinquished his speaking time and announced that he would submit his comments in writing. The fathers applauded.

There is only one way in which I can make sense out of this morning's session. That is by the assumption that from somewhere behind the scenes the word has come down, "There is to be no vote on religious liberty or the Jews." Whether it has come down from the coordinating commission, or the pope, or from someone *speaking* for the pope, or from someone *presuming* to speak for the pope, I have no way of knowing. But I see no other way to explain the total shift in atmosphere and the apparent handcuffing of otherwise vigorous and courageous men.

Even though many people are upset about this, there seems to be nothing they can do, no rule of procedure by means of which one of the fathers can rise to a point of order. All that is needed is a call for the vote, already promised, on the acceptability of Chapters Four and Five for detailed discussion. But the call for the vote is not forthcoming.

*   *   *

There is a kind of last-ditch hope in Bar-jonah that some of the progressive cardinals can get through to the bottleneck, if there is one, and open the question up again before Monday. But many of the Council fathers acknowledge themselves without resources to act. One bishop: "We're all for Chapters Four and Five, but we don't have any procedural means to get a vote." Another bishop: "The big boys [the cardinals] are exerting all the pressure they can." A *peritus* (to me): "If you're willing to get up on the Council floor and tell the fathers what this delay will mean in the non-Catholic world, I'll put your speech in Latin for you." I've indicated to various *periti* that if any Council fathers need convincing about how crucial it is for the Council to go on record on these two matters, various observers are ready to talk at any time, to any group, anywhere. But on the Council floor . . . ?

* * *

It hurts me to make what must sound like harsh judgments about the Council. I wish they were not true, and perhaps from a longer perspective they will seem trivial. But at the moment they are far from trivial. It is not as a carping critic that I express disappointment, but as one who in the last nine weeks has seen such moments of splendor and greatness in the Council that I expect more of it in late November than I did in early October. At one time in my ecumenical life I could have reacted to this morning's session with the words, "What did you expect?" I can't say that now. Or, if the question is put to me, I can only answer, "Much more . . . and I will *continue* to expect much more."

* * *

Even in my present state of mind, however, I would have allowed the intervention of Bishop Pinera of Chile. The *schema,* he said, in its concern for inner renewal should put more emphasis on poverty, humility, and concern for social justice. Our profession of faith should be reflected in our outer life. It should lead Catholics to get rid of signs of wealth such as titles, fine garb, ceremonies, expensive modes of living. No wonder the Protestant groups in South America attack the poor, when the Protestant missionaries are willing to live among the poor in dire poverty themselves. Catholics must learn this lesson from their separated brethren.

Who can be anything but humbled by a speech like this? I must remember that if there are men in the church who are engaged in behind-the-scenes maneuverings, there are also men like Bishop Pinera — and much as I decry the former I must thank God for the latter.

Some good things were said in the other interventions, of course, but the point is that they were not new things, and could have been omitted or drastically condensed. It was helpful to have a man of Cardinal Frings's eminence say that, whatever the Catholic Church may think of the advisability of mixed marriages, it must acknowledge the validity of mixed marriages contracted in the presence of a non-Catholic minister and must remove all ecclesiastical penalties for such a marriage. It is well to be reminded that some bishops still look on ecumenism as a "return" to Rome. I am encouraged if a French bishop wants warmth of heart to characterize our ecumenical relationships. I am glad that more Melchites want relaxation of the rules against Catholic participations in non-Catholic services. I agree with an Italian bishop that ecumenism should not lead to indifferentism. I rejoice that an Indonesian bishop wants us to share a common Bible, even though I am amazed at his suggestion that it should be the Latin Vulgate. I am glad a Spanish bishop wants more charity. I appreciate a Brazilian bishop suggesting that inner renewal must be Catholicism's first ecumenical direction.

But, with the exception of Bishop Pinera, I still think Bishop D'Souza made the most creative contribution of the morning when he relinquished his speaking time.

Friday, November 29

Just to show how hard I am taking things these days, I dreamed last night that the Holy Office had issued a condemnation of Hans Küng's *The Council in Action,* citing at least one theological error on every single line. Things aren't quite that bad of course, but there is a mounting feeling of frustration over the fact that the moderators simply won't ask for the vote on Chapters Four and Five. The seats are emptier than at any time thus far in the Council and the halls and bars are filled with bishops who seem to realize that the debate is not going in new directions.

The mass this morning was St. Chrysostom's liturgy in Greek, which took over an hour, and by the time Felici had finished all his announcements it was 10:40 A.M. — a pretty late starting hour for a council that convenes at 9:00. However, there were a couple of important announcements, and one of them was very encouraging. After announcing that the third session would go from about September 14 to about November 20, 1964, Felici read the names of those elected to the conciliar commissions by yesterday's vote. In spite of Felici's earlier plea that the fathers elect men close enough to Rome to attend meetings easily, the spread of bishops elected is from all over the world. Out of forty-two bishops elected, only one is an Italian. It is not being anti-Italian to say that this fact symbolizes a real revolution, and the real beginning of a new day in the Catholic Church. The conciliar commissions are being internationalized, even if the Curia isn't — and remembering Pope Paul's speech of September 21, we can expect Curia appointments in the future to follow this new pattern as well. On the crucial Theological Commission, all four of the new members can be called progressives, and two of them, Bishop Ancel of Lyon and Abbot Butler, head of the English Benedictines, have been ecumenically active. The election of Butler is particularly significant, since he is the author of one of the alternative statements on Mary which builds on a Biblical foundation; one of the main functions of the Theological Commission will be to prepare a new Mariological statement for the next session. A good many other ecumenically minded bishops were elected to various posts: Baudoux of Canada, de Provencheres of France,

D'Souza of India, and others. Two Americans who have been active in ecumenical affairs in the United States were elected to the Secretariat for Christian Unity, Bishop Helmsing of Kansas City, and Bishop Primeau of Manchester, New Hampshire.

These elections are a genuine ray of hope in the ecumenical picture and encourage me to believe that if temporary setbacks are being experienced now they will be offset in the future if men like these can come to dominate the commissions to which they have been elected.

*   *   *

In his intervention this morning, Bishop Goody of Australia told a story which illustrates how "involved" non-Catholics feel in what is going on here. Just before Bishop Goody left for Rome the corresponding Anglican bishop gave him a sizable purse to help defray his expenses in coming to the Council, because, as the Anglican said, "We non-Roman Catholics expect such great things from the Council."

He was followed by Bishop Helmsing of Kansas City, whose intervention demonstrated the extent of his ecumenical concern, and made me doubly glad of his election to the Secretariat for Christian Unity. He described the distinction in Chapter Three between the "churches" of the East and the "communities" of the West as "invidious," and then went on to suggest reasons why the word "church" should be used throughout the chapter: (1) The word is in common usage, and "ordinary decency and politeness" (spoken in booming English) demand that Catholics use the word the Protestants themselves use. (2) The word need not be used univocally, i.e., it can have different meanings in different contexts. (3) When there were schisms in Biblical history, between the northern and southern Kingdoms, for example, it was never denied that the Spirit was working through the prophets of the northern Kingdom; similarly it must not be denied that the Spirit is working through the separated brethren. (4) It is not enough to view the separated brethren individually. Catholics must view them in terms of their churches, in which they hear the Word of God, receive baptism, have a life of grace, and gather for corporate worship to the praise of God. While they do not, by Catholic standards, have the fullness of eucharistic doctrine, they do have strong eucharistic devotion, and by it they give witness to Christ and to His coming.

This was bracing, but there was more to come. At the end of his intervention, speaking "in my name and in the name of many of the fathers," Bishop Helmsing asked directly what had happened to the vote that had been promised on Chapters Four and Five. Where is the vote? The moderators are empowered at any time to interrupt the discussion and call for the vote. Let it be done now.

This was greeted with applause from the rear of the *aula*. It represented the first time anybody had had the courage even to attempt a direct breakthrough of the procedural impasse. Would the question be answered? Would the plea be heard? Would the challenge be acknowledged? From the moderator came no reply, and no acknowledgment of the question, but only the impassive announcement of the next speaker: *Loquatur nunc Excellentissimus. . . .*

This was clearly the handwriting on the wall, and I plunged into Bar-jonah looking for shoulders to cry on. I had to offer mine. The most joy that could be extracted was the fact that at least somebody had had the courage to ask on the floor the question everybody has been asking off the floor. But if another person says to me, "The mills of God grind slowly," all I will be able to respond will be, "They certainly do."

And yet—I must also report that at this very moment, when we have just gotten clear evidence that this session will end indecisively, there was also clear evidence of a resurgence of hope among the bishops and *periti*. Other themes began to dominate our discussion: This may be a temporary setback, but the direction of the Council is clear; it may be better to have the next nine months to drive home the importance of Chapters Four and Five so that there can really be significant debate next fall; the elections to the commissions are much more important evidence of the Council's mind than the reversal on the Jews and religious liberty. There is a faith in the church, and in the ability of the church to weather all storms and crises, that is most impressive. The real source of the Catholic Church's greatness, I would guess, is that it can command this kind of loyalty.

It has only one disadvantage. It makes reformation awfully slow.

❊   ❊   ❊

I took part in a BBC television broadcast this afternoon. Having been told that I would have four minutes, I prepared a statement that I pared to the bone to keep within the allotted time, only to discover that the setting was to be a conversation rather than a speech. The very able and kindly priest supervising the filming said, "Throw away your notes and trust God." I did both, and found that, in trying to assess Vatican II in four minutes of conversation, my immediate disappointments are considerably assuaged by all the creative things that have happened earlier in the fall. So even if the British public didn't learn a great deal, I had a sense of perspective restored to me. Maybe that's what comes from trusting God.

❊   ❊   ❊

A number of observers are proposing to "boycott" the Tuesday session, which is commemorating the Council of Trent, because Trent produced so many anathemas of Protestant theology. I don't particularly like Trent either, but if we stayed away from everything in the Council with which we have theological difficulties, we'd have to be away 80 per cent of the time. I do not imagine that Catholic observers at a World Council gathering would walk out if a day were devoted to interpreting the Protestant Reformation. My feeling is that, since I am here as an observer, my job is to observe everything I can. To decide in advance that nothing can be done creatively about Trent, particularly in the light of the amazing job of reinterpretation in which Catholic historians are engaging, is to close oneself off from any real possibility of observing inner reform and renewal. If the day is an ecumenical disaster, I will say so. But I forfeit the right to say anything, if I do not even turn up. So I will be there, armed with my third notebook and fourth ballpoint pen.

The Last Three Days
(December 2 − 4)

No vote on Chapters Four and Five – the last press panel – commemoration of Trent – the bishops' "faculties" – the two promulgations – the concluding papal discourse

Monday, December 2

I arrived early this morning and discovered that, while there was no reason to hope for a vote on Chapters Four and Five, Cardinal Bea will give a speech asserting that written emendations for those chapters will be accepted by the Secretariat along with emendations to Chapters One through Three, and that a promise has been given that Chapters Four and Five will be discussed at the beginning of the third session.

Let this promise be shouted from the housetops for the next nine months.

The interventions once again covered the whole gamut of Catholic reactions to ecumenism. Cardinal Ruffini, who quite unaccountably had not yet spoken on Chapter Three, began by reassuring us genially that, although he might have seemed throughout the Council to be untranquil, he was really very tranquil in his heart. Realizing that ecumenism was here to stay, he wanted to issue some warnings. It must be made clear to all that Christ founded only one church, which is the Roman Catholic Church. This church is infallible and it cannot fail. Nevertheless, people have seceded from it and the result has been misery for all. The hope must be that the separated brethren will once again embrace Roman Catholicism, for, like a mother, the church is waiting for her children to return. The faithful should be instructed so that they can engage in ecumenical dialogue to this end, and all should pray to God and to Mary that the separated brethren will once again acknowledge the supremacy of the Roman pontiff.

These sentiments are as far removed as possible from modern ecumenical currents, but I really think the old boy meant it as a generous gesture of good will, and the fathers must have, too, for they applauded him when he had finished.

Bishop Green of South Africa raised the question of Anglican Orders, declared invalid last century by the papal document *Apostolica Curae*. There is a new situation today, he said, and the matter must be reconsidered, "without fear and with a certain audacity."

Here is another instance of going beyond what the *schema* itself explicitly discusses, and in a direction that even a short time ago would have been looked upon as extremely *avantgarde*.

Not so, however, Bishop Muldoon of Sydney. While his first point was a recognition that the description of the "sixteenth-century communities" is inadequate, his second point went completely against the grain of most of the ecumenically oriented interventions. He chastised the fathers for spending so much time urging the Catholic Church to confess its sins and ask the forgiveness of non-Catholics. Those who have been urging this quote the pope, he said, but they quote him wrongly. For in his allocution of September 29, the pope did *not* say that Catholics were guilty. He said only, "*If* we are in any way to blame . . ." *If, if*. Let those fathers who want to confess their sins do so in the privacy of the confessional, rather than proclaiming them on the Council floor to the whole world.

Technically, of course, Muldoon is right. The pope *did* say, "*If* . . . ." Indeed, at the time of his allocution a number of the observers expressed the fear that the gesture was a half-hearted and conditional one. I find no grounds whatever to accept this interpretation, particularly in the light of his unambiguous statement to us on October 17: "We grant pardon and ask it in return." It is significant, too, that in the dozens of times the words of the opening allocution have been cited on the Council floor, every other bishop has accepted the words as a straightforward confession of sin and plea for forgiveness, both human and divine.

We had familiar themes in most of the other interventions: There must be "diversity in unity"; legislation about corporate worship and mixed marriages must be changed; the descriptions of the separated brethren in Chapter Three must be made more precise; and Abbot Butler insisted, against Muldoon, that Catholics must openly confess their responsibility for the divisions of Christendom, lest they resemble the Pharisee who said, "Lord, I thank thee that I am not as other men."

But two new suggestions did emerge. Bishop D'Mello of India made the very creative proposal that before adjournment the fathers and the observers stand together and say the *Pater Noster*, as the pope had done with the observers. And Archbishop Hermaniuk, recently elected to the Secretariat for Christian Unity, suggested setting up mixed theological commissions, one consisting of Catholics and Orthodox, another of Catholics and Protestants, to explore problems of division and unity, and recommended a search for ways in which the Catholic Church could work more actively with the World Council of Churches.

In a few moments the interventions ended and Cardinal Bea, as head of the Secretariat which had proposed *De Oecumenismo*, was given the privilege of making some summary comments. The fathers crowded to the front of the *aula* to hear him, emptying the coffee bars in a matter of seconds, for here was the moment at which it would be learned what, if anything, could be salvaged concerning Chapters Four and Five.

It was clear, Bea began, that the whole church agreed on the importance of ecumenism, and that the vote on the first three chapters indicated "moral unanimity." Arriving at the prickly matter of the treatment of Chapters Four and Five, he said, "We all regret that it was not permitted to us to have at least a foretaste of a discussion concerning these chapters also." After assuring the fathers that discussion of Chapters Four and Five was omitted solely because of lack of time, and for no other reason, he asked, "Could a vote have been taken to admit Chapters Four and Five as a basis for discussion?"

To this question one might perhaps answer in the affirmative. Nevertheless, I think we should be grateful to the Venerable Fathers, the Moderators, because they wished to give ample opportunity for speaking on the three fundamental chapters to prevent creating the danger that someone might say that a hasty vote was taken on these three chapters and on the two others which treat of matters that are sufficiently difficult. . . . What is deferred is not suppressed. . . . The discussion which it was not permitted to accomplish here, will be held in the next session of the Council.

He concluded by urging the fathers to send in their comments on *all five* chapters, so that these could be used in preparation for the next session.

What does this add up to? On the most optimistic reading, it is a rather modest victory. The important thing, of course, is the promise that Chapters Four and Five will be discussed next session. But there is no assurance that they will be returned for discussion in their present form, and this is what a vote would have ensured.

The notion that there was "not enough time" for a vote was rendered even more curious by the fact that, when Bea had finished, the moderator called on Bishop Hengsbach to give the introductory speech on the *schema* on the laity, a *schema* that will not be discussed by the fathers for at least nine months.

When Hengsbach had finished, Agagianian engaged in words of thanks to all present: the pope, the presidents, the other moderators, the coordinating commission, the *periti*, the secretary-general, the undersecretaries, the observers, and the auditors. Each group was accorded a handsome round of applause.

And then, suddenly, Cardinal Tisserant was leading the fathers in the *Angelus,* and the working sessions of Vatican II, session two, had ended.

*   *   *

The last press panel was held this afternoon in the basement of the USO building at the far end of the Via della Conciliazione. It would be hard to exaggerate the importance of these panels and the high quality they have maintained throughout the Council. The panels have been open, frank, informative, and creatively opinionated. They have given no impression that the Catholic Church was trying to "hide" anything, but rather that it wanted to give as full a picture as possible of what really went on in the *aula.*

Fr. John Sheerin of the Paulists has been the moderator, presiding every day behind a green ping-pong table, and deflecting each question to the panel member most qualified to deal with it. For his efforts, the journalists today gave him a gold-plated ping-pong paddle, the First Annual John Sheerin Award, presented amid loud applause and a number of comments about the adriotness of the panels' handling of the questions.

I would have liked to comment on the exceptionally adroit footwork of the newsmen as well, who knew how to phrase a question so that it could elicit an answer deeper than the reports of the official press releases. Many of the reporters were veteran newsmen, and many others were priests working for diocesan newspapers. Between them, the two groups managed to cover the journalistic waterfront pretty effectively. Questions positively dripping with innocence had a whole lifetime of journalistic or theological knowhow behind them.

Item: "Sir, since *De Ecclesia* was debated for so long, it is clear that the Theological Commission has a great deal of work to do, redrafting the *schema* on the basis of written and oral suggestions. May we assume, therefore, that the Commission is meeting on a more or less around-the-clock basis, in order to get the work done?"

Answer: [which the reporter knew very well but wanted publically verified]: "As you know, commissions meet only when called by the chairman. At present, the Theological Commission is meeting one afternoon a week."

Item: "Sir, it was remarked some time ago that when the liturgy *schema* was approved by the fathers, there was great applause at the announcement. Can we assume that there was a similar response this morning when it was announced that the Communications *schema* had been approved?"

Answer: [which the reporter had previously heard from people leaving the *aula* but wanted publically verified]: "The applause for the Communications *schema* was very feeble and died out almost immediately."

The questions, in other words, were as innocent as doves, but behind them lay the wisdom of the serpent. Lest anyone take offense at such an assessment, it should be remembered that we have it on high authority that the combination is pleasing to the Almighty (Matthew 10:16).

The prize, however, for an astute combination of innocence and wisdom, undoubtedly goes to that member of the panel who, toward the end of one session, casually remarked, "Of course, the whole matter may have to be reconsidered by the Holy Father in view of the fight this morning on the steps of St. Peter's."

Period.

In the split second of electric silence that followed, one could feel seventy-four reporters instinctively lunging toward the vacuum created by this remarkable bit of understatement. And how much better that they soon got a correct account (from an eyewitness of the incident on the steps of St. Peter's) than that they should later have had to piece together the wild and exaggerated rumors that were already beginning to circulate among the coffee bars and other bars of Rome.

Tuesday, December 3

Today was an "open session." An open session means TV cameras, diplomats, extra contingents of Swiss guards, and all the trappings of a Renaissance court. Various military types "stand guard," relieving one another periodically, and other men, right out of the seventeenth century, stand at attention, swords handy in case of an uprising of the *plebs*. The pope is carried around the church on a hugh gold throne resting on the shoulders of a dozen stalwart men. Bishop Dante, the master of ceremonies, presides over everything like a mother hen fussing with her chickens, shoving people here and there, motioning to priests during the prayers to move elsewhere, putting pillows under the pope's feet, removing pillows from under the pope's feet, and continually waving for this and that.

When I saw this for the first time last fall, it was new, colorful, and mysteriously interesting. Today I find it antiquated, strange, and rather distressing. The reason is not that I have become "anti-Catholic," but just the contrary: I have heard so many wonderful speeches in this very *aula* pleading for a rejection of pomp, for an identification of the church with the destitute, and for an image of the church as servant rather than master, that it is doubly distressing to find the closing sessions of the Council even more ornate than the opening one. There is something incongruous about "the servant of the servants of God" being carried about on a gold throne. For all I know, thrones may be part of the furniture of heaven, but they seem incongruous as part of the equipment of the saints on earth. I wonder about the reaction of the bishops who have spoken with such power against the worldliness and vanity of the church, and have called the church back to an imitation of her Lord, who, during *His* earthly pilgrimage, had nowhere to lay His head.

One bit of hierarchical differentiation, however, has disappeared. Since the cardinals wear purple instead of bright red during the advent season, which has just begun, it is hard to tell a cardinal from an ordinary bishop. It is also interesting at an "open session" to see where the cardinal-presidents and cardinal-moderators sit when they are not occupying their special desks at the front of the *aula*. Doepfner sits next to Koenig, which is appropriate, but Frings is next to Spellman, and Suenens is next to Ottaviani. If politics makes strange bedfellows, the cardinalate makes strange seatmates.

✻   ✻   ✻

After mass, Cardinal Urbani of Venice gave an address commemorating the four hundredth anniversary of the conclusion of the Council of Trent. The speech was more creative than I had anticipated. Almost anything could have been done with Trent, and certainly some speakers would have gloried in all the anathemas against Protestant theology. No attempt was made to extol Trent as the summation of Catholic wisdom. Indeed, Urbani insisted, the present Council represents certain advances over Trent. The very composition of its members indicates advance at three points: (a) "The presence of representatives of Christian brethren still separated from us is specially dear"; (b) the greater number of heads of religious orders is an advance; and (c) "the presence of the laymen in this assembly is a further point of contrast, full of hope for the future."

After emphasizing that Trent was a council in which there was great liberty of expression, and emphasizing also that the dogmatic canons subsequently promulgated are unchangeable, Urbani nevertheless went on to comment that those canons "always offer, to those who examine them with care, the possibility of further analysis and of more accurate investigation by which their contents may be more fully revealed and the breadth of their application increased."

This is a particularly significant statement. For the last couple of decades, the most creative voices in Catholic scholarship have been engaging in a massive reassessment of Trent's decrees, with results that can be very important for the ecumenical dialogue. Urbani's speech certainly shut no doors in that direction, but implied that they should be opened even wider.

What, then, is the most important thing Trent says to the Catholic Church today? Urbani singled out the theme of the *pastoral* duty of the bishops. The fulcrum of the restoration of the church was to be "nothing other than the episcopate, not, to be sure, divorced from the Roman Pontiff, but rather in union with him." The stress was to be on making bishops independent of political influence and concern for rank and privilege, so that they could tend to the care of souls.

Surely with the observers in mind, Urbani went on to say, "We express our confidence in the sincere search for truth. . . . We state our confidence in dialogue which is always possible with men of good will; hence we imply our trust in the intrinsic effectiveness of the truth when presented without dissimulation of hypocrisy, without compromise or equivocation, without subterfuge or falsification. We are confident in the power of dialogue as the ecumenical premise for religious unity and universal peace."

I had arrived this morning ready for anything. And I left encouraged, even uplifted, by the fact that the anniversary of Trent had been handled in a forward-looking manner rather than a backward-looking one. Some of us were criticized for attending the session. Cardinal Urbani will probably never know that his speech got us off the hook.

*   *   *

The morning, however, was not yet over. The next item on the agenda was the reading of a *motu proprio* from the pope to the bishops, a letter to be called *Pastorale Munus*, restoring to the bishops certain "faculties" (or powers of authority) that in the course of time have been appropriated by the Curia. As Felici read the list of these faculties in Latin, the net effect began to sound more and more impressive. By the time the list was complete, the pope had granted forty "faculties" and eight "privileges" to the bishops, all concerning matters for which they used to have to get permission from Rome, but can now do or grant on their own authority. If I may employ a somewhat irreverent image, the pope's letter sounded like an end run around the Curia, or perhaps a forward pass over Curial heads into the arms of 2200 eligible episcopal receivers, or maybe even a power play right through the middle of the line.

When I saw a translation of the text later in the day, however, I was forced to some second thoughts, for on the most generous interpretation *Pastorale Munus* does not represent a very sweeping reform. Most of the permissions have long since been granted to missionary bishops, and many of the items are insignificant, such as power to permit "pious women to wash altar linens" without appealing to Rome for authorization. One or two of the permissions may be important, such as "the right to permit the reading and retaining of forbidden books to those who need this authorization for the discharge of their duties or the pursuance of their studies." On the whole, however, to return to my previous image, the general effect is that of a wide end run, rather spectacular, but not advancing very far beyond the line of scrimmage.

To put the matter another way, the letter is important *as a symbol.* In it, the pope is restoring to the bishops certain faculties that are theirs, rather than the Curia's, and in so doing he is lending support to decentralization and to the belief that pope and bishops rule the church, rather than pope and Curia. This is an important symbol in the light of all the assertions of the conservatives that the collegiality vote had no meaning. But the *content* of the symbol is not very far-reaching. If the bishops were hoping for a significant realignment of church authority in the pope's letter, I doubt if they got it.

On the other hand, as one observer remarked, "If out of forty faculties, most of which seem trivial, even one or two are important, that represents significant progress." If one argues that "the church moves slowly," there is cause for encouragement that movement was recorded this morning;

if one argues that in this day and age the church must move more rapidly, there is cause for disappointment that the church is still only on the threshold of significant action.

❊ ❊ ❊

Another symbol must be mentioned. Before today's session concluded, comments were addressed to the pope by two of the lay auditors at the Council. Until today, the lay auditors have been "silent," with no opportunity to speak before the Council fathers. Now the principle has been established that they can properly have a voice in conciliar proceedings, and I will be most surprised if this principle is not extended next fall (when the *schema* on the laity is under discussion) to permit lay auditors to speak during the working sessions as well as the public sessions. Indeed, if the Council goes on long enough, it may even be that the voice of an observer will be heard in the *aula* as well as in the coffee bar.

Wednesday, December 4

A few days ago I expressed the hope, reflecting the sentiment of many of the liturgical experts, that on the day of the promulgation of *De Sacra Liturgia*, the principle of concelebration incorporated in the *schema* could be practiced by the Council fathers. This was expecting too rapid a pace of reform, for not only was there no concelebration, there were not even lay communicants. The latter have been a very important symbol at the regular sessions of the Council, and I am sorry their presence was not manifested before the TV cameras for the benefit of the faithful everywhere.

Nevertheless, today was a moment of history, for it witnessed the first conciliar promulgations by the Roman Catholic Church since 1870. And the last promulgations before 1870 were back at the time of Trent – 1563.

As at the opening session last fall, the cardinals, heads of religious orders, and representatives of the bishops, went one by one up to the papal throne and made their act of submission. After this, Archbishop Felici read the text of *De Sacra Liturgia* preparatory to a final vote by the fathers in the presence of the pope. (Actually, he read only the introductory paragraph of each chapter, on the wise and time-saving assumption that by this time the fathers were acquainted with the text.) The fathers voted, the ballots were collected by the clerks, and then fed into the computors.

For about twenty minutes, while we were waiting for the computors to disgorge the results, nothing happened. After a bit, the choir sang (and it must be recorded that the music of *Ave Maris Stella* is particularly lovely). From time to time the rest of us sang such hymns as *Christus Vincit*, with which everyone in Rome is familiar. If the words and the setting could have been changed, I would have been reminded of nothing so much as a Wednesday night hymn-sing in a Methodist Church.

When the computors had done their task, Felici reported the results to the pope, and the results were overwhelming: The fathers had approved *De Sacra Liturgia* by a vote of 2147 *placet*, to 4 *non placet*. (Knowing the antagonism of two highly placed members of the American hierarchy to the original *schema*, many people asked, "I wonder who cast the other two negative votes?") It is a stunning fact that this degree of unanimity has been achieved on a document that represents such thorough-going reform at the very heart of the life of the church.

The way in which the *schema* was promulgated, however, may be as important as the fact of its promulgation. Before this morning there had been a great deal of speculation about the formula the pope would use in the act of promulgation. Who would be promulgating — the pope alone, or the pope *and the bishops?* The answer to this question would be a good indication of the status of the collegiality question. The answer was not apparent in the manual distributed at the beginning of the morning. But when it came to the actual words of promulgation, the formula went, "Paul, the servant of the servants of God, *in union with the fathers of the Coun-*

cil. . . ." As Père Laurentin commented later about this wording, "Collegiality took a great step forward. This was the theological event of the morning." This fact must not be lost in all the attention that will quite properly be given to the text of *De Sacra Liturgia* as a constitution of Vatican Council II.

An identical procedure was followed with the Communications *schema:* Felici read the text, the fathers voted, we had a congregational hymn-sing, the vote was announced, the *schema* was promulgated this time as a "decree," which is a less solemn definition than a "constitution." It did not receive the overwhelming assent that its companion did.

Even this morning there were 164 *non placets.*

*   *   *

The morning concluded with the pope's final discourse. The text was far less significant than the opening allocution in September had been, much of it being simply an account of what the Council had achieved. The one point at which the pope looked up and gestured with his hands was at the words, "Even now our hearts are moved by the sight of the esteemed observers who have been invited to this gathering and who have so graciously accepted the invitation." After praising the work of the Council he went on to indicate its unfinished tasks. Three areas were cited: a treatment of divine revelation (a *schema* distributed to us but not discussed this fall), the question of episcopacy, and the question of the Blessed Virgin, who is to be treated in the *schema* on the church. His reference to Mary was the only point in his prepared text which elicited applause.

I am pleased that these emphases were cited, for they all have ecumenical significance, but I cannot help wishing that certain other emphases had been cited as well, and I must record the burning hope that at least four of them will not be slighted when session three begins. (1) We have just completed two weeks of discussion of the Catholic Church and

ecumenism; is not this one of the most crucial of the unfinished tasks? (2) We have just left the question of the Jews
and of religious liberty dangling in mid-air; should not this
unfinished business receive the highest priority at the beginning of the next session? (3) We have heard numerous
requests for treatment of "the church and the modern world,"
at the next session; is not this a matter of urgent concern for
a Council pledged to *aggiornamento?* (4) The *relatio* to the
schema on the laity has already been given; must not extended discussion be devoted to this subject as well?

Let no Council father relax his vigilant insistence that
these subjects, too, receive attention before the Second Vatican Council has completed its work.

When the pope had completed his prepared text, he indicated that there was still more to come. In what was obviously a surprise to almost everyone in the *aula*, he announced
that he would make a pilgrimage to Palestine on January
4–6, 1964. This brought forth wild applause, as did his request for the prayers of the faithful as he embarked on the
journey. I hope great good can come from such a trip, as an
encouragement to the churches of the Eastern rites, to the
Orthodox, and also to the Jews. Indeed, I hope this will be
only the first of similar pilgrimages by the pope to all parts
of the world. I am all for a spirit of internationalization, from
the humblest subdeacon to the "servant of the servants of
God."

*   *   *

I've been exposed to a bit of internationalization myself
in the last three months: San Francisco, Seattle, Winnipeg,
London, Glasgow, Iona, Geneva, Rome, Assisi, Montecassino,
Salerno, Florence, New York, Washington, Los Angeles, San
Francisco. But if I am going to be completely honest I must
confess that when I got off the last plane — when I saw Peter
and Mark, openly glad to see their old man back; Alison,
offering me her most special hug; Tommy, carrying my type-

writer clear out to the car before asking, "What did you bring me?"; and Sydney, younger-looking I am sure than when I left — the thing that pleased me most of all was the realization that all roads lead to home.

Vatican II, Session Two:
A Preliminary Assessment

Signs of hope – causes for concern – before session three

Vatican II, session two, began on September 29 with an opening allocution by Pope Paul. It closed on December 4, about 610 speeches later, with a concluding discourse by Pope Paul. In between those two papal speeches, the bishop of Rome let the other bishops do all the talking. If one asks how much finished business their talking brought them to, the answer has to be, in terms of their total agenda, "Not very much." But if one remembers that Vatican II is not yet over, and is only in recess until September 14, it is clear that a great deal has been accomplished that will have significant effect on subsequent sessions of the Council.

To attempt an evaluation of the second session within a week of its recess is, of course, a dangerous business, and the true "meaning" of the session will not be discernible for a long time. But there is value, perhaps, in recording some immediate impressions while the events are still fresh, even though those involved in them (whether as bishops, auditors, or observers) are likely to be suffering from a combination of conciliar hangover and ecumenical battle fatigue.

I do not think it is the latter ailments but the events themselves that have produced a certain change of mood in my own assessment of the possibilities of far-reaching reform by Vatican II. I went to Rome in September filled with buoyant optimism. I left Rome in December filled with chastened optimism. The optimism remains: The Council is going to do many things for the genuine renewal of the Roman Catholic

Church, and whatever renews one part of Christendom is beneficial to the rest. But the optimism is tempered by a more realistic assessment of the fact that this renewal is going to take longer, and be harder to achieve, and be less sweeping, than I had originally hoped. There were many times when it seemed perfectly clear to me what the Holy Spirit and I wanted to have happen on the Council floor, but the message didn't get through to the Council fathers. Sometimes — and this is more disturbing — the message got through to most of them, but a minority was able to block a clear expression of His working. For years I have known about presbyterian obstructionists. Now I know a bit more about episcopal obstructionists, some of whom not only wear purple but even cardinal red.

*   *   *

Nevertheless, optimism concerning the final impact the whole Council will have is greater than certain disappointments concerning the immediate impact this session of the Council will have. A few indications can suggest why this is so:

1. Where the ecumenical dialogue is concerned there is reason for hope. Ecumenism is in the Catholic Church to stay. The day on which *De Oecumenismo* was introduced for discussion in a Council of the Roman Catholic Church was a historic day in Christian history. And the morning, not long thereafter, when the first three chapters of the *schema* were overwhelmingly accepted as a suitable basis for detailed discussion inaugurated a new era in Christian history. With less than 100 dissenting votes, 2200 Council fathers pledged themselves to serious discussion of the nature of their relationship to the "separated brethren," and while it is clear that there are going to be remaining pockets of resistance to the notion, it is now clear that the vast majority of bishops are eager to foster ecumenical dialogue on many

levels. Such concern is no longer *avant-garde;* it is central
and normative for the Catholicism of the future.

Moreover, it is clear that many of the fathers want to go
further than the relatively cautious *schema* itself. Taking a
cue from the *schema's* insistence that the first ecumenical
step must be the inner renewal of the Catholic Church, a
number of bishops took a further cue from Pope Paul's opening allocution and insisted that the *schema* should be
amended to include specific reference to the responsibility of
the Roman Catholic Church for the guilt that has led to a
divided Christendom. Other bishops wanted greater possibilities for sharing in corporate worship than are now possible.
Still others — from Europe, missionary lands, and Eastern
rites churches — pressed for changes in the laws concerning
mixed marriages, since the church's intransigent stand here
has had many harmful effects on ecumenical encounter. And
a significant number, both from America and Europe, felt
that the *schema's* use of the term "communities" was too pale
a term by which to describe those branches of Christendom
that emerged in the sixteenth century, and argued that the
schema should use the word "churches" to describe non-
Catholic groups in the West as well as those in the East. An
ecumenical ferment is stirring beyond anything one might
reasonably have expected even a few months ago.

2. The Council's most substantial achievement to date, and
possibly one that will stand as the most substantial achievement of the entire Council, is the recently promulgated constitution *On the Sacred Liturgy.* This is a document breathing
reform in almost every line, and at the final vote on the day
of promulgation it received only four negative votes. The
constitution provides for extensive use of the vernacular in
all of the sacraments, including the mass, much greater liturgical participation by the laity, further opportunities for
concelebration and communion under both species, greater
stress on Scripture and sermon, reform of the breviary, and
many similar changes. The intent throughout is to ensure
that worship is the act *of the people,* and not simply a specta-

cle performed for them by the priest. The constitution opens many doors that can later be pushed even wider, and does not bind the church to a new liturgical rigidity.

3. The outcome of the vote on the treatment of Mary was ecumenically important. To be sure, the vote was disturbingly close, but it nevertheless committed the Council to a significant course of action. Rather than retaining a separate *schema* dealing with Mary, the fathers voted to incorporate a chapter on Mary into the *schema* on the church. Mary, in other words, is to be seen *within* the context of the church. Had the vote gone the other way, it would have given free reign to continued independent Mariological development, and would have led in the unmistakable direction of seeing the church in the context of Mary — which is a very different thing from seeing Mary in the context of the church. The proposal now is to write a new chapter with a Biblical orientation, so that Mary, who for so long has been ecumenically divisive, can be a possible means of ecumenical rapport. Certainly, such a move will force Protestants to re-examine in a fresh and nonpolemical way the Biblical materials that deal with Mary, and see where they lead.

4. Even more important to the ecumenical situation was the famous "five questions" vote of October 30, certainly the most significant action of the entire session. In a deliberate effort to go beyond the one-sided and incomplete teaching of Vatican I about the teaching authority of the bishop of Rome, Vatican II has committed itself to a doctrine of "collegiality," i.e., to a view that authority in the church was given not only to Peter (and his successor, the bishop of Rome) but to all the apostles (and their successors, the other bishops). It is pope *and* bishops who hold rule in the church, and neither can be properly understood without the other. This decision does not, of course, resolve the Protestant difficulties concerning infallibility, but it does put them in a very different context, and it clearly dispels some of the stereotypes most Protestants (and many Catholics) have had about papal monarchialism and "one man rule" ever since the definition

of Vatican I in 1870. Indeed, if this vote had gone the other way, I venture the guess that it would have meant the end of really serious ecumenical discussion between Catholicism and the rest of Christendom. But the vote was decisive on each of the five questions.

5. The Council made clear that its members wanted to hear what the non-Catholic observers thought. I had no idea that our presence would be taken as seriously as it was. Particularly during the discussion on ecumenism, it was apparent that many bishops wanted to know what Protestant reactions were to statements in the *schema* about Protestantism, and wanted to elicit Protestant opinions on how the *schema* could be improved. Thus, although we had no direct "voice" on the Council floor, we did indeed have an indirect voice through the many contacts that were possible with the fathers and their indispensable strong right arms, the *periti*.

6. Another encouraging fact about the Council was the prophetic concern of the bishops for the state of the world. Cardinal Meyer of Chicago spoke about sin in the church and the need for the church to acknowledge its sin publicly. Cardinal Suenens of Belgium reminded the church that grace is not dispensed solely through the hierarchy, and that the fathers must be prepared for "charisms" within the church in most unlikely places. Bishop McGrath of Panama pointed out that the church must be concerned about the needs of man's body if it is to be concerned about the needs of his soul. Bishop Primeau of New Hampshire stressed the need for the church to give the laity a more active part in its life and quit treating the laity like "dumb sheep." South American bishops urged the church to identify more directly with the plight of the poor and dispossessed. Cardinal Gracias of India pleaded again and again for the church to concern itself with the poor, the illiterate, and the hungry. Bishop Philbin of Ireland reminded the fathers that "remedial charity" is not enough, and that the church's task is not to bind up the wounds of those harmed by the world, so much as to trans-

form the world so that the wounds will not be inflicted in the first place.

These are typical of the voices *in* the Council. Not until the Council is finally over, of course, will we know to what degree they have become the voice *of* the Council.

7. It was encouraging to discover that the majority of the fathers were clearly in favor of a strong statement supporting full religious liberty for all men, whether they are Catholics or not. When Bishop DeSmedt of Bruges had finished his long introduction to the chapter on religious liberty, he received the loudest applause given to any speech during the Council. It was also encouraging to discover that the American hierarchy overwhelmingly favors such a statement and will give it strong support. (This, indeed, may be the place where the contribution of the American hierarchy will be most significant. For American bishops can say to those who are fearful of a doctrine of religious liberty, "Not only is this right, but it also works.")

*   *   *

But here is the point at which account must be taken of the *chastened* optimism that must safeguard too euphoric an assessment of Vatican II. Indeed, the fate of the religious liberty chapter is a good example of the fact that not all is well in Vatican City.

1. It is true that the majority of the Council fathers wished to adopt a statement affirming religious liberty. But it is also true that they were not permitted to do so. The fact is doubly disappointing since the proposed statement certainly includes within it all the things a non-Catholic wants to hear the Catholic Church say on the matter. But the last week of the Council was clouded by the growing realization that no vote would be called for. The Council fathers were presented with a creative opportunity — and they backed away from it. If this seems a harsh judgment, it can be put in even harsher terms. The harsher truth is that a minority within the Coun-

cil was able to thwart the manifest will of the majority, not only in relation to the proposed statement on religious liberty but also in relation to the proposed statement on the Jews. I do not pretend to know all the factors that were involved behind the scenes, but one cannot avoid the conclusion that from somewhere came the word, "No vote on religious liberty or the Jews" — and there was no vote. Strong voices and strong men seemed powerless in the face of this, and so the Council ended on a note of unresolved ambiguity. I hasten to add that the setback is only a temporary one, but it is disturbing all the same. Believers in religious liberty must see to it that session three does not indulge in further equivocation on this issue, which, as Cardinal Ritter so rightly pointed out, is a precondition for any genuine trust in ecumenical life.

2. Another disappointment was the Council's second piece of "finished business," the decree *On Instruments of Social Communication*. Where the Liturgy constitution is creative, the Communication decree is disappointing. On the one hand it is banal and innocuous, with nothing fresh to say, and is thus unworthy of a church council. On the other hand, it has implications that can give rise to censorship, boycott, news management, and Catholic cultural ghettos. The modern man, reading it, will not be particularly impressed by the church's attempt to speak to the modern world. A total of 503 fathers voted against the *schema* when it was proposed, and even at the promulgation session it received 194 negative votes. Nevertheless it stands as half of the Council's public achievement to date. It will later be surrounded by more creative documents, but in the meantime it can only be an embarrassment to the church.

3. No matter how solidly ecumenism may have made its way into the life of the Catholic Church, it still means a variety of things to a variety of bishops. To a number of them it simply involves making the church more attractive, so that non-Catholics can "return" with a minimum of pain. It need hardly be pointed out that such a concept does not have a real future among non-Catholics. Ecumenical activity must

involve a genuine reaching out from both sides, a mutual contrition and a mutual forgiveness, a willingness for both partners to walk along a new path together, not quite sure where it will lead, but willing to walk with a certain amount of risk because of the assurance that the Holy Spirit is taking the lead. Protestants must not be too impatient if it takes awhile for this notion to penetrate certain Catholic minds, but they must also not be too willing to settle for anything less.

4. A final area of disquiet is focused in the way minorities can frustrate the will of majorities, thereby slowing the re-forming pace of the church. The example of the religious liberty chapter has already been cited. To give another example, after 80 per cent of the fathers had voted to affirm the principle of "collegiality," various members of the minority continued to rise almost daily to insist that the vote had no meaning, that it had decided nothing, that there really was no such thing as collegiality, and that the matter would be decided not by the Council fathers but by the Theological Commission charged with rewriting the *schema* on the church. When one reflects that those voicing this opinion included both the chairman and vice-chairman of the Theological Commission itself, it is clear that much time may pass before such a group is going to produce a document pleasing to the 80 per cent who persist in the feeling that their vote somehow signified something. Such tactics can delay for an almost indefinite period the creative results of the Council.

❖   ❖   ❖

All of this suggests that the period between now and the next session will be the most crucial period in the history of the Council. Without resorting too dramatically to the "good-guys-bad-guys" way of interpreting the Council, it must be said that the last ten days of the session demonstrated that the progressives were not so much in control of things as might have been assumed after their strong victory in the "collegiality" vote. The conservatives somehow rallied, and thwarted conciliar acceptance of statements on religious liberty and the Jews. They obviously hope to tone down any subsequent statement on "collegiality" so that it will lose its significance.

Before the second session of the Council, I thought it could go only one way — forward. Now I realize that it could go another way — backward. I believe it will move forward, but I do not believe it will do so automatically. It will do so only as the progressive forces marshal their resources and determine their line of action, only as bishops voice their convictions openly and as laymen prod their bishops to do so. It is not a matter of becoming wholly impatient, but it *is* a matter of cultivating "holy impatience," of realizing that if significant reform of the church is not achieved now — while there is a Council in session — there may not be another such opportunity in our lifetime.

And if non-Catholics cannot *directly* help the Council fathers in the noble work of reform, we can at least continue to indicate to them the directions in which we hope reform will go, and we can, even more significantly, sustain and reinforce them with our prayers, praying on their behalf the prayer they offered each morning at the beginning of their labors:

They are present, Holy Spirit of God; they are present, conscious indeed of the burden of sin, but gathered together especially in Thy name. Go to them, and be with them: deign to enter into their hearts. Teach them what to do and how to proceed; and show them what they should accomplish, that with Thy help they may be able to please Thee in all things. Be Thou the beginning of their judgments and bring them forth, Thou Who alone has the name of God, along with the Father and His Son. Do not, Thou Who lovest order above all things, permit them to undermine justice in any way. Let not ignorance lead them astray. Let not the desire to please turn them away from their duty. Let not bribery or favoritism corrupt them. Unite them, instead, effectively to Thyself with the gift of Thine Own grace. Grant that they may be one with Thee and that they may not deviate from the truth. As they have gathered together in Thy name, so may they maintain in all things a proper piety and a fitting moderation that in the Council their thinking may not fail Thee in any way. . . .

Appendices

Appendix A: For Ready Reference

A Brief Glossary of Latin Terms

Adsum – "I am present" – the form of recording one's attendance at daily sessions of the Council

Adsumus – "We are present" – opening words of the prayer recited by all the Council fathers at the beginning of each daily session

aula – the "hall" of St. Peter's in which the sessions are held

Carissime observatores – "beloved observers" – a salutation sometimes used by ecumenically minded bishops

de jure divino – "by divine right" – a crucial phrase in the discussion of the power of a bishop: Is it "by divine right" or only by human consent of the pope?

Dixi – "I have spoken" – the conclusion of a conciliar speech

Exeunt omnes – "All must leave" – words spoken at the beginning of each session, ordering those without proper credentials to depart

in genere – "in general" – refers to broad discussion of a topic before proceeding to detailed discussion

Loquatur nunc . . . et accedat ad microphoniam . . . – formula used by the moderators to announce the next speaker and the one immediately following him

peritus (plural, *periti*) – an "expert," a theologian appointed to assist the Council fathers with their theological deliberations

placet – an affirmative vote

non placet – a negative vote

placet juxta modum – an affirmative vote "with modifications" which must be submitted in writing along with the ballot

relatio – an introductory speech presenting a new *schema* for discussion *schema* (plural, *schemata*) – a "draft," a document proposed for discussion to the Council fathers. The following *schemata* were discussed during Session Two:

De Beata Maria Virgine – On the Blessed Virgin Mary

De Ecclesia – On the Church

De Episcopis ac de Diocesium Regimine – On Bishops and the Ruling of Dioceses

De Instrumentis Communicationis Socialis – On Instruments of Social Communication

De Oecumenismo – On Ecumenism

De Sacra Liturgia – On the Sacred Liturgy

sub secreto – "under pledge of secrecy" – refers to all Council documents, the texts of which may not be divulged to the public

Venerabiles patres – "Venerable fathers" – the salutation at the beginning of conciliar speeches

Appendix B:

Bishop DeSmedt's Introduction to the chapter of *De Oecumenismo* on "Religious Liberty" (November 19)

Very many Conciliar Fathers have insistently demanded that this Sacred Synod clearly explain and proclaim the right of man to religious liberty. Among the reasons given, four principal ones should be listed:

1) *Truth:* The Church must teach and defend the right to religious liberty because there is question of truth, the care of which was committed to her by Christ;

2) *Defense:* The Church cannot remain silent today when almost half of mankind is deprived of religious liberty by atheistic materialism of various kinds;

3) *Peaceful Social Life:* Today in all nations of the world, men, who adhere to different religions or who lack all religious belief, must live together in one and the same human society; in the light of truth, the Church should point the way toward living together peacefully;

4) *Ecumenism:* Many non-Catholics harbor an aversion against the Church or at least suspect her of a kind of Machiavellianism because we seem to them to demand the free exercise of religion when Catho-

lics are in a minority in any nation and at the same time refuse and deny the same religious liberty when Catholics are in the majority.

Religious liberty is such a grave problem in modern society that it can not be omitted in a pastoral decree on Ecumenism. Therefore, we submit to your deliberations this fifth chapter of our schema on Ecumenism. The Secretariat for Promoting Christian Unity, to the best of its ability, has carefully watched over the preparation of this material.

Since we are treating of a most difficult question and at the same time one of great importance in modern life, the authors of the schema cherish the hope that your attention and pastoral consideration will emend what needs emendment and perfect what is still imperfect in the schema now offered to you.

The term "Religious Liberty" has a definite meaning in our text. In the forthcoming discussion, great confusion might arise if any of the Fathers give to the expression a meaning that differs from the one intended by the text.

When religious liberty is defended, it is not asserted that it is proper for man to consider the religious problem according to his own whim without any moral obligation and decide for himself according to his own will whether or not to embrace religion (religious indifferentism).

Nor is it affirmed that the human conscience is free in the sense that it is as it were outside of the law, absolved from any obligation toward God (laicism).

Nor is it said that falsehood is to be considered on an equal footing with truth, as though there were no objective norm of truth (doctrinal relativism).

Nor is it admitted that man in any way has a quasi-right to maintain a peaceful complacency in the midst of uncertainty (dilettantistic pessimism).

If anyone were to insist upon giving any of the aforesaid meanings to "Religious Liberty," he would attribute to our text a meaning which neither the words nor our intention possess.

What therefore is meant in the text by "Religious Liberty"? Positively, religious liberty is the right of the human person to the free exercise of religion according to the dictates of his conscience. Negatively, it is immunity from all external force in his personal relations with God, which the conscience of man vindicates to itself.

Religious liberty implies human autonomy, not from within certainly but from without. From within, man is not freed of the obligations toward the religious problem. From without, his liberty is offended when obedience to the dictates of his conscience in religious matters is impeded.

At this point, two questions must be asked: 1) can each man claim for himself religious liberty as a sacred right given to him by God?

2) is there, and to what extent is there, a duty on the part of others to recognize the aforesaid religious liberty?

Our decree, since it is pastoral, tries to treat the present matter especially from the practical point of view and, after the manner of John XXIII, will carefully strive to remove the whole question from that world of abstractions which was so dear to the nineteenth century. The question is put therefore regarding real man in his real dealings with other men, in contemporary human and civil societies.

I

The first pastoral problem which must be examined now by this Sacred Synod is this: *how must Catholics because of their faith conduct themselves toward men who do not belong to the Catholic faith?* We propose the following answer for your deliberations:

1) All Catholics are invited by Christ to strive by prayer, penance, witness and evangelizing in the Holy Spirit to bring our non-Catholic brothers to the blessing of the evangelical light and of the life of the Church. The sacred, absolute rights of God as well as the evangelical and natural truths must always and everywhere be honored and observed by them.

2) They must abstain from all direct and indirect coercion. Although God wills all men to be saved and to come to the knowledge of the truth, the disciples of Christ may not infringe upon the religious liberty of the individual person. On the contrary, they must respect and esteem the right and duty of non-Catholics to follow the dictate of their own conscience even when, after sincere and sufficient study, it errs in good faith.

What is the reason of faith why non-Catholics can be forced by no one to admit the Catholic doctrine against their conscience? This reason is found in the very nature of the act of faith. For this act, on God's part, is a supernatural gift which the Holy Spirit most freely gives to whom and when he wills; and, on man's part, it is and must be an assent which man freely gives to God.

3) All Catholics are bound, by the command of the Lord, to love and to help their non-Catholic brothers with a sincere and active charity.

II

At this point, the schema takes a step forward and asserts that each and every man, who follows his conscience in religious matters, has a natural right to true and authentic religious liberty. In this second part, it is proposed that the Sacred Synod solemnly demand religious liberty for the whole human family, for all religious groups, for each human person whether his conscience be sincere (rectam) and true or sincere and false concerning faith, provided only that he sincerely follow the dictate of conscience. Therefore, a general principle is laid down: *no human person can be the object of coercion or intolerance.*

What is the reason why observance of religious liberty is demanded of all? The human person, endowed with conscious and free activity, since he can fulfill the will of God only as the divine law is perceived through the dictate of conscience, can obtain his ultimate end only by prudently forming the judgment of conscience and by faithfully carrying out its dictate.

From the nature of things, in forming this judgment, whereby man tries freely to conform to the absolute demands of God's rights, neither any other man nor any human institution can take the place of the free judgment of man's conscience. Therefore, the man who sincerely obeys his own conscience intends to obey God himself, although at times confusedly and unknowingly, and is to be considered worthy of esteem.

When religious liberty is violated, then the very freedom of the human person is violated in its principal matter, in a fundamental demand, in man's ordination to the supreme and ultimate end. The greatest injury is to prevent a man from worshipping God and from obeying God according to the dictate of his own conscience.

III

The schema takes still another step forward and enters upon a most difficult question. Religious liberty would be fruitless and empty if men were not able to carry out the dictate of their conscience in external acts whether in private life, in social life, or in public life, or if human persons were prevented from forming religious groups whose members could worship the Supreme Deity by common and social acts and lead a religious life.

Here, however, there arises a most difficult problem. For, if a human person carries out the dictate of his conscience by external acts, there is danger of violating the rights and duties of another or of others. Since man is a social being and since in the human family men are subject to error and to sin, the conflict of rights and the conflict of duties cannot always be avoided.

From this it is evident that *the right and duty to manifest externally the dictate of conscience is not unlimited, but can be and at times must be tempered and regulated for the common good.*

This ordering of the common good must be done juridically in human society and belongs to public authority (potestati publicae). "One

of the fundamental duties of civil authorities, therefore," we read in
Pacem in Terris [trans. NCWC rev. #62], "is to coordinate social relations in such fashion that the exercise of one man's rights does not
threaten others in the exercise of their own rights nor hinder them in
the fulfillment of their duties. Finally, the rights of all should be effectively safeguarded and, if they have been violated, completely restored."

How is public authority to carry out this duty? In establishing order
for the common good, public authority can never act contrary to the
order of justice established by God. As St. Thomas says: "Human law
is truly law to the extent that it is in accordance with right reason; and
therefore it is evident that it is derived from the eternal law. In so far as
it departs from reason, it is a so-called "wicked law," and therefore is
not truly a law but a kind of violence" (i – ii, q. 93, a. 3, ad 2um).

Recent Roman Pontiffs again and again have bewailed the fact that
not a few governments have gone too far in this matter, ignoring and
violating religious liberty. In our own day, there are some regions in
which tolerance in religious matters has been so little observed that
the Supreme Pontiff, Paul VI, in his allocution to the Fathers of the
Second Vatican Council on September 29, 1963, said, speaking of the
violated right to religious liberty:

"Because of sufferings of this kind, with what sadness are We affected, and how deeply We are grieved, when We behold that in some
territories religious liberty, together with the other principal rights of
man, is suppressed by the principles and arts of those who do not tol-
erate opinions different from theirs on politics, on races of men, or on
religion of any kind. We are sorrowed also by the many injuries which
are done to those who would like to profess their religion honestly and
freely."

IV

In order that we might clearly understand the doctrine of the Church
on the extent and limits of the civil power's duty relating to religious
liberty, we must, in a few words, develop the history of this doctrine.
Bear with me, Venerable Fathers, if I seem to make more than just
demands on your patience. But the Secretariat for Promoting Christian
Unity is convinced that many difficulties and confusions can be avoided
in the study of the schema if, before the discussion begins, I show very
briefly what the Supreme Pontiffs since the time of Pius IX have taught
concerning the duties of public authority in religious matters.

On the question of religious liberty, the principal document is the
encyclical "Pacem in Terris," in which Pope John XXIII especially
developed these two points of doctrine: 1) by the law of nature, the

human person has the right to the free exercise of religion in society
according to the dictates of a sincere conscience (conscientia recta)
whether the conscience be true (conscientia vera), or the captive either
of error or of inadequate knowledge of truth and of sacred things. 2) To
this right corresponds the duty incumbent upon other men and the
public authority to recognize and respect that right in such a way that
the human person in society is kept immune from all coercion of any
kind (cf. AAS 55, 1963, p. 299; p. 264 and pp. 273 – 274).

Moreover, this doctrine must be understood as the contemporary
terminus of a process of evolution both in the doctrine on the dignity
of the human person and in the Church's pastoral solicitude for man's
freedom. This doctrinal evolution took place according to a two-fold
law:

1) *Law of continuity:* The Church's doctrine and solicitude are always self-consistent, always remain the same. This perennial doctrine
can be expressed in the words of Pope John: "The dignity of the human person demands this, that in his actions man should enjoy his own
counsel and freedom" (ibid. p. 265). This doctrine has its deepest roots
in the Sacred Scriptures which teach that man was made to the image
of God. From this doctrine stems the continual pastoral solicitude of
the Church for man's true freedom.

2) *Law of progress:* The ecclesiastical magisterium adapts, explains,
and defends genuine doctrine according to the demands of errors which
are spread and according to the needs which arise from the development of man and of society. By this progress, the mind of the Church
is led to search more deeply into doctrine and to understand it more
clearly.

In this way, there has arisen in two areas a distinction which no one
has explained more clearly than Pope John XXIII in his encyclical
Pacem in Terris: 1) A clearer distinction between false *philosophical
teachings* and the endeavors and institutions which these ideologies
give rise to or nourish. While on the one hand the ideologies are always to be condemned, on the other hand the economic, social and
civil institutions which have arisen therefrom can contain something
that is good and worthy of approval. 2) A clearer distinction between
errors and the person who errs in good faith. While on the one hand
errors must always be rejected, on the other hand the man in error
"does not cease to be endowed with human nature, nor does he ever
lose his dignity as a person, due consideration of which must always
be maintained" (ibid. pp. 299 – 300).

These two laws of continuity and progress must be kept before our
eyes always when the documents of the Apostolic See are read and
interpreted.

V

In this way the door is opened to a correct understanding of many pontifical documents which in the nineteenth century treated of religious liberty in such words that this liberty appeared as something that had to be condemned. The clearest example is found in the encyclical "Quanta Cura" of Pius IX, in which we read: "From this completely false concept of social rule (naturalism), they do not hesitate to foster that erroneous opinion which is especially injurious to the Catholic Church and the salvation of souls, called by our predecessor Gregory XVI "deliramentum," namely that the freedom of conscience and of cults is the proper right of each man, and this should be proclaimed and asserted in every rightly constituted society" (ASS 3, 1867, p. 162).

As is evident, this freedom of conscience is condemned because of the ideology of the rationalists who founded their conclusions upon the principle that the individual conscience is under no law, and, therefore, is subject to no divinely given norms. (Cf. Syllabus, prop. 3, ASS 3, p. 168.) Freedom of worship is condemned also when it is based upon religious indifferentism (ibid., prop. 15, p. 170). Finally, there is condemned that separation of the Church from the State which is based upon the rationalistic principle of the juridical omnicompetence of the State, according to which the Church is to be incorporated into the monistic organism of the State and is to be subjected to its supreme authority (ibid., prop. 39, p. 172).

To understand these condemnations correctly, we must see in them the constant doctrine and solicitude of the Church concerning the true dignity of the human person and his true liberty (law of continuity). For the ultimate basis of human dignity lies in the fact that man is a creature of God. He is not God himself, but an image of God. From this absolute dependence of man upon God there flows every right and duty of man to claim for himself and for others true religious liberty. For man is subjectively bound to worship God according to the sincere dictate of his own conscience (juxta rectam suae conscientiae normam) because objectively he is absolutely dependent upon God.

In order, therefore, that his absolute dependence upon God might not be infringed in any way, man must not be impeded in any way by others or even by public authority from freely practicing his religion. Therefore, in opposing the philosophical and political tenets of laicism, the Church was fighting for the dignity and true liberty of the human person. In accordance with the law of continuity, then, the Church, in spite of changing conditions, has remained consistent both in the past and in the present.

Leo XIII had already started this doctrinal development when he distinguished clearly between the Church, the People of God, and the civil society, a terrestrial and temporal people (cf. Immortale Dei, ASS 18, 1885, pp. 166 – 167). By this means, he opened the way to a new affirmation of the due and lawful autonomy which belongs to the civil order and to its juridical dispositions. Because of this, it was possible to take a step forward (law of progress) toward a new judgment on "modern freedoms."

These freedoms can be tolerated (cf. ibid., p. 174; Libertas Praestantissimum, ASS 20, 1887, pp. 609 – 610). And yet they were to be *tolerated* only. The reason was evident. For at that time in Europe, the regimes which proclaimed the modern freedoms, religious liberty among them, consciously drew their inspiration from the laicist ideology. There was danger, therefore – and Leo XIII sensed this – that the civil and political institutions of this kind of republic, since they were of laicist orientation, would lead to such abuses that they would necessarily do violence to the dignity and true liberty of the human person. In accordance with the law of continuity, what was dear to Leo XIII is always dear to the Church – the safeguarding of the human person.

With the rise of State-Totalitarianism in its various forms, Pope Pius XI brought the pastoral and doctrinal development to a new height. There is no longer any danger, as there was in the nineteenth century, that the false concept of liberty might do violence to human dignity. There is a new danger, that every kind of human and civil liberty, and above all religious liberty, will be destroyed. For this reason, the Church is beginning in a new way to manifest her concern, which through the centuries has never wavered, for human liberty and dignity. With the increase of her pastoral concern, the Church's doctrine continues to develop.

Faithfully observing the law of continuity, Pius XI maintained the unstinting opposition of the Church to anti-religious laicism. "Those things which Pius X condemned we also condemn; as often as there is in 'laicism' any meaning or purpose that is harmful or contrary to God or religion, we condemn laicism, and openly declare that it must be condemned, as alien to God and religion" (Maximam gravissimamque, AAS 16, 1924, p. 10).

But observing the rule of progress no less, Pius XI introduced a new distinction which was of great importance for a deeper understanding of Catholic doctrine. He made a distinction between the "freedom of consciences" and the "freedom of conscience." The latter he rejected as "equivocal," as often used by the laicist to signify "an absolute independence of conscience, which is an absurdity in man who was created and redeemed by God"; the former however, "freedom of consciences," he accepted, stating that he would joyfully fight the good fight for "freedom of consciences" (Non abbiamo bisogno, AAS 23, 1931, pp. 301 – 302).

Moreover, Pius XI not only fought for the religious liberty of the faithful, but he was at the same time compelled to show the pastoral concern of the Church on a wider basis. For not only Christian, but human reality was at stake, if we can rightly distinguish between two things that are in reality one.

By way of new advances, Pius XI developed a truly liberal and Christian doctrine when he taught: "man as a person possesses God-given rights which must remain immune from all denial, privation, or interference on the part of society" (Mit brennender Sorge, AAS 29, 1937, p. 159). And he continues in no ambiguous words: "The believer possesses the inalienable right to profess his faith and to practice it in a proper way. Laws which interfere with or render difficult this profession and practice are in contradiction to the natural law" (ibid., p. 160). No one, who understands the condition of the times and the purposes of this encyclical, can fail to understand the universal intent of this statement.

Deeply sharing the pastoral solicitude of his predecessor, Pius XII developed further and expanded his doctrine (law of progress). One thing he kept before his mind, the human person, created by God, redeemed by Christ Jesus, yet placed in stringent circumstances and surrounded on all sides by dangers.

In this context of doctrine and pastoral solicitude (law of continuity) must we read the text which in this matter is supreme. Enumerating "the fundamental rights of the person" which must be recognized and respected in every well-ordered society, he repeats the doctrine of Pius XI and vests it with new authority, affirming "the right to the private and public worship of God, including religious 'actio caritativa'" (Nuntius radiophonicus 24 Dec. 1942, AAS 35, 1943, p. 19).

The Roman Pontiff did not propose this doctrine as a tenuous opinion or as a theory belonging to the schools. On the contrary, he carries the doctrine to its juridical conclusions so that it becomes a principle according to which just limits are placed on public authority: "The chief duty of any public authority is to safeguard the inviolable rights that are proper to men and so to provide that each one might more easily fulfill his duties" (Nuntius radiophonicus 1 June, 1941, AAS 33, 1941, p. 200).

Here we must recall especially the doctrine of Pius XII on the limitation of the State, because it deals with the suppression of errors within society: "Could it be that in certain circumstances He (God) would not give men any mandate, would not impose any duty, and would not even communicate the right to impede or to repress what is erroneous and false? A look at things as they are gives an affirmative answer." Then, having cited the example of divine providence, he proceeds: "Hence the affirmation: religious and moral error must always be impeded, when it is possible, because toleration of them is in itself immoral, is not valid absolutely and unconditionally. Moreover, God has not given even to human authority such an absolute and universal command in matters of faith and morality. Such a command is unknown to the common convictions of mankind, to Christian conscience, to the sources of revelation, and to the practice of the Church" (Ci Riesce, AAS 45, 1953, pp. 798 – 799).

This declaration (law of progress) is of the greatest importance for our question, especially if we keep in mind what was in the past held concerning the role of the State.

At the end of this historical development comes the encyclical "Pacem in Terris." This document comes forth as the ripe fruit of a slow process of growth which has taken place within the Church, under the light of the Holy Spirit, throughout the whole of the last century.

Our schema had already been prepared and had been studied by the Central Commission and by the Commission for Coordination when Pope John, on April 11 of this year, published his last encyclical "Pacem in Terris." We believe that our text is in complete conformity with his pellucid doctrine, which was received within the Church and outside of the Church with unprecedented praise.

We now submit this text for your consideration. In the historical conspectus of this doctrine, we have shown that, in the pontifical documents, along with continuity, we must look for a progressive spelling out of doctrine. It is evident that certain quotations from the Popes, because of a difference of words, can be put in opposition to our schema. But I beseech you, Venerable Fathers, not to force the text to speak outside of its historical and doctrinal context, not, in other words, to make the fish swim out of water.

Let our document be studied as it stands. It is not a dogmatic treatise, but a pastoral decree directed to men of our time. The whole world is waiting for this decree. The voice of the Church on religious liberty is being waited for in universities, in national and international organizations, in Christian and non-Christian communities, in the papers, and in public opinion — and it is being waited for with urgent expectancy.

We hope that it will be possible to complete the discussion and the approbation of this very brief, but very important, decree before the end of this second session. How fruitful our work would appear to the world if the Conciliar Fathers, with the voice of Peter's successor, could announce this liberating doctrine on religious liberty!

Venerable Fathers, we will add our labors to yours. Our Secretariat will study your emendations most attentively and also with the utmost speed. We will work day and night. But our hope is in the Lord. May Jesus Christ assist all of us with His grace. If at the end of this session He asks of us: "Young men, do you have any fish?," seeing the faith and good will of this Council, He might say to their successors what once He said to the Apostles: "Cast the net to the right of the boat: and you will find" (Jn. xxi, 6).

Appendix C:

In Memoriam: Gustave Weigel, S.J.

Until Roman Catholic ecumenism really got off the ground during the pontificate of Pope John, its adherents tended to be located in Europe. One could talk about Yves Congar, Abbé Couturier, George Tavard, Karl Adam, Gregory Baum and others. When asked who were their counterparts in this country, ecumenically minded Protestants would start off enthusiastically, "Well, there's Father Weigel . . ." and discover that they had just about exhausted the list.

The fact that ecumenism has entered American Catholicism to stay should not blind us to the long, lean years when most of it was borne on the broad and capable shoulders of Gustave Weigel, S.J. Indeed, he carried this weight so effectively and made his time and energy available to Protestant groups with such staggering generosity that his heart quietly stopped beating early in January, while this book was being written.

The ways of providence are mysterious, but both Catholics and Protestants, confronted with the completely unexpected death of the great-hearted man whom many called "Gus," can agree that there was probably no man on either side of the divide we could less afford to spare. His voice is needed in these crucial days not only to describe the Council but to interpret it, and to act as a prod, spur and catalyst to those "open-door minds," as he so ably described them, within his communion.

His was an "open-door mind." This did not mean that he sat lightly to Roman dogma. Indeed, he was more conventional and orthodox in his theology than many Protestants who knew him chiefly through his hearty good spirit and broad humanity were aware. But he did not have a fixed and narrow mind; he was always open to new currents. Those who saw him in action at the Council could not doubt that his convictions were those of the "open door" fathers, who wanted to relate "the faith once delivered to the saints" to the modern world, the non-Catholics and the future — three things feared above all else by the "closed-door" group.

His attitude toward ecumenism was not static but constantly enlarging. Shortly before his death he talked of the possibility of a follow-up volume to *An American Dialogue*. It was suggested that he write an initial chapter entitled *"Retractiones."* He was all for this, acknowledging that he had grown and changed in his estimate of the ecumenical task; what he had thought in 1960 was no longer a sufficient index of what he thought in 1963.

Those who saw him at the Council often commented on how tired he appeared to be. In retrospect, we can see that he gave himself so unstintingly to the task of interpreting the Council to the non-Catholic observers and the press that he quite literally wore himself out. He will be unable to provide that interpretation at the third session, and this is a loss for all Christendom. But those who knew his devotion to the possibilities of renewal that the Council has opened up can believe that he will be very close to St. Peter's, cheering the Council on from the same corner of heaven in which Pope John has been engaged in an identical enterprise.

R.M.B.

Reprinted with the permission of *Christianity and Crisis*, February 3, 1964

INDEX OF NAMES